†Owen J. Blum, O.F.M. (1912–98),
published frequently on Peter Damian
and assisted in the critical edition of the
Letters published in the series Monumenta
Germaniae Historica. **Irven M. Resnick** is
professor of philosophy and religion, and
Chair of Excellence in Judaic Studies, at
the University of Tennessee at Chattanooga.

THE FATHERS
OF THE CHURCH

MEDIAEVAL CONTINUATION

VOLUME 7

THE FATHERS
OF THE CHURCH

MEDIAEVAL CONTINUATION

PETER DAMIAN
LETTERS
151–180

Translated by

†OWEN J. BLUM, O.F.M.
Quincy University, Quincy, Illinois

and

IRVEN M. RESNICK
University of Tennessee, Chattanooga, Tennessee

THE CATHOLIC UNIVERSITY OF AMERICA PRESS
Washington, D.C.

Copyright © 2005
THE CATHOLIC UNIVERSITY OF AMERICA PRESS
All rights reserved
Printed in the United States of America

The paper used in this publication meets the minimum requirements of the
American National Standards for Information Science—Permanence of Paper
for Printed Library Materials, ANSI z39.48 - 1984.

LIBRARY OF CONGRESS CATALOGING-IN-PUBLICATION DATA
Peter Damian, Saint, 1007–1072.
    [The letters of Peter Damian.
    (The Fathers of the Church, mediaeval continuation ; vv. 1–3, 5–7)
    Translation of the Latin letters of Peter Damian.
    Includes bibliographical references and indexes.
    Contents: [1] 1–30—[2] 31–60—[3] 61–90—[5] 91–120—[6]
121–150—[7] 151–180.
    1. Peter Damian, Saint, 1007–1072—Correspondence.   2. Christian
saints—Italy—Correspondence. I. Blum, Owen J., 1912–1998. II. Series:
Fathers of the Church, mediaeval continuation ; v. 1, etc.
BX4700.P77A4 1998   270.3   88-25802
ISBN 0-8132-0702-9 (v. 1)
ISBN 0-8132-0707-X (v. 2)
ISBN 0-8132-0750-9 (v. 3)
ISBN 0-8132-0816-5 (v. 5)
ISBN 0-8132-1372-X (v. 6)
ISBN-13: 978-0-8132-1425-2 (v. 7)
ISBN-10: 0-8132-1425-4 (v. 7)

CONTENTS

INTRODUCTION

by Irven M. Resnick

This volume concludes the series of Peter Damian's *Letters* in English translation. *Letters* 151–170 were written between 1067 and 1070, in the years before Damian's death on February 22, 1072. *Letters* 171–180 are not datable. Several of the *Letters* in this volume are fragmentary or reconstructed from fragments (*Letters* 163, 173, and 175) found in the *Collectanea* of Damian's disciple, John of Lodi. *Letter* 178 was discovered in an eleventh-century manuscript and first printed in the twentieth century.

Among these *Letters* are some of Damian's most passionate calls to promote the ideals of the eremitic life, wherein he indicates his understanding of the proper relationship between cenobites and hermits. These include *Letter* 152, in which Damian defends as consistent with the spirit and the letter of Benedict's *Rule* his practice of receiving monks into the eremitic life who had abandoned their cenobitic communities. Another defense of the ideals of the hermitage is found in *Letter* 153 (previously *opusculum* 13 and subtitled "On the Perfection of Monks"[1]), which is a lengthy exhortation to the monks of Pomposa to struggle to achieve religious perfection.

Pomposa was a venerable and ancient monastic community that Damian knew well. As a young man, not long after he had entered the hermitage of Fonte Avellana, Damian had been sent to Pomposa by his prior to instruct the monks there. He was impressed by the Benedictine community's effort to combine cenobitic practices and eremitic ideals. It was a community with an enviable library, and it was there that Damian composed his first literary work, entitled *Against the Jews* (*Letter* 1) in

---

1. *De perfectione monachorum.*

1040–41.[2] In *Letter* 153, written approximately twenty-five years after his first visit, Damian laments a general decline in religious fervor. From this general complaint, he passes to a discussion of the requirements of monastic life, and a description of its offices. He also encourages his fellow monks at Pomposa (and elsewhere, since Damian knew his letters circulated among a larger audience) to pass beyond the minimum standards established in the *Rule* of St. Benedict, to the higher and more demanding vocation of the eremitic life. The standards of the eremitic life demanded a rigorous penitential discipline focused on prayer, solitude, fasting, and self-flagellation, which Damian often recommends to monks as well. The cenobitic monastery, he remarks, was established by Saint Benedict as a sort of primary school for learning obedience to the *Rule;* but, claims Damian, Benedict always viewed the hermitage as the culmination of the monks' struggles and aspirations. The "gentler" regimen in cenobitic houses Damian viewed as an accommodation to human infirmity, but one that hermits regularly surpassed. Despite the instruction Damian himself had offered to the monks at Pomposa a quarter-century earlier, in this letter he reproves those monks who devote themselves more to the study of the works of the Latin grammarians and to secular literature than to the *Rule* of Benedict, their spiritual guide. Instead, he urges the monks to shed tears of compunction, which represent the first step of spiritual renewal. And, finally, Damian outlines the duties of the monastic officers—the abbot, prior, lector, cellarer, and others—and elaborates upon the proper training of novices.

Damian develops some of the same themes in his *Letter* 161 (previously *opusculum* 43, subtitled "In Praise of Flagellation"[3]), addressed to Abbot Desiderius of Monte Cassino. Monte Cassino, the venerable and ancient font from which Benedictine spirituality flowed, was another community Damian visited often and knew well. He was on especially friendly terms with its abbot, Desiderius, who later was named Pope Victor III (d.

---

2. *Antilogus contra Judaeos* (FOTC, MC 1.37–83).

3. *De laude flagellorum et ut loquuntur disciplinae.*

1087). Despite (or perhaps because of) their friendship, in *Letter* 161 he chastises the community for having abandoned the practice of public flagellation on Fridays, which it had employed previously. Damian describes this scourging as a salutary practice that renders the monk a more perfect image of Christ himself. If they will not share his suffering, Damian wonders, how will they share his glory?

Also well known is *Letter* 165 (previously *opusculum* 12, subtitled "On Contempt of the World"[4]). This letter is addressed to a hermit, Albizo, and to a monk, Peter. Written in August 1069, after Damian's participation in two Roman synods at which his best efforts seem to have been frustrated, the letter laments the deplorable condition of this world, which seems to be rushing toward its destruction and end. Monks who had vowed to renounce the world, he complains, have reneged on their promises and involve themselves in worldly affairs. He enumerates their many sins and judges that as the integrity of the monastic profession has weakened, so too has the world fallen even deeper into an abyss of sin and corruption. Carried away by his denunciation of these false monks, who ought to have served the Church as a model of religious perfection, he paints a picture of unrelenting worldly corruption that must be a prelude to final disintegration.

The Roman synods mentioned above were called during the pontificate of Alexander II. Although Alexander had previously allowed Damian to be relieved of his responsibilities as Cardinal-bishop of Ostia in order to return to a life of contemplation at Fonte Avellana, Damian had continued to serve the Holy See as a papal legate when called upon. He was also a very influential figure in the Church, whom Alexander himself praised as "the eye and immovable support of the Holy See."[5] Roman intrigues and money's influence on ecclesiastical politics, however, left him yearning all the more for the solitude of his hermitage. In *Letter* 165 he urges his recipients not to abandon the

---

4. *De contemptu saeculi.*
5. "Petrum videlicet Damianum, Ostiensem Episcopum: qui nimirum et noster est oculus et apostolicae sedis immobile firmamentum." *Diploma Alexandri II, de legatione S. Petri Damiani in Gallias* (PL 145.857B).

monastery or hermitage, as others have done, but to take refuge there within their fortress while the world outside their walls paves the way for the advent of Antichrist.

Although the letters described above were concerned above all with monastic life, Damian was equally concerned to address the moral condition of the larger Church. *Letter* 162, addressed to the archpriest of the canons of the Lateran, and chancellor of Pope Alexander II, represents the last of Damian's four tracts condemning clerical marriage (Nicolaitism) or concubinage and exhorting the secular clergy to celibacy. Like the servants at the altar in the Jerusalem Temple, who had to abstain from sexual contact, the priests of the Church, he insisted, must adopt the practice of celibacy to serve at the altar of the Lord. Damian's condemnation of Nicolaitism also informed his rejection of Cadalus, the antipope Honorius II (see *Letters* 154 and 156), who was said to support clerical marriage, and it therefore cast him into the center of a storm of ecclesiastical (and imperial) politics from which Damian never completely extricated himself.

ABBREVIATIONS

Burchard	Burchard of Worms, *Decretorum libri XX.* PL 140.537–1058.
CCL	*Corpus Christianorum, Series Latina.* Brepols, 1954– .
CJC	*Corpus Juris Canonici.* Ed. E. A. Friedberg, 2 vols. Leipzig, 1879–1881.
CCCM	*Corpus Christianorum, Continuatio Mediaevalis.* Brepols, 1971– .
CSEL	*Corpus Scriptorum Ecclesiasticorum Latinorum.* Vienna.
DA	*Deutsches Archiv für Erforschung des Mittelalters*
DTC	*Dictionnaire de théologie catholique.* 15 vols. Paris, 1903–1950.
FOTC	The Fathers of the Church. New York and Washington, D.C., 1947– .
FOTC, MC	The Fathers of the Church, Mediaeval Continuation. Washington, D.C., 1989–.
Gaetani	*S. Petri Damiani . . . Opera omnia.* 4 vols. 1606–1640. Later editions will be cited by year of publication.
Hinschius	Pseudo-Isidore, *Decretales Pseudo-Isidorianae et capitula Angilramni,* ed. P. Hinschius. Leipzig, 1863.
HJb	*Historisches Jahrbuch*
Itala	*Itala: Das Neue Testament in altlateinischer Überlieferung.* Ed A. Jülicher. 4 vols. 1963–1976.
Jaffé	*Regesta Pontificum Romanorum.* Ed. P. Jaffé. 2d ed. Corr. S. Loewenfeld, F. Kaltenbrunner, P. Ewald. Graz: Akademische Druck- und Verlagsanstalt, 1956.
LThK	*Lexikon für Theologie und Kirche.* 11 vols. Freiburg, Basel, Rome, Vienna: Herder, 1993–2001.

Mansi	*Sacrorum conciliorum nova et amplissima collectio.* Ed. Joannes Dominicus Mansi. 53 vols. Paris, 1900–1927.
MGH	Monumenta Germaniae Historica
Auct.ant.	Auctores antiquissimi
Capit.	Capitularia regum Francorum
Const.	Constitutiones et acta publica imperatorum
Epp.	Epistolae (in Quarto)
LL	Leges (in folio)
NCE	*The New Catholic Encyclopedia,* 2d ed. 2003.
Nom. hebr.	Jerome, *Liber interpretationis hebraicorum nominum,* ed. P. de Lagarde, CCL 72 (1959).
PG	*Patrologia Graeca.* Ed. J.-P. Migne. Paris, 1857–1886.
PL	*Patrologia Latina.* Ed. J.-P. Migne. Paris, 1844–1855.
RE	*Real-Enzyklopädie der Classischen Altertumswissenschaft.* Ed. Pauly-Wissowa.
Regino	Regino of Prum, *De ecclesiasticis disciplinis et religione Christiana libri duo.* PL 132.185–370.
Sabatier	*Bibliorum sacrorum Latinae versiones antiquae.* Ed. P. Sabatier. 3 vols. 1743.
SC	Sources chrétiennes. Paris, 1942– .
Vulg.	*Biblia sacra iuxta vulgatam versionem.* Ed. Robert Weber. 2 vols. 2d ed., 1975.

SELECT BIBLIOGRAPHY

Sources

Albertus Magnus On Animals: *A Medieval Summa Zoologica.* Trans. Kenneth F. Kitchell and Irven M. Resnick. 2 vols. Baltimore: Johns Hopkins University Press, 1999.

Alexander II, Pope. *Epistolae et diplomata.* PL 146.1279–1436.

Ambrose. *De Abraham.* Ed. Charles Schenkl. CSEL 32/1. Prague, Vienna, Leipzig: F. Tempsky (1896) 500-638.

———. *De incarnationis Dominicae sacramento.* PL 16.817–46.

———. *De institutione virginis.* PL 16.305–35.

———. *De obitu Theodosii Imperatoris.* Ed. Otto Faller. CSEL 73/7. Vienna: Hoelder-Pichler-Tempsky (1955) 370–401.

Augustine. *De civitate Dei.* Ed. B. Dombart and A. Kalb. CCL 47 and 48 (1955).

———. *De diversis quaestionibus octoginta tribus.* Ed. A. Mutzenbecher. CCL 44A (1975).

———. *De haeresibus.* CCL 46, 13/2. Turnholt: Brepols (1969) 283–345.

———. *De natura et origine animae.* Ed. Charles F. Urba and Joseph Zycha. Vienna: F. Tempsky; Lepizig: G. Freytag (1913) 303–420.

———. *De trinitate libri XV.* Ed. W. J. Mountain and F. Glorie. 2 vols., CCL 50 and 50A (1968).

———. *De utilitate credendi.* Ed. Joseph Zycha. CSEL 25/1. Prague and Vienna: F. Tempsky; Leipzig: G. Freytag (1891) 1–48.

———. *Quaestionum in Heptateuchum libri VII.* Ed. I. Fraipont. CCL 33 (1958) 1–377.

———. *Sermones.* Ed. C. Lambot. CCL 41 (1961).

Bede. *De temporum ratione liber.* Ed. C. W. Jones. CCL 123B (1977).

Benedicti regula. Ed. R. Hanslik. CSEL 75 (1977).

Burchard of Worms. *Decretorum libri XX.* PL 140.537–1058.

Canones apostolorum. Ed. C. H. Turner. In *Ecclesiae occidentalis monumenta iuris antiquissima. Canonum et conciliorum Graecorum interpretationes latinae* (1899–1939).

Die Chroniken Bertholds von Reichenau und Bernolds von Konstanz 1054-1100. Ed. Ian S. Robinson. MGH, Scriptores rerum Germanicarum, n.s. 14. Hanover: Hahnsche Buchhandlung, 2003.

Cicero. *De inventione rhetorica.* Trans. H. M. Hubbell. Loeb Classical Library 2. Cambridge, MA: Harvard University Press, 1949.

Claudius of Turin. *Quaestiones XXX super libros Regum.* PL 104.623–810.

Collectio Dionysio-Hadriana. PL 67.39–346.

Diogenes Laertius. *De vitis . . . clarorum philosophorum.* Ed. Otto Holtz. Leipzig: Tauchnitz, 1895.

Epiphanius. *Adversus haereses* [*Panarion*]. In *Epiphanii . . . Opera.* Ed. G. Dindorfus. 3 vols. Leipzig: T. O. Weigel, 1859–1861.

Eutropius. *Breviarium ab urbe condita.* Ed. H. Droysen. MGH Auct.ant. 2 (1879).

Gallia Christiana in provincias ecclesiasticas distributa. Ed. Monachorum Congregationis S. Mauri ordinis S. Benedicti [the Maurists]. 1744. Repr. Westmead, Farnborough, Hants, England: Gregg International, 1970.

Gelasius I. *Tractatus.* Ed. A. Thiel. *Epistolae Romanorum pontificum genuinae* 1 (1867–1868) 510–607.

Gennadius. *De scriptoribus ecclesiasticis.* PL 58.1053–1120.

———. *Liber de ecclesiasticis dogmatibus veteris.* PL 58.979–1000.

Gregory I. *Dialogi.* 3 vols. Ed. A. de Vogüe. SC 251, 260, and 265 (1978–1980).

———. *Homiliae xl in Evangelia.* PL 76.1075–1312.

———. *Moralia.* Ed. Mark Adriaen. CCL 143, 143A (1979); 143B (1985).

———. *Registrum epistolarum.* 2 vols. Ed. P. Ewald and L. M. Hartmann, MGH Epp. 1 and 2 (1891/1899). Ed. D. Norberg, CCL 140 (1892) (cites from MGH).

———. *Règle Pastorale.* Ed. Floribert Rommel [French]. Trans. Charles Morel. SC 381–382. Paris: Éditions du Cerf (1992).

———. *Sermones de vetero Testamento.* Ed. Cyril Lambot, O.S.B. CCL 46, 11/1. Turnholt: Brepols (1961).

Horace. *Carmina.* In *The Odes and Epodes.* Trans. C. E. Bennett. Loeb Classical Library 33. Cambridge, MA: Harvard University Press, 1952.

Innocent I. *Epistulae.* PL 20.463–612.

Isidore of Seville. *De haeresibus liber.* Ed. Angel Custodio Vega. Scriptores ecclesiastici hispano-latini veteris et medii aevi, fasc. 5. Madrid: typis augustinianis Monasterii Escurialensis, 1940.

———. *Etymologiarum sive originum libri XX.* Ed. W. M. Lindsay. Oxford, 1911.

———. *Quaestiones. In Exodum.* PL 83.287–322.

———. *Quaestiones. In Numeros.* PL 83.339–60.

Jerome. *Commentariorum in Matheum libri quattuor IV.* Ed. D. Hurst and M. Adriaen. CCL 77 (1969).

———. *Epistulae.* 3 vols. Ed. I. Hilberg. CSEL 54–56 (1910–1918). See especially *Epist.* 58 (*ad Paulinum*) in CSEL 54 (1910).

———. *Liber interpretationis hebraicorum nominum.* Ed. P. de Lagarde. CCL 72 (1959) (cited here as Jerome, *Nom. hebr.*, with text divisions).

John the Deacon. *Sancti Gregorii Magni vita.* PL 75.59–242.

Juvenal. *Saturae.* Ed. A. E. Housman. Cambridge: Cambridge University Press, 1931.

Leo I. *Epistulae.* PL 54.551–1218.

———. *Sermons.* Trans. René Dolle. 2d ed. SC 22/1–2, 74, 200. Paris: Éditions du Cerf (1961–1973).

Odorannus of Sens. *Ad Everardum monachum, de tribus quaestionibus.* In *Opera omnia,* ed. Robert-Henri Bautier, Monique Gilles, Marie-Elisabeth Duchez, and Michel Hugo. Paris: Éditions du Centre National de la Recherche scientifique, 1972.

Petrus Damiani. *Die Briefe des Petrus Damiani.* 4 vols. Ed. K. Reindel. In MGH *Die Briefe der deutschen Kaiserzeit* (1983–1993) (=Reindel, *Briefe*).

———. *Sermones.* Ed. G. Lucchesi. CCCM 57 (1983).

Poenitentiale Egberti. Ed. F. W. Wasserschleben. *Die Bussordnungen der abendländischen Kirche* (1851) 231–47.

Pseudo-Isidore. *Decretales Pseudo-Isidorianae et capitula Angilramni.* Ed. P. Hinschius. Leipzig, 1863.

Pseudo-Jerome. *Quaestiones hebraicae in librum Regum et Paralipomenon.* PL 23.1329–1402.

Regino of Prum. *De ecclesiasticis disciplinis et religione Christiana libri duo.* PL 132.185–370.

Turner, C. H., ed. *Ecclesiae occidentalis monumenta iuris antiquissima. Canonum et conciliorum Graecorum interpretationes latinae.* 2 vols. Oxford: Clarendon Press, 1899–1939.

Victorius of Aquitaine. *Cursus paschalis annorum DXXXII ad Hilarum archidiaconum ecclesiae Romanae.* Ed. Th. Mommsen. MGH Auct.ant. 9 (1982). Reprinted by Krusch, *Studien zur christlichen ma. Chronologie. Die Entstehung unserer heutigen Zeitrechnung I. Victorius.* Ersatz der fehlerhaften Ausgagen Mommsens in den M. G. (Aus Abh. Berlin, Jahrgang 1937, Nr. 8, 1938).

Virgil. *Georgica.* Ed. R. A. B. Mynors. Oxford: Clarendon Press, 1990.

Literature

Blum, Owen J. *St. Peter Damian: His Teaching on the Spiritual Life.* The Catholic University of America. Studies in Mediaeval History N.S. 10 (1947).

———. "Alberic of Monte Cassino and a Letter of St. Peter Damian to Hildebrand." *Studi Gregoriani* 5 (1956): 291–98.

Browe, Peter. *Die häufige Kommunion im Mittelalter.* Münster: Regensbergsche Verlagsbuchhandlung, 1938.

Bruyn, D. de. "Une lettre inédite de S. Pierre Damian." *Revue bénédictine* 31 (1914–19): 92–93.

Bynum, Caroline Walker. *Holy Feast and Holy Fast: The Religious Significance of Food to Medieval Women.* Berkeley, Los Angeles, London: University of California Press, 1987.

Čâernik, Peter. "Per la storia del lessico economico medievale: le 'epistolae' di Pier Damiani (1043–1069)." *Studi medievali* 40/2 (1999): 633–80.

Dictionnaire Encyclopédique de la Bible. Turnholt: Brepols, 1987.

Dressler, Fridolin. *Petrus Damiani. Leben und Werk.* Studia Anselmiana 34. Rome: Herder, 1954.

Duchesne, Louis. *Fastes épiscopaux de l'ancienne Gaule.* 2 vols. Paris: Fontemoing, 1910.

Fournier, Paul. "Études critiques sur le Décret de Burchard de Worms." *Nouvelle revue historique de droit français et étranger* 34 (1910): 41–112; 213–21; 289–331; 564–84.

Gilchrist, John. "*Simoniaca heresis* and the Problem of Orders from Leo IX to Gratian." Pages 209–35 in *Proceedings of the Second International Conference of Medieval Canon Law at Boston, 1963.* Ed. Stephan Kuttner and J. J. Ryan. Monumenta iuris canonici C1, 1965. Vatican City, 1964.

———, ed. *Diversorum patrum sententie sive Collectio in LXXIV titulos digesta.* Monumenta iuris canonici 1. Vatican City, 1973.

———, trans. *The Collection in Seventy-Four Titles: A Canon Law Manual of the Gregorian Reform.* Mediaeval Sources in Translation 22. Toronto, 1980.

Grundmann, Herbert, ed. *Gebhardt Handbuch der Deutschen Geschichte.* 9th ed. Stuttgart: Union Verlag Stuttgart, 1970.

Jestice, Phyllis. "Peter Damian Against the Reformers." In *The Joy of Learning and the Love of God. Studies in Honor of Jean Leclercq.* Ed. E. Rozanne Elder. Cistercian Studies Series 160. Kalamazoo, MI: Cistercian Publications, 1995. Pp. 67–94.

Leclercq, Jean. "Simoniaca heresies." *Studi Gregoriani* 1 (1947): 523–30.

Lokrantz, Margareta. *L'opera poetica di S. Pier Damiani.* Studia Latina Stockholmiensia 12. Stockholm, 1964.

Lucchesi, Giovanni. *Clavis S. Petri Damiani.* Faenza, 1970 (=Lucchesi, *Clavis*).

———. "Per una vita di San Pier Damiani. Componenti cronologiche e topografiche." In *San Pier Damiano nel IX centenario della morte (1072–1972),* vols. 1 (1972) 13–179 (Nos. 1–153) and 2 (1972) 13–160 (Nos. 154–231) (=Lucchesi, *Vita*).

Meyer, Heinz and Rudolf Suntrup. *Lexikon der mittelalterlichen Zahlenbedeutung.* Münstersche Mittelalter-Schriften 56. München: W. Fink, 1987 (=Meyer-Suntrup, *Lexicon*).

Michel, Anton. *Papstwahl und Königsrecht, oder, Das Papstwahl-konkordat von 1059.* Munich: M. Hueber, 1936.

Mittarelli, Johanne-Benedicto and Anselmo Costandoni, eds. *Annales Camaldulensis Ordinis Sancti Benedicti.* Venice: 1756. Repr. Westmead, Farnborough, Hants, England: Gregg International, 1970.

Mombritius, Boninus. *Vita s. Silvestri* in *Sanctuarium seu vitae Sanctorum.* New ed. by the Monks of Solesmes [Monachi Solesmenses]. 2 vols. Paris: Fontemoing, 1910.

Neukirch, Franz. *Das Leben des Petrus Damiani.* Göttingen: Gebrüder Hofer, 1875.

Noonan, J. T. *The Morality of Abortion.* Cambridge, MA: Harvard University Press, 1970.

Pelster, Franz. "Der Dekret Bischof Burkhards von Worms in Vatikanischen Hss." *Miscellanea Giovanni Mercati* 2, *Studi e Testi* 122 (1946): 114–57.

Pierucci, Celestino and Alberto Polverari. *Carte di Fonte Avellana* 1. Thesaurus ecclesiarum Italiae 9.1. Rome: Edizioni di storia e letteratura, 1972.

Reindel, Kurt. "Studien zur Überlieferung der Werke des Petrus Damiani I–III." DA 15 (1959) 23–102; 16 (1960) 73–154; 18 (1962) 317–417 (=Reindel, *Studien*).

Resnick, Irven M. "Odo of Tournai and Peter Damian. Poverty and Crisis in the Eleventh Century." *Revue bénédictine* 98, 1/2 (1988): 114–40.

Ryan, J. Joseph. *Saint Peter Damiani and His Canonical Sources. A Preliminary Study in the Antecedents of the Gregorian Reform.* Pontifical Institute of Mediaeval Studies. Studies and Texts 2. Toronto: Pontificum Institutum Studiorum Mediae Aetatis, 1956 (=Ryan, *Sources*).

Silvestre, Hubert. "Nouveaux témoignages médiévaux de la 'Littera Pythagorae.'" *Le moyen âge* 79 (1973): 201–7.

———. "Pour le dossier de l'Y pythagoricien. Nouveaux témoignages." *Le moyen âge* 84 (1978): 201–9.

Spijker, Ineke van 't. *Fictions of the Inner Life: Religious Literature and Formation of the Self in the Eleventh and Twelfth Centuries.* Disputatio 4. Turnholt: Brepols, 2004.

Struve, Tilman. "Die Romreise der Kaiserin Agnes." *HJb* 105 (1985): 1–29.

Werner, Ernst. "Pietro Damiano ed il movimento popolare del suo tempo." *Studi Gregoriani* 10 (1975): 287–315.

Wilmart, André. "Une lettre de S. Pierre Damien à l'impératrice Agnes." *Revue bénédictine* 44 (1932): 125–46.

CONCORDANCE

Since the new edition of Damian's letters in Kurt Reindel, *Die Briefe der Petrus Damiani*, MGH Die Briefe der deutschen Kaiserzeit (München, 1983) has assigned new numbers in chronological order, the old system of number for *epistolae* and *opuscula* is now outmoded. To correlate the new with the old, the following concordance is herewith provided. There is no longer a distinction between "letters" and "works," and *Letters* 171–180 are placed at the end of the series because they are undatable.

MGH (Chronological) Numeration in Earlier Editions

Reindel	Migne Number	Reindel	Migne Number
1	opusc. 2 and 3	27	epist. 6, 24 = opusc. 48
2	epist. 7, 15	28	opusc. 11
3	epist. 3, 2	29	epist. 6, 15
4	epist. 3, 3	30	epist. 4, 4
5	epist. 4,2	31	opusc. 7
6	epist. 6, 6	32	epist. 4, 13
7	epist. 3, 5	33	epist. 1, 4
8	epist. 5, 12	34	epist. 4, 10
9	epist. 6, 28	35	epist. 5, 6
10	epist. 6, 23	36	epist. 5, 17 = opusc. 8/2
11	epist. 2, 19	37	epist. 6, 7
12	epist. 4, 6	38	opusc. 16
13	epist. 1, 1	39	epist. 5, 9 = opusc. 27
14	epist. 4, 7	40	opusc. 6
15	epist. 8, 4	41	Ad Heinricum
16	epist. 1, 2	42	Ad Odalricum
17	opusc. 10	43	epist. 7, 1
18	opusc. 14	44	epist. 6, 30 = opusc. 51
19	opusc. 8/1	45	epist. 5, 8
20	epist. 7, 2	46	epist. 1, 5
21	epist. 8, 8	47	epist. 4, 14 = opusc. 26
22	epist. 4, 5	48	epist. 2, 1
23	epist. 8, 9 = opusc. 58	49	epist. 2, 5
24	epist. 6, 14 = opusc. 29	50	opusc. 15
25	epist. 8,7 = opusc. 42/2	51	epist. 7, 14
26	epist. 1, 3	52	epist. 2, 4

Reindel	Migne Number	Reindel	Migne Number
53	Ad Iohannem	97	epist. 2, 2 = opusc. 31
54	epist. 6, 18 = opusc. 46	98	epist. 1, 18 = opusc 24
55	epist. 6, 19	99	epist. 3, 6
56	epist. 6, 27	100	epist. 6, 5
57	epist. 1, 10 = opusc. 20	101	epist. 3, 7
58	epist. 3, 4	102	epist. 2, 15 = opusc. 34/1
59	epist. 3, 9 = opusc. 25	103	epist. 6, 2
60	epist. 1, 7	104	epist. 7, 5 = opusc. 56
61	epist. 1, 6 = opusc. 17	105	epist. 6,8 = opusc. 21
62	epist. 4, 11	106	epist. 2, 14 = opusc. 33
63	epist. 2, 9	107	epist. 1, 16
64	epist. 7, 9	108	epist. 1, 17 = opusc. 23
65	opusc. 5	109	epist. 1, 19 = Vita
66	epist. 7, 19 = opusc. 50		Rodulphi et Dominici
67	epist. 7, 11 = opusc. 57/1	110	opusc. 9
68	epist. 7, 12 = opusc. 57/2	111	epist. 3, 8 = opusc. 39
69	epist. 2, 3 = opusc. 22	112	epist. 4, 3 = opusc. 18/2
70	epist. 5, 16 = opusc. 42/1	113	epist. 6, 4
71	epist. 7, 4	114	epist. 7, 16 = opusc. 18/3
72	epist. 1, 9 = opusc. 19	115	epist. 4, 16
73	epist. 4, 1	116	epist. 6, 10
74	epist. 4, 12	117	epist. 6, 17 = opusc. 45
75	epist. 2, 8	118	epist. 6, 35 = opusc 55
76	epist. 6, 31 = opusc. 53	119	epist. 2, 17 = opusc 36
77	epist. 5, 5	120	epist. 7, 3
78	epist. 6, 11 = opusc. 44	121	epist. 5, 1
79	epist. 1, 8	122	epist. 1, 11
80	epist. 4,17 = opusc. 40	123	epist. 6, 21 = opusc. 47
81	opusc. 1	124	epist. 7, 6
82	epist. 2, 12	125	epist. 6, 3
83	epist. 8, 5	126	epist. 2, 20 = opusc. 37/1
84	epist. 5, 7	127	epist. 2, 21 = opusc. 37/2
85	epist. 8, 3	128	Ad Ambrosium et
86	epist. 2,18 = opusc. 52		Liupardum
87	epist. 4, 9	129	epist. 5, 14 and 5, 15
88	epist. 1, 20	130	epist. 7, 7
89	epist. 1, 21 and opusc. 4	131	epist. 6, 13
90	epist. 2, 13	132	epist. 6, 26 = opusc. 49
91	epist. 3, 1 = opusc. 38	133	epist. 6, 34
92	epist. 6, 16 = opusc. 59	134	epist. 6, 36
93	epist. 8, 13	135	Ad Cinthium
94	epist. 8, 14	136	epist. 8, 12
95	epist. 2, 11	137	epist. 6, 33 = opusc. 54
96	epist. 1, 15	138	epist. 5, 2

Numeration of Earlier Editions in MGH

Migne Number	Reindel	Migne Number	Reindel
epist. 2, 19	11	epist. 5, 14	129
epist. 2, 20 = opusc. 37/1	126	epist. 5, 15	129
epist. 2, 21 = opusc. 37/2	127	epist. 5, 16 = opusc. 42/1	70
epist. 3, 1 = opusc. 38	91	epist. 5, 17 = opusc. 8/2	36
epist. 3, 2	3	epist. 5, 18	177
epist. 3, 3	4	epist. 5, 19 = opusc. 28	spuria
epist. 3, 4	58	epist. 6, 1 = opusc. 43	161
epist. 3, 5	7	epist. 6, 2	103
epist. 3, 6	99	epist. 6, 3	125
epist. 3, 7	101	epist. 6, 4	113
epist. 3, 8 = opusc. 39	111	epist. 6, 5	100
epist. 3, 9 = opusc. 25	59	epist. 6, 6	6
epist. 3, 10 = opusc. 34/2	168	epist. 6, 7	37
epist. 4, 1	73	epist. 6, 8 = opusc. 21	105
epist. 4, 2	5	epist. 6, 9	176
epist. 4, 3 = opusc. 18/2	112	epist. 6, 10	116
epist. 4, 4	30	epist. 6, 11 = opusc. 44	78
epist. 4, 5	22	epist. 6, 12	152
epist. 4, 6	12	epist. 6, 13	131
epist. 4, 7	14	epist. 6, 14 = opusc. 29	24
epist. 4, 8	157	epist. 6, 15	29
epist. 4, 9	87	epist. 6, 16 = opusc. 59	92
epist. 4, 10	34	epist. 6, 17 = opusc. 45	117
epist. 4, 11	62	epist. 6, 18 = opusc. 46	54
epist. 4, 12	74	epist. 6, 19	55
epist. 4, 13	32	epist. 6, 20	150
epist. 4, 14 = opusc. 26	47	epist. 6, 21 = opusc. 47	123
epist. 4, 15	174	epist. 6, 22	158
epist. 4, 16	115	epist. 6, 23	10
epist. 4, 17 = opusc. 40	80	epist. 6, 24 = opusc. 48	27
epist. 5, 1	121	epist. 6, 25	169
epist. 5, 2	138	epist. 6, 26 = opusc. 49	132
epist. 5, 3	163	epist. 6, 27	56
epist. 5, 4 = part of		epist. 6, 28	9
opusc. 18/1	162	epist. 6, 29	166
epist. 5, 5	77	epist. 6, 30 = opusc. 51	44
epist. 5, 6	35	epist. 6, 31 = opusc. 53	76
epist. 5, 7	84	epist. 6, 32	142
epist. 5, 8	45	epist. 6, 33 = opusc. 54	137
epist. 5, 9 = opusc. 27	39	epist. 6, 34	133
epist. 5, 10	147	epist. 6, 35 = opusc. 55	118
epist. 5, 11 = opusc. 41	172	epist. 6, 36	134
epist. 5, 12	8	epist. 7, 1	43
epist. 5, 13	141	epist. 7, 2	20

Migne Number	Reindel	Migne Number	Reindel
epist. 7, 3	120	opusc. 13	153
epist. 7, 4	71	opusc. 14	18
epist. 7, 5 = opusc. 56	104	opusc. 15	50
epist. 7, 6	124	opusc. 16	38
epist. 7, 7	130	opusc. 17 = epist. 1, 6	61
epist. 7, 8	144	opusc. 18/1 = epist. 2, 10	162
epist. 7, 9	64	opusc. 18/2 = epist. 4, 3	112
epist. 7, 10	154	opusc. 18/3 = epist. 7, 16	114
epist. 7, 11 = opusc. 57/1	67	opusc. 19 = epist. 1, 9	72
epist. 7, 12 = opusc. 57/2	68	opusc. 20 = epist. 1, 10	57
epist. 7, 13	148	opusc. 21 = epist. 6, 8	105
epist. 7, 14	51	opusc. 22 = epist. 2, 3	69
epist. 7, 15	2	opusc. 23 = epist. 1, 17	108
epist. 7, 16 = opusc. 18/3	114	opusc. 24 = epist. 1, 18	98
epist. 7, 17	151	opusc. 25 = epist. 3, 9	59
epist. 7, 18	143	opusc. 26 = epist. 4, 14	47
epist. 7, 19 = opusc. 50	66	opusc. 27 = epist. 5, 9	39
epist. 8, 1	145	opusc. 28 = epist. 5, 19	spurium
epist. 8, 2	155	opusc. 29 = epist. 6, 14	24
epist. 8, 3	85	opusc. 30 = epist. 8, 11	146
epist. 8, 4	15	opusc. 31 = epist. 2, 2	97
epist. 8, 5	83	opusc. 32 = epist. 2, 7	160
epist. 8, 6	179	opusc. 33 = epist. 2, 14	106
epist. 8, 7 = opusc. 42/2	25	opusc. 34/1 = epist. 2, 15	102
epist. 8, 8	21	opusc. 34/2 = epist. 3, 10	168
epist. 8, 9 = opusc. 58	23	opusc. 35 = epist. 2, 16	159
epist. 8, 10	170	opusc. 36 = epist. 2, 17	119
epist. 8, 11 = opusc. 30	146	opusc. 37/1 = epist. 2, 20	126
epist. 8, 12	136	opusc. 37/2 = epist. 2, 21	127
epist. 8, 13	93	opusc. 38 = epist. 3, 1	91
epist. 8, 14	94	opusc. 39 = epist. 3, 8	111
epist. 8, 15	171	opusc. 40 = epist. 4, 17	80
opusc. 1	81	opusc. 41 = epist. 5, 1	172
opusc. 2	1	opusc. 42/1 = epist. 5, 16	70
opusc. 3	1	opusc. 42/2 = epist. 8, 7	25
opusc. 4	89	opusc. 43 = epist. 6, 1	161
opusc. 5	65	opusc. 44 = epist. 6, 11	78
opusc. 6	40	opusc. 45 = epist. 6, 17	117
opusc. 7	31	opusc. 46 = epist. 6, 18	54
epist. 8/1	19	opusc. 47 = epist. 6, 21	123
opusc. 8/2 = epist. 5, 17	36	opusc. 48 = epist. 6, 24	27
opusc. 9	110	opusc. 49 = epist. 6, 26	132
opusc. 10	17	opusc. 50 = epist. 7, 19	66
opusc. 11	28	opusc. 51 = epist. 6, 30	44
opusc. 12	165	opusc. 52 = epist. 2, 18	86

Letters That Are Not Found in Migne

LETTERS
151–180

LETTER 151

Peter Damian to Rainerius II, marquis of Monte S. Maria, a dependency of Tuscany. As a penance for sins that the marquis had confessed to Damian, the latter ordered him to go on a pilgrimage to Jerusalem. Rainerius demurred, citing the difficulties and dangers of the long journey. Using several contemporary *exempla,* Damian explains that while the way is long and perilous, God in his goodness will provide for his safety.

(1067)

O SIR RAINERIUS, the illustrious marquis, the monk Peter the sinner sends his greetings.

(2) For the sins you confessed to me, noble sir, I have enjoined you to travel to Jerusalem, and thus appease divine justice by the penance of this long pilgrimage. But since, according to Scripture, you have no idea what tomorrow will bring,[1] you are putting off this matter until later; and while fearing the uncertainties of the journey, you are not providing for yourself a secure city in which you might live. And so, in your case we see the pronouncement carried out that says: "He who watches the wind never sows, and he who keeps his eye on the clouds never reaps."[2]

(3) Obviously, I maintain a certain restraint and regularity in assigning this kind of penance, so that I do not indiscriminately deny permission for this journey to all who come to me for counsel, nor do I let down the barriers for all who wish to go. Indeed those who live under a rule, and properly observe the dictate of the canonical or monastic life, I persuade to persevere in the vocation in which they find themselves, and not to neglect necessary tasks in favor of those left to our free choice. In this regard, John says: "Hold fast what you have, and let no one rob

1. Cf. Jas 4.14.   2. Eccl 11.4.

you of your crown."[3] But I exhort those who serve the world in the military, or who are dedicated to the service of God, but are unfaithful to their profession, to undertake this journey as a sort of spiritual exile, and to make satisfaction to the awesome judge, whose laws and commands they have not observed at home while engaged in the stress of everyday living. By wandering about in this fashion on their pilgrimage, they may provide for themselves a quiet dwelling in their homeland.

(4) Therefore, my dear friend, do not conjure up every possible thing you can invent or imagine, and like a woman do not fear misfortunes that might happen unexpectedly, but "trust in the Lord and do good."[4] For often, the more anxious we are because of our dependence on human reason, the more readily divine goodness comes to our aid; and when we despair of human comfort we often become aware of God's assistance.

(5) And now to say a few words about the pilgrimage with which we are concerned. It came to my attention from the report of my brother and fellow monk, Richard,[5] a man of upright life and sterling honesty, that this very year eight men are returning from Jerusalem, having fulfilled the vow they had been so piously intent on making. But as they walked through uninhabited regions, and had been suffering for four days without food, as one man they began to beg God's mercy to help them in their great necessity, and that "he who gives food to all his creatures,"[6] should not deny them at least some nourishment in their hour of need. Just as they had finished praying, they saw a loaf of bread of enormous size and marvelous brightness lying in the road. They wondered at this sight before their very eyes, not unaware, to be sure, that something of such great weight could not have fallen unnoticed from the pack of him who carried it. They at once recognized this bounty as evidence of God's goodness, and since there were eight of them, they divided the bread, divinely provided for them, into just that many

3. Rev 3.11.   4. Ps 36.3.
5. At the time of this letter, Richard was still a simple monk. But in 1070 he was the *rector* of the monastery of Camporeggiano, on which see Peter Damian, *Letter* 169.5.
6. Ps 135.25.

pieces. With this bread they satisfied their hunger in such agreeable and sufficient fashion, that never again, as long as they lived, did they ever enjoy such delicious and abundant food.

(6) Our same brother Richard told me of another event which I cannot pass over in silence. He related that our brother Agius, a man advanced in years and outstanding for his religious observance, when still a layman used to pray fervently in the church of blessed Michael the Archangel that stood near Siponto on Monte Gargano. He and his brother, also a layman, had only one horse which both of them rode, each taking his turn, and thus they lightened the fatigue of the journey. But when he saw that their fellow travelers needed help to carry their baggage, he told his brother that they should both discontinue riding their beast, and out of charity to their companions offer it to carry their bags. However, as they were exhausted from this long and difficult trip, they stopped for a while to get some rest. While they were refreshing themselves with food, brother Agius, whom I mentioned before, broke up some bread into a cup of wine, and setting it down beside him, postponed his meal for a while, and fell asleep.

(7) While they were both napping, robbers suddenly came upon them, and snatching their horse and everything else that they had, made off. One of them, however, remained behind, and gulped down brother Agius's bread and wine. At that, he experienced an intolerable pain, and until he was able to vomit up everything he had swallowed, he had no relief from the deadly distress he felt in his stomach. Then jumping up with surprising agility, he quickly ran after his companions, and persuaded them that unless they at once returned the animal to the servant of God, they would never elude the danger of divine vengeance that threatened them. Terrified before heaven, they immediately went back to the man of God, with tears in their eyes begged forgiveness for their reckless deed, and restored the horse along with everything else that they had taken. And so, God's protective goodness was not so far away, that he could not help those[7] whom he saw devotedly engaged in serving him.

7. Cf. Ps 21.20.

(8) Bonizo, another brother of ours, a holy man long in the
service of God, who had already lived many years in the hermitage, and whose weakness, brought on by old age, did not
cause him to mitigate the rigors of his austere life, as he himself
told me, once suffered shipwreck as he was returning by sea
from Jerusalem. In the angry waves the ship went down, and all
his companions were lost in the wild storm. But he took hold of
a sack that was filled with baled cotton,[8] and riding on it amid
the rolling waves for almost three days and two nights, like a
man fighting for his life, he battled the sea and held death at
bay. Then it happened that several oarsmen in their boat came
cutting through the waves, saw him from some distance away,
and after generously rescuing him and giving him something
to eat, treated him most kindly. And so, he who managed to
save Paul, adrift for twenty-four hours on the open sea,[9] also
kept this brother afloat amid the wash of contending waves, lest
he be swallowed up by the storm. And he, by whose power the
voracious beast discharged Jonah from his maw,[10] also commanded a gentle sea to support this man, not allowing him to
drown, but bringing him to safety.

(9) Therefore, noble sir, meditate on these and similar flowers of heavenly mercy, do not depend on your own ability, but,
as is only proper, place your trust in the unfailing protection of
him who is almighty. Our ignoble body is afraid, but the native
ardor of a courageous soul is already on fire. Set out, be up and
doing, and join the fight, for he who rewards our determination will lead the pilgrimage. It is your task to take on this journey, but it is God who directs the steps of those who search for
him. He who causes the generous heart to love, brings our
good works to fruition. And he who encourages the human
spirit to do well, undoubtedly will fulfill the vows that our piety
suggests to us.

8. This is one of the earliest references to cotton *(bombax)* in Western literature. Cf. *Mittellateinisches Wörterbuch* 1, 1515–16, s. v. *bombyx;* also J. F. Niermeyer,
Mediae latinitatis lexicon minus (Leiden, 1976), 101, s. v. *bombyx.*
    9. Cf. 2 Cor 11.25.
    10. Cf. Jon 2.11.

LETTER 152

Peter Damian to abbot J——. Responding to the charge that he was in violation of the *Rule* of St. Benedict in accepting monks who left the monastery to enter the eremitical life, Damian defends his actions as those of a true Benedictine. Benedict, he states, wrote the *Rule* for cenobites, that is, for beginners in the spiritual life. Far from forbidding their withdrawal to hermit living, he advised, taught, and exhorted them to do so after their probation period in the monastery. There seems little doubt from this letter that Damian considered himself and his congregation to be in the family of "our holy father St. Benedict," and that Fonte Avellana and its dependent hermitages were fulfilling the instructions of the *Rule* and living in the tradition of the founder.

(After 1067)

 O SIR J——,[1] the venerable abbot, the monk Peter the sinner sends the affection of sincere charity.

(2) With proper gratitude, venerable father, I have received the letter from your holiness, to which, as the subject requires, I here briefly reply. For you are angry with me, and complain that I am accepting your monks into the hermitage contrary to the precepts of our holy father, St. Benedict, who decreed that those who leave some other known monastery should not receive entrance into the houses of strangers.[2] With all due respect, I can easily overcome the obstacle of this reproach, since this holy man obviously established monasteries subject to the rules that he prescribed, but claimed no authority over hermits. For after enumerating four kinds of monks, he immediately added: "Therefore, omitting all reference to

1. Some have thought that this letter was addressed to John of Fécamp; cf. G. Lucchesi, *Vita* 2, p. 153, n. 83.
2. Cf. *Benedicti regula* 61.13 (CSEL 75.157).

these, let me now, with the Lord's help, lay out regulations for that most valiant type, the cenobites."[3] And so, he who set about legislating only for the group known as cenobites, clearly indicated that he did not have an order of hermits in mind. But let me here quote this holy man's very words, so that we may be sure whether he was writing about cenobites or hermits. "Let the abbot be careful," he said, "never to receive in residence a monk of some other known monastery as a member of his community without the consent of his abbot."[4] Since he was speaking to the abbot of a monastery, and not to the prior of a hermitage, he plainly shows that whatever he wrote was not intended for hermits, but was rather enjoined on cenobites.

(3) Now that I have already clearly demonstrated that St. Benedict did not forbid a monk of another monastery to be received into a hermitage, let me now show that he even promoted such a practice, namely, that a monk should leave the monastery for the hermitage. What follows are not my words, but those of our common father: "The second type," he said, "are the anchorites or hermits, that is, those who are not in the first fervor of their conversion, but after long probation in a monastery, have learned how to fight against the devil, trained by the help of many brethren. They go out well armed from the ranks of the community to single combat in the desert. They are able now to live in safety without the help of others, and by their own strength and God's assistance to fight against the temptations of both the flesh and the mind."[5] From these words, therefore, one can obviously gather that the beneficent teacher not only did not forbid a brother to depart from a monastery for the hermitage, but even advised, taught, and with a certain amount of persuasion, encouraged it.

(4) In fact, he even sanctions a brother after long probation in a monastery, to learn how to fight in a hermitage against the machinations of the clever tempter. In his former surroundings he begins the struggle, assisted by the support of the community, so that later he might strive constantly and untiringly by his

3. *Benedicti regula* 1.13 (CSEL 75.20).
4. *Benedicti regula* 61.13 (CSEL 75.157).
5. *Benedicti regula* 1.3–5 (CSEL 75.18–19).

own strength, not succumbing to the onslaught of carnal vices or mental temptations. There he was a raw recruit, but here he is a knight. There, as one who was green and unformed, he was accustomed to combat under the direction of a drillmaster, but here at full strength, he does not shrink from the fight or refuse single combat as a champion of Christ. There, like a boy, he plays at training for combat, but here with a sure hand he buckles on his weapons for battle, and does not fear to engage in hand-to-hand fighting. There he was a man coming from the world, like one entering the small town of Zoar after leaving Sodom; but when he passed over to the hermitage, with Lot he now went up into the hill country.[6]

(5) Therefore, for one wishing to reach the heights of perfection, the monastery must be transitional, and not a place to stay; not a home, but a hostel; not the destination we intend to reach, but a quiet stop along the way. Indeed, one registers as a cleric, that the bishop may select him for promotion to ecclesiastical orders; one enters the schools of the grammarians, that when he becomes proficient in the arts he may depart. And lastly, one strives to learn the ordinances of the law, that he might engage in actions at court and perform brilliantly in the tribunals of judges. And just as these do not intend to spend their life in what they are presently doing, but undoubtedly have another goal in mind, so also a monk who is not impeded by age or infirmity, remains physically in the monastery, but with all the strength he can muster should strive toward entering the hermitage. And thus, while intending like a noble tree to strike roots in the desert, he disciplines himself for a time in the monastery by the practice of obedience to the *Rule*, so that his life in the monastery might be nothing more than a preparation for the hermitage, and everything that he first practices in his life as a monk might tend to this higher purpose. So it was that Jacob served Laban as a shepherd for fourteen years only with the intention of marrying Rachel. Yet first he received Leah as his wife, but with all his love he yearned for the embrace of the beautiful Rachel.[7]

6. Cf. Gen 19.30.   7. Cf. Gen 29.20–30.

(6) Consequently, in these words of the holy *Rule* that I cited above, it is clearly stated that while St. Benedict takes a man into the monastery, he leads him to the hermitage. There, indeed, he gives him a home, but by his exhortation invites him to go elsewhere. Here he teaches him to begin his engagement in spiritual combat, but he instructs him to perfect the process there. Here he admonishes him to take up arms as a recruit, so that there he might not hesitate to cut down the ranks of the enemy and oppose the barbarous attacks of the vices.

(7) But perhaps it may be said that I am doing violence to the words of this holy man, and am construing them as I see fit, depending rather on assumptions than allowing truth to support me in this interpretation of his words. So, let us once again ask this most blessed man what he thinks about this point under discussion, to explain more plainly why these words of his, cited above, are found in the very introduction to the holy *Rule*. Let us now see how he brings this same *Rule* to its conclusion. There he says: "We have written out this *Rule* in order that, by practicing it in monasteries, we may show that we have attained some degree of virtue and the starting point of monastic life. But, for him who would hasten to a monastic life of perfection, there are the teachings of the holy Fathers, by observing which a man is led to the summit of perfection."[8]

(8) You see, then, that the eminent teacher established the beginning of the religious life in the monastery, but urged the one installed in it on to higher goals of piety, so that he might there begin to lead a God-fearing life, and adjust his moral attitudes in this enclosure of piety, and after fortifying himself by spiritual exercise climb to the heights of perfection like one abandoning milk for solid food. Now, an animal is conceived in its mother's womb that it might emerge. And certainly, the mother must abort if the fetus does not come to term. But we seem to wish that the womb should always remain distended, and that the child once conceived should not break free. A child is unfavorably endowed, if its teeth do not come forth from the gums when it is some years old, and its knees do not

---

8. *Benedicti regula* 73.1–3 (CSEL 75.180).

grow strong and allow it to walk. And what is more, since the *Rule* for cenobites gives evidence that it does not contain perfection, but clearly sends him who would be perfect to eremitical orders, why do we consider it of small account to climb to the heights of perfection ourselves, and, besides, prevent others from advancing to that which is better?

(9) When John saw Jesus walking by, he exclaimed: "Look, there is the Lamb of God."[9] And then the evangelist promptly added: "And the two disciples heard him say this, and followed Jesus."[10] What objection could John have, I ask, as he evidently preferred Jesus to himself, and his disciples indeed followed the better man? Therefore, if the *Rule* that leads the way directs those who flock to it to leave for the hermitage, how dare anyone living under the *Rule* object? For now it is as clear as day that he who protests against those who seek entrance into the hermitage, undoubtedly rebelliously opposes the *Rule* and contradicts it; and in depriving the words of the *Rule* of their authority, condemns the author of the holy *Rule* himself. The true mother hands over her son that he might live, while the false one asks that the sword of state should cut it in two.[11] Barzillai, who was eighty years old, mindful of the welfare of his son Chimham, did not ask him to provide for the support of his lame old age. And while he was in the service of King David, he did not refuse to help his destitute son.[12] Anthony sent Hilarion away, that alone he might rise to greater heights.[13] We hermits love the monks as we do asses, or certainly like deer. For men love these animals, not to benefit the animals, but for their own sake, that is, to provide meat for their own bodies, or that they might benefit from their labor. Men care for them for their own welfare, but are not concerned whether animals live or live poorly. As far as this is concerned, in order to obtain the monks' service we too consider an improvement in their welfare of little importance.

(10) Of this, moreover, we are certain: that blessed Benedict was a man devoted to life as a hermit, and that he undoubtedly

9. John 1.36.   10. John 1.37.
11. Cf. 1 Kgs 3.16–28.   12. Cf. 2 Sam 19.31–41.
13. Cf. Jerome, *Vita Hilarionis* 3 (FOTC 15.246–47).

wanted us to be what he was. And since, as he himself declared that "every man has his proper gift from God, one this gift and another that,"[14] but that "this is something which not everyone can accept,"[15] he first normatively established the smooth way of the monastic life there, so that, bruised by the strokes of discipline and strengthened by the practices [of the *Rule*], we might more easily climb to the highlands of the hermitage. And so, Benedict followed exactly the example of Paul. How shall we act, since he was an apostle and yet he urged people to marry? "Let each man," he said, "have his own wife and each woman her own husband. The husband must give the wife what is due to her, and the wife equally must give the husband his due."[16] But a little farther on he says: "I should like you all to be as I am myself."[17] Therefore, the apostle intended one thing, and taught another. He wished us to be celibate as he was himself because of the excellence and value of resplendent chastity, but he ordained that people should marry, because he feared the danger threatening our weak nature. By wishing me to be like him, he invited me to go higher; by offering marriage, he provided a support to keep me from falling. For his part, he was inclined toward the former, but unwillingly granted the latter. He preferred that I be what he was, rather than become what he was not. He wished that in every way I should remain close to him, rather than become a total stranger far from him. And just as blessed Paul preferred the unmarried state to monogamy or bigamy, and still allowed men to marry lest the weak lapse into concubinage, so also St. Benedict, while more readily wishing us to be what he was, that is, followers of the hermit life, still thought it better for us weak and feeble men to live less nobly in the haven of the monastery, than to perish in the stormy waves of a shipwrecked world.

(11) Therefore, the brothers who practice stability by living in the monastery are to be tolerated, but those who with a spir-

---

14. *Benedicti regula* 40.1 (CSEL 75.110); 1 Cor 7.7.
15. Matt 19.11. This quotation is not found in any critical edition of the *Regula*.
16. 1 Cor 7.2–3.
17. 1 Cor 7.7.

it of fervor transfer to the hermitage should receive the highest praise. The former, to be sure, seek shelter behind the shield of God's protecting hand, while the latter go forth into the field of battle and are awarded the badge of victory. The former defend what is theirs, but the latter bring back the spoils. With God as their defender, the former are invincible, but the latter are content each day to tread on the necks of their enemies. Ensconced within their walls, the monks battle to keep their attackers from entering, but the hermits drive the threatening ranks of the enemy far from their lines and force them to flee. And what more shall I say? The monks, indeed, are set apart from the world, but the hermits already speak familiarly with God, to whom they are joined by the intimate bonds of his love for them. The former guard the bronze altar,[18] the latter now enter the Holy of Holies.

(12) But now to add an epilogue at the conclusion of this letter, since I am accused of accepting monks from a known monastery, it becomes clear as day that in so doing, I am in no way giving offense to St. Benedict. For just as he did not impose on us who live in the hermitage certain tasks to perform, so too there is nothing at all that he forbade or enjoined us to avoid. And so, as I made sufficiently clear above, this celebrated teacher not only did not refuse a brother permission to move from the monastery into a hermitage, but he actually encouraged, promoted, and urged it. And to show beyond doubt how great his desire was in this regard, he set it at the beginning of his *Rule*, and spoke of it as he brought the *Rule* to a close. With this idea he began his holy book, and on this note, to increase the effect, he concluded it, so that it would seem that he was commanding it throughout the whole text. Moreover, while it is the norm for beginners who are learning to write, that they recommend the topics about which they will write, to catch the attention of the hearer, St. Benedict, not only at the outset of his *Rule*, but also at the end, depreciated his whole work by lightening and annulling it, so as to make the order of cenobites somewhat inferior to the eremitic life.

18. Cf. 2 Kgs 16.14–15.

(13) And thus, that brothers might ascend from monastic life to the hermitage, you should exhort them, and we must lovingly receive them, lest, which God forbid, like enemies we should appear to be torn away from this blessed man by schismatic dissension, but be truly recognized as his disciples, and in one spirit agree with him and among ourselves.

LETTER 153

Peter Damian to abbot Mainard of Pomposa (?).[1] In this exhortation to the monastic life, Damian pursues an extended explication of biblical texts that, understood allegorically, refer one to the struggle for spiritual perfection. He outlines the ideal monastic life, explains its requirements and its offices, and encourages his fellow monks to pass beyond the minimum standards established in the *Rule* of St. Benedict for the higher and more demanding calling of the eremitic life.

(after 1067)

O THE VENERABLE abbot lord M., and to the holy community, the monk Peter the sinner sends the obedience of most devoted service.

(2) Even though it may be impossible for a poor debtor to pay all that he owes, nevertheless to offer what little he has constitutes a release from the debt. Often, indeed, a peasant who has borrowed money lent at interest, who has brought to his creditor a gift of garden vegetables, is then absolved from the signed note of his obligation. And so accordingly I, who owe so much to your kindness, send this poor letter. Poor, I say, from my rustic manner, and not from its content, which has to do with the signs of the divine will, and which is a faithful deposit concerning deeds both old and new.

(3) Certainly you are not unaware, my brothers, of what I mention with tears, how far our order has fallen away from holy fervor, or rather how our order does not cease to fall further downward every day, as, having forgotten already almost all of the precepts from neglect, we seem to be content with only the outer garment of its profession. For we live in a worldly manner

1. For a discussion of the letter's addressee, variously identified in the manuscripts, see Reindel, *Briefe* 4, p. 13, n. 1.

under the guise of religion, and, having violated the spirit of the discipline, as we abandon ourselves to currents of illicit pleasures, we even possess in vain the name of monks since we have departed from the title of our nobility. We are like an illegitimate child who rejoices that he is known by his father's name, while the degenerate nature of his origin holds him back, by law, from inheritance. Now both Ishmael and all the sons of Keturah were said to be Abraham's sons, without distinction. But when the laws of succession became known, the inheritance was delivered whole in its entirety to Isaac,[2] namely, to the legitimate son; the concubines' sons received only gifts. "Bastard slips," says Solomon, "shall not provide deep roots."[3] Nor, I beg you, should you take what I say as an insult to yourselves. For you know well that kindling is best arranged where at least a spark of fire seems to remain. Who is so foolish as to blow on a spot from which he thinks all the heat has completely expired? Moreover, unless I expected better things from you through the grace of Christ, I would consider it useless, having put aside other tasks, to pursue you with a letter of exhortation.

(4) For this reason, beloved, with Christ's aid gather yourselves in strength, and fervently, or, rather, manfully and not sluggishly or torpidly, bear his service, on whose shield you swore, so that the foundations of your conversion,[4] which still occupy a sort of middle position, may not return through your negligence to nothing (may God forbid), but may instead achieve the height of perfection through the persistence of your abiding fervor. Remember what is said to the angel of the church of Sardis: "Be watchful and strengthen the things that remain that are ready to die, for I have not found your works full before my God."[5] Since he did not find his works full before God, he claimed that even those things that had already been done well were about to die. If what is dead in us is not kindled to life, then even what is held to be still alive, as it were, is extinguished. He who does not consummate what has been

2. Cf. Gen 21.9–21; 25.1–6.
3. Wis 4.3.
4. That is, the beginnings of the monastic life.
5. Rev 3.2.

done loses what he has accomplished. What good is it if a body begins to be formed in a mother's womb, and yet does not attain the fullness of natural growth? It is not hidden from you of what child it is said: "A woman, when she is in labor, has sorrow because her hour has come, but when she has borne a child she no longer remembers the anguish, for joy that a human being is born into the world."[6]

(5) God, who examines the deeds of every person and office, of every rank and order, on a balance of careful examination, and who has different scales for each order, clearly does not approve a work that has been aborted. Did he not have an appropriate balance for weighing the deeds of a king, and did he not place on it the acts of the one for whom he wrote on the wall with a hand: "Your kingdom is weighed in the balance, and is found wanting"?[7] And immediately after he added: "Your kingdom is divided and is given to the Medes and the Persians."[8]

(6) If God almighty took away from him both his life and kingdom for no crime other than that he did not find in him the fullness of good work befitting a king, what should he think of us, who even promised to scale the heights of perfection in our monastic profession, and yet still lie in the valley of our imperfection in a torpor of idleness? Is it only in order not to lose all that he acquired in some past labor that a man does not strive with all his might to complete what he aims at? What use is it, I ask you, for someone to have completed a part of a journey if he does not reach the destination? Moreover, if someone has greatly enraged the king and can return to his favor only if he weighs out one hundred pounds of silver, and is certain that after this debt owed to the royal court has been satisfied, he will receive not only favor, but also the official tokens of some great rank, will he not be foolish to allow the loss of ninety-nine pounds which have already been paid to the public treasury because he did not satisfy the debt with one pound remaining due? Is it not better for a person to pay fully the little that re-

6. John 16.21.   7. Dan 5.27.
8. Dan 5.28.

mains, to receive both favor and rank, than to lose what has already been given and, what is even more terrible, to remain subject to the king's displeasure?

(7) We have given, brothers, if I may say it boldly, we have given ninety pounds of silver to Christ our king, for whose sake we have abandoned possessions and spurned marriage, avoided the eating of meat, looked with horror upon the glory and pomp of the world, and exchanged the splendor of worldly dress for a humble garment. These are great things, these are difficult things, I confess, and they ought to be rewarded with great gifts of heavenly recompense. But something yet remains with which the appointed weight has to be completed, before one deserves to be admitted to the treasure house of the eternal king. You ask what this is? It occurs to me, actually, that I should answer you with this: obedience, love, joy, peace, patience, and the other virtues, which the preacher to the Gentiles enumerated.[9] But I want to treat this very briefly so that your mind will retain it more easily and, in this way, more perfectly. It is nothing else but this: zeal for God and mortification of self. For if the apostolic word should live in us, where it says: "Always bearing in our bodies the mortification of Jesus,"[10] then since carnal love will have no place to diffuse itself within us, necessarily all our delight, because it has been lifted up, will transfer itself to God, and our passion that is rising up will live there because it will have no place for diffusing itself within us. Moreover, a man who is prudent and intent upon safeguarding his salvation always keeps watch with such care to check the vices that he binds completely his loins and his reins, his belly and his sides, with the girdle of mortification. Certainly this occurs when a greedy gullet is kept in check, when an insolent tongue is restrained by silence, when the ears are shut to slanders, when the eye is prevented from looking upon illicit things, when the hand is bound so that it does not strike out cruelly, and the foot, lest it wander about aimlessly, when one resists the heart lest it envy the happy prosperity of another, lest

9. Cf. Gal 5.22–23.
10. 2 Cor 4.10.

one desire what is not his own by avarice, lest he separate himself from fraternal love by wrath, lest he arrogantly raise himself above others, or consent to titillating pleasure from delight, lest he oppress himself either too much in grief or, seduced by gladness, relax too much. Since the human mind is not able to remain entirely empty or unoccupied with love of something, when it is everywhere surrounded with a wall of virtues, it is necessarily carried off above itself because it is never permitted to expand around itself.[11]

(8) In this way, when our mind begins to rest in its Creator, and to taste the most profound delight from that sweetness, then it rejects whatever it judges is contrary to the divine law, and abhors whatever departs from the rule of supernal justice. Clearly, from this true mortification is born; from this it happens that a person bearing the cross of his Redeemer seems dead to the world. Thus, he will take no pleasure in the absurdities of fables nor agree to drift off in idle conversation, but frees himself for hymns and spiritual songs, seeks out a remote place, desires a refuge, considers the workshops where people speak together and the cloisters of the monastery to be like a public market. He searches out secret places, rejoices in unfrequented places, and, so far as he is able, he avoids human conversation that he may more freely stand in the presence of his Creator.

(9) Here, after a man has demolished the cities of the enemy, after he has trodden on the necks of those kings hiding in the cave and brought them to ruin, after he has overturned the kingdoms of the sea, the plains, and the mountains, what is left then except to possess the promised land in tranquil peace with a triumphant Joshua?[12] Otherwise, what use is it that after abandoning Egypt we have crossed the divided Red Sea, if we are confined in the desert now for a period of forty years and

11. For the importance of this notion for Damian that the mind is like a room that must be filled with the right content or furnishings in order to promote appropriate thoughts or meditations, see the discussion in Ineke van 't Spijker, *Fictions of the Inner Life: Religious Literature and Formation of the Self in the Eleventh and Twelfth Centuries*, Disputatio 4 (Turnholt: Brepols, 2004), 40–43.

12. Cf. Josh 11.12–13.

can neither return to the fleshpots nor enter the land flowing with milk and honey by right of possession?[13] We are sleeping, we snore, and we waste away in a torpor of slothfulness.

(10) Rightly, then, the very same thing that that Joshua spoke to the seven tribes that had not yet obtained their possessions is said to us as a reproach: "How long are you indolent and slack, and do not go in to possess the land which the Lord, the God of your Fathers, has given you?"[14] Certainly he is a foolish soldier who is content to be victorious if earlier he has not pursued the fight; he is too soft if he strives to achieve victory before he goes out to the battle. The farmer is frustrated if before he has sweated to sow he seeks to thresh, since it is well known that whoever wants to gather the grain necessarily must first root out the bushes and the brambles. And in truth the divine voice says to sinful man: "Your earth will bring forth thorns and thistles";[15] for this earth to be fertile for crops, however, let it first endure the mattock and the ploughshare, so that after it has been cultivated with various afflictions and by the discipline of a perfect penance, it may be adorned with the fecundity of all the virtues just as with a crop of abundant fruits.

(11) Joshua actually urged the sons of Joseph to this type of agriculture, figuratively speaking, when he said to those who complained that a slender portion had been their lot: "You are many; go up into the woodland and cut down room for yourself in the land of the Perizzites and the Raphaim, because the possession of the mountain of Ephraim is too narrow for you."[16] Now, if I may relate this to the matter at hand, not inappropriately, he who has decided to be content with the *Rule* of the blessed Benedict alone has limited himself to the narrow possession of the mountain of Ephraim. But listen to how the new Joshua urges you on to the mountain and commands you to hurry toward a broader area of your possessions: "We have described this Rule," he says, "so that observing it somewhat we may show ourselves to have either an honorable character or the beginning of conversion."[17] Behold the mountain of

13. Cf. Exod 16.3.   14. Josh 18.3.
15. Gen 3.18.   16. Josh 17.15.
17. *Benedicti regula* 73.1 (CSEL 75.179).

Ephraim. But seeing that he thought this possession to be a narrow one, he then sends them beyond to places that are at once higher and broader: "For another who hastens to perfection, there are the teachings of the saints, that is, the *Conferences* and *Institutes of the Fathers*,"[18] etc. Since we know that these are well known to you, we judge that it is superfluous to add anything here.

(12) But since we are ignoble and lukewarm we never strain to reach the heights, but would that we at least cultivate assiduously the narrow places of this small mountain, so that no precepts fall into neglect in any corner of this same *Rule* that might be left unfurrowed by the plough of our labor and effort. For wherever we see harsher or somewhat higher precepts, we are as afraid to introduce the plough of our sweat there as onto a rugged mountain or into living rock. We want to be counted among the ranks of soldiers, but we do not take care to have the insignia of virtue. We present the appearance of integrity to the eyes of men, but we neglect to hold on to the reality in the sight of the hidden Judge. For there are some who cross over to the order of a new religious life who, and I cannot say this without pain, nevertheless never abandon the old ways of their former life. Indeed, these are clearly Gibeonites, and not Israelites.[19] For it is well known that the Gibeonites, terrified by a fear of death, came to the Israelite people with cunning and deceit, clothed themselves in old clothes, and even carried dry bread, skins, sacks, shoes, and all manner of old things, and in this way life was given back to them by a treaty they procured; however, as a consequence, after the fraud was brought to light, Joshua, once he had discovered the deceit, condemned them under a curse and established by a perpetual law that they should be water carriers and hewers of wood.

(13) Moreover, who are these Gibeonites, who cross over to the Israelites from fear of death, but those who take refuge in

18. *Benedicti regula* 73.2 (CSEL 75.180). That is, the *Institutes* and *Conferences* of John Cassian, composed between 419–426 C.E. The *Institutes* outline the rules and customs of Egyptian monasticism, whereas the *Conferences* contain interviews or dialogues with the well-known hermits of the Egyptian deserts.

19. Cf. Josh 9.3–27.

the soldiery of divine service not from a love of perfection but
trembling for the enormity of their crimes? Some of them are
changed not in the mind but only in their outer garment; they
carry dry bread to eat, because they still do not know the unleavened bread of truth and sincerity.[20] They are clothed with
old garments because, still rooted in the old man, they do not
know how to put on the new man, who is created after God in
justice and the sanctity of truth.[21] Moreover, all that they do
seems hardened with age, because they persist in the vices of
the old life, paying no attention to the apostle, who commands:
"Be renewed," he says, "in the spirit of your mind."[22] Nor does
this passage apply to them, which says: "The old things are
passed away, and behold all are made new."[23] Coming to a new
way of life only in a superficial way, indeed they persist in the
old, since they show no improvement and no new way of living
in their habits. Such as these, then, are punished by a curse,
and they are in no way permitted to share the inheritance with
the Israelites. For it is not said of their number: "You are called
to this, that you may inherit a blessing."[24] Water, however, is
tasteless, and wood is hard. Therefore, they are commanded to
hew wood and to carry water because, unacquainted with the
taste of spiritual intelligence, they are employed in the harsh
and senseless tasks of outward labor. In fact, they seem to confer some benefit on the church by serving in external things,
but because they live as slaves they are unable to possess an inheritance among the Israelites.

(14) Nevertheless, some of these people, if they have been
frequently admonished, if the full rigor of correction is applied
to them, if the punishment that is inflicted on the wicked is exposed to them, if then the terror of the dreadful last judgment
is raised before them, pass from slavery to freedom and rise up
with the others to establish a right to hereditary possession.
Those tribes who were first assigned the task of cursing at the

20. Cf. 1 Cor 5.8. "Unleavened bread": *azima*. The Latin use of *azimes*, or unleavened bread, during the celebration of the Eucharist was a source of controversy separating Latin and Greek Christians, and contributed to the schism of
1054.

21. Cf. Eph 4.24.   22. Eph 4.23.
23. 2 Cor 5.17.   24. 1 Pet 3.9.

command of Moses and later by Joshua following after him, symbolize them. Thus Scripture attests: "The entire people and all the elders and the leaders and the judges stood on either side of the ark before the priests who carried the ark of the covenant of the Lord, both the stranger and he that was born among them, half of them by Mount Gerizim and half by Mount Ebal."[25] Now those who stood by Mount Gerizim blessed the doers of the law, whereas those who were by Mount Ebal cursed the transgressors of the law.[26] What do those who discharge the office of blessing signify if not those who doubtlessly take refuge in divine service not from fear of punishments but from hope of heavenly rewards and a love of perfection, who bless God without ceasing with works of a holy life? And what do those signify who are appointed to curse if not those who neither burn with a love of perfection, nor yearn with a desire for heavenly glory, but merely guard what is commanded in the law in order to evade the punishments of Gehenna?

(15) They are sent to curse so that while they curse they may themselves return to a sense of what is right and, contemplating the punishments that are established in the Scriptures for sinners, restrain themselves by fear from the perversity of sinning. From this it is plain that the tribes that were appointed for blessing are the more noble, namely, because they are the sons of wives, whereas those appointed for cursing are base, the sons of maidservants, that is, Gad and Asher, Dan and Naphtali, among whom were Reuben, who dishonored his father's bed, and Zebulon, the last son born to Leah.[27]

(16) One must note, too, that all are reported to have stood about the ark of the covenant because none, whether noble or base, and for that reason fervent or lukewarm in the love of God, withdraw from holy Church. Now this was commanded by Moses, but only long after was it put into execution by Joshua. What does Moses represent if not the law, and what does Joshua represent if not the Gospel? Not only did the Old Law proclaim that a blessing is due to the just and that a curse is to be applied

25. Josh 8.33–34.
26. Cf. Deut 27.12–13.
27. Cf. Deut 27.13, 1 Chr 5.1, and Gen 30.20.

to sinners, but the grace of evangelical reformation also makes
this clear. But although the former may be noble and, for that
reason, discharge the office of blessing, and those that are
more base are terrified by fear of a curse, nevertheless because
they both contend against the enemy in common cause, because they work to lay claim to the promised land for themselves with the earnestness of shared labor, all are admitted to
a portion at the same time and will be co-heirs with one another without distinction in law. Nevertheless, it is more distinguished that we, fervent and strong, be identified by the titles
of nobles, than that we be found soft and forced to suffer punishment in some degenerate ignobility.

(17) Let us flee from Ebal, let us condemn so much the
more the Gibeonites in order not to burden ourselves with the
condition of a slave, entangled in externalities, and let not the
torpor of idleness sentence us to live among the ignoble sons,
restrained by the fear of Gehenna alone. Let us lay claim to our
inheritance with the arms of virtue, so that we may expand the
boundaries of our possession by the sweat of assiduous labor.
But perhaps some idle people will answer with what Scripture
reports that the sons of Joseph said then: "We cannot," they
said, "go up to the mountains, for the Canaanites who dwell in
the low lands have chariots of iron."[28] Indeed some people seek
the heights, but they fear those who dwell in the low lands, because they strive to hasten to the summit of the virtues but they
despair of the power to overcome the impulses of the vices of
the flesh to which, nevertheless, one is not allowed ignobly to
yield, but rather one must respond: "You are a people great in
size and strength, and you will not have one lot only, but you
will pass to the mountain and cut down wood and make yourself room to dwell in and you will be able to proceed farther."[29]
Rather, to provide courage to the timid, God almighty himself
calls out: "I am," he says, "he who will cut them off from the
face of Israel."[30] And Joshua exhorts the warriors of the heavenly army, and promises them an easy victory over the enemies:

28. Josh 17.16.
29. Josh 17.17–18.
30. Josh 13.6. Damian's passage truncates the Vulg.

"Do not be afraid," he says, "nor be dismayed; take courage and be strong; for the Lord will disperse all your enemies against whom you fight."[31]

(18) In addition, beloved, if I may speak to you familiarly as to confederates of one mind in Christ, we know that a certain custom is observed in several monasteries, which we humbly encourage you to renounce. For there are some directors of the brothers who, attributing more to the monastic rule than is fitting, impose no penance whatsoever on those coming from the world even if they have gravely sinned, except to command them to guard the common order of the monastery. Anyone who knows anything understands how thoughtless, how inhuman, how utterly undiscerning this is. For these men leave their pupils in the base condition of the Ebalites, as they deprive them of a zeal for repentance, as they fail to teach them to climb to the heights after the debt has been discharged by the love of perfection, but they teach them instead to languish in a torpor of degenerate idleness, always seized by a fear of punishments and bound by a concern for what has been lent at interest, so that they do not bless the Lord safely with those who stand beside Gerizim, but instead they fear the darts of curses with the sons of the maidservants around Ebal. One who does this does not recognize the difference between ten thousand talents and a hundred pence.[32] Now if one considers the law of discretion, then the more any person is burdened with offenses the more he must be burdened with a greater weight of satisfaction. Indeed, the debtor who has borrowed an ounce discharges his debt more easily than one who has borrowed a pound, nor must a person who has stolen a sheep be forced to make the same reparation as one who has stolen an ox.

(19) Now, if we pay careful attention, we find that also the apostles themselves, the leaders of the Christian teaching and those foremost in our discipline, had different tasks among themselves according to the sins of their former life. For Paul, because he involved himself cruelly in Stephen's murder,[33] endured more pains of suffering than the others, whereas Peter

---

31. Josh 10.25. Damian departs slightly from the Vulg.
32. Cf. Matt 18.23–28.   33. Acts 7.58–59.

wiped out the stain of marriage with the blood of martyrdom, and John, because he was chosen as a virgin, was loved more than all the rest,[34] and since he withdrew from the world while still in boyhood, he committed no grave sin, but passed from the world not suffering the pains of martyrdom but sweetly and quietly, as if sleeping. And although the distinguished preacher says: "I am the least of the apostles, who am not worthy to be called an apostle, because I persecuted the church of God,"[35] although he chastised his body and brought it into submission,[36] although he accepted nothing from the Gospel which he conceded to others, but lived by the labor of his own hands,[37] although he labored more than all the rest, yet he feared that he had not understood.[38] If he, I say, did not trust in his apostleship among such magnificent works of virtue, how much do we who are unhappy and wretched presume to trust in our monastic life of idleness? Whosoever soberly takes refuge in the order of this religion puts an end to evil deeds.

(20) But what does it profit a person to cease from the commission of sins if he does not strive to wipe away those that have been committed, by the satisfaction of a severe penance? But if one does not perhaps believe me, let him investigate what blessed Pope Gregory has to say about this in his book *On Pastoral Care*, where he says: "Those who have abandoned their sinful ways yet do not weep must be admonished, lest they think that those sins have already been absolved which they do not cleanse with tears, even though they have ceased to add to them."[39] These precepts are so fully, so clearly and reasonably set out there that anyone who carefully reads them through can, based on this one, have no doubt concerning the rest; however, we think that they ought not to be included here because we want to avoid the weariness of an extended treatment. And in truth how can one be secure concerning a pardon for his crimes who, when coming to a place of penance, does not attend to penance?

---

34. Cf. John 21.20–22.   35. 1 Cor 15.9.
36. Cf. 1 Cor 9.27.   37. Cf. 1 Cor 4.12.
38. Phil 3.13.
39. Gregory I, *Regula pastoralis* 3.30 (SC 382.482).

(21) But perhaps you object that the *Rule* does not enjoin a special fast on one coming from the world, beyond the common fast. We easily reply to this that the blessed Benedict set forth his precepts for monks, yet he did not overturn the sacred canons that pass judgment on sinners, but rather confirmed all the Catholic writings. Clearly he gave precepts for living to those undergoing conversion to the religious life, but he did not remit penance for sinners; otherwise, those who are still in their youth and those who come to the religious life having guarded themselves against grave sins can murmur and justly complain if they are compelled to abide by the same mode of living as those who are heavily burdened by crimes. Now if we ought never to undergo any fast or penance other than what is prescribed in this holy *Rule*, then why is it commanded there: "The fast may be broken by the prior for the sake of the guests, unless it is a special fast day"?[40]

(22) Now go, read, run through and turn over the pages, investigate them carefully, and show me where this special day for fasting, which is mentioned here in passing, is commanded by the authority of the holy doctor. And when you cannot find it, you will have to confess that the holy man wanted us to observe not merely what he wrote down, and he did not annul the edicts of the Fathers who preceded him when he established his own. But lest someone attack me for rashness, like one who undervalues and passes judgment while disparaging our holy order, we credit our holy profession with so much that we confess that it is nothing less than a second baptism and a second rank of the apostolic order. But I say what the prince of the apostles said when he spoke to certain ones who wished to come to conversion: "Do penance and be baptized each and every one of you."[41] By what determination is he safe who neglects to weep over sins already committed when the highest pastor of the church even believed that penance ought to be added to the sacrament that principally dismisses sins? Certainly the holy *Rule* has been drawn up with so much discretion and

---

40. *Benedicti regula* 53.10 (CSEL 75.136).
41. Acts 2.38.

specially tempered with a scale of such moderation for those
who abandon the world with a free will and love of perfection
to boot, and not for those who, terrified by the enormity of
their crimes, are compelled to flee the world from necessity. It
was set out for those, I say, who come from love of obedience
and not for those who are drawn by fear of Gehenna, for those
who desire to grow in grace, and not for those who want to
avoid punishment. This is clearly inferred at the very beginning
of the *Rule*, if one pays attention carefully to who it is to whom
the Holy Spirit directs his words.

(23) I say the Holy Spirit. For it was not in order to burst
forth with words aimed at usurping for himself the chair of the
teacher, and particularly the privilege of the tender Father, that
the holy man, a laborer of such great humility, said: "Listen, my
son, to the precepts of the Master and incline the ear of your
heart, and willingly receive the admonition of the tender Father."[42] Rather, the Holy Spirit made his servant the organ of
his own voice, as he did similarly when he began to cry out
through Isaiah in the very introduction to the beginning of the
prophecy, saying: "I have nourished and exalted children."[43]

(24) Let us see, then, to whom he directs the words when he
begins to write, for what sort of person he intends the power of
the speech that follows. For he says: "To you, now, my speech is
addressed, whosoever you are, who takes up the very strong
and bright weapons of obedience, renouncing his own desires,
to fight for the lord Christ, the true king."[44] One knows that the
school of this *Rule* was established more for learning obedience
than for performing penance, as far as we can determine from
the words of the holy man, not to exclude either sinners or just
persons or to reject any kind of people, but because it disposes
all its power and effort to teach the precepts of obedience.

(25) As we write these things, certainly we are not unaware
that we offend certain brothers, namely, those who think that
absolution for crimes and the realization of the virtues stems
from the religious way of life alone. But let it be enough for us

42. *Benedicti regula*, prol. (CSEL 75.1).
43. Isa 1.2.
44. *Benedicti regula*, prol. (CSEL 75.1–2).

to reply that when we set forth these things we do not wish to cast a snare on anyone, as the apostle says,[45] but merely to urge him on to what is good. Let me explain why, however, I draw out these things at such length, since it does not seem irrelevant. Once a certain brother came to us from a monastery, and confessed the sins he had committed in lay life. If I remember rightly, he had to do seventy years of penance, as were required, it seemed to us, according to the decrees of the sacred canons. He had already been in the habit of religion for seven years, and when we asked him how much penance he had already performed for these sins, he replied that he had confessed all of these to the lord abbot, but that he had imposed on him no penance beyond that which was the common practice of the monastery, because he claimed that conversion to the religious life alone fully sufficed for the absolution of all his sins. What shall I say? I confess that the matter greatly displeased me. I looked down, I trembled, and I cried out that the man had been deceived, that certainly he had not yet made a beginning at the penance which he could have already completed with various types of afflictions.

(26) Let these and the many other things which deceived people misunderstand, while without knowledge they think they are acting properly, displease you, beloved ones, and so that you can correct them with a free authority in the other things that they ought not do, show them that these things ought to be held in contempt, while you yourselves more cautiously avoid them. But let us return to the matter at hand. The holy *Rule* has been made like a full, spacious mansion, capable of taking in all types of people, boys as well as old men, the strong and the weak, the delicate and those who differ in various ways by a difference in their practices. We ought not to deceive ourselves with a foolish sense of security, then, nor arbitrarily claim all the indulgence of the *Rule* as if for our use alone. For although a public thoroughfare may be open to every traveler, he is an uncouth wayfarer who attempts to take up the whole of it with steps spaced widely apart. The spring

45. Cf. 1 Cor 7.35.

that flows in the center is the sum of individual springs, but he
who wants to lay claim to the whole for his own use acts in an
insolent manner.

(27) Accordingly, we are speaking about the relaxation of
the holy *Rule* and exhort each brother who is concerned about
his own salvation to return to an awareness of his own capabili-
ty, and to assume for his own use from the *Rule's* relaxation not
so much what is permitted as what is necessary. Indeed, what is
commanded by authority is one thing, while what is mercifully
indulged is something else. But what is commanded is not neglected without sin, whereas what has been conceded as an indulgence is a good if it is relaxed, but it is not an evil if it is fulfilled. But if we pay attention carefully to the words of the *Rule*
itself, we easily prove what we wish to say. For when he says
someplace: "Making allowance for the weakness of the infirm,
we believe that one hemina[46] of wine suffices for each individual per day. However, let those to whom God grants the ability
to endure abstinence know that they will have their own proper
reward."[47] Now how is what he says about wine for monks different from what the apostle says about the embrace shared by
spouses? "I speak this, however," he says, "by indulgence, not by
commandment."[48] Then he adds there: "For I would that all
people were even as myself, but each one has an individual gift
from God, one after this manner, another after that."[49]

(28) The apostle wanted one thing, then, and permitted another. He wanted all people to be just as he was himself, that is,
strangers to marital concerns, but since he could not persuade
all of this, driven by necessity he permitted marriage, determining that it is better for them to lie on a marriage bed, like those
who are weak, than to break their necks falling into the pit of
wanton behavior. But blessed is he who listens to the apostle
commanding what he wishes, rather than to him allowing what
he does not. In the same way, the author of the holy *Rule* permits one thing out of necessity, owing to the weakness of those

46. A *hemina* is equal to about one-half pint.
47. *Benedicti regula* 40.3–4 (CSEL 75.111).
48. 1 Cor 7.6.
49. 1 Cor 7.7.

who are frail, but commands another by authority with the balanced judgment of discretion. Now when he says, "Although we read that wine is not at all proper for monks,"[50] and elsewhere when he says, "Although the life of the monk ought always to be a Lenten observance, nevertheless because this is a virtue of the few,"[51] and many other things like this, it is just as if to say: I show you the heights, but seeing that you are limping along on weak knees I take you through the plains. If, however, someone should have the strength, would he not abandon the lowlands, which unwillingly I have allowed to him, and would he not take to the heights, which I desire? For certainly it is better for a soul to be saved in Zoar than for it to be consumed by brimstone in the fire of Sodom. "For it is better to marry than to be burnt."[52] But how much more glorious it is to climb the mountains than to lie in the obscure baseness of little Zoar![53]

(29) To return once again to our concern, it is certainly better to live in the spiritual order slothfully than to perish completely in a worldly life. But how much finer is it to destroy quickly all signs of the vices and to hasten to the peak of the virtues with burning desire, than to slumber away under the torpor of idleness with the security only of the religious order we have adopted. It is as if the promulgator of the holy *Rule* should say to his listeners: you who take advantage of what I allow indulgently do not sin, but you who do not take advantage will receive a reward; indeed, having accepted compassion you do not incur a penalty, but having renounced it for God's sake you will achieve the crown. This applies to those not burdened with any special crime; otherwise, whoever is mindful of the fact that he has committed illicit acts must now abstain in turn from even licit things, and one who has pridefully committed things that are prohibited ought now humbly to give up concessions. Now there are many who live soft and sweet lives who, if ever they are exhorted to undertake the way of even a slightly stricter path, they then plead an argument for their defense, as

50. *Benedicti regula* 40.6 (CSEL 75.111).
51. *Benedicti regula* 49.1–2 (CSEL 75.130–31).
52. 1 Cor 7.9
53. Cf. Gen 19.20–23.

one of them says: "I live as I am commanded to do, I maintain the mandates of my law when I make use of concessions"; then, to appear like the victor who fights from a higher position, he leaps forth boldly. He asks, the *Rule* does not remove the freedom to do these sorts of things, does it? Does it not allow me to do these things? Truly, one who argues this way has not yet learned to distinguish between the writer's desire and what he is forced to allow, and has not recognized that some things are permitted as an indulgence, and others are commanded as an order.

(30) This person certainly will die in the desert, because while he dwells ignobly in the desires of his flesh he does not exert himself to obtain the land that is his by right with laborious battles. Or else he is stuck with the people of Reuben and Gad before crossing the Jordan,[54] and he does not deserve to possess the land of milk and honey with the other tribes after their triumph for the reason that he has placed a limit on his effort, and he believes that, though still engaged in a journey, he already dwells at home, and he does not reach the portion of his inheritance where there is true rest and secure tranquility.

(31) Finally, our entire way of life and renunciation of the world strives for nothing other than rest. But this rest is only acquired if first a person is engaged in the various labors of its battles, so that, through the grace of contemplation, the mind is directed to catching sight of the truth, once the din of every disturbance has ceased. But since this rest, as has been said, is only attained through labors and battles, how does one who has not yet descended to the battles that have been appointed in our midst attain this rest? Now, how can one enter the royal hall if he has not yet crossed through the arena that is outside? How has one who has not learned to sow seed, who has not pruned the branches of the vines, who has never broken up clods of earth with a hoe, who has not furrowed new fields with a plough, how will he be able to lay up grain in a storehouse, once it has been separated from the chaff, or remove grape skins from the pipes filled with new wine?

54. Cf. Num 32.1–5.

(32) Besides, it is well known that Laban had two daughters; Jacob, who wanted the younger of them in marriage, nevertheless could not come to her embrace until unwittingly, and for that reason unwillingly, he received the older one.[55] But because I mention the matter to ones who know all about it, I need not elaborate with many words. Now Laban means "cleansing." However, who turns to God, unless to be cleansed by the grace of absolution from the blackness of sins that is left behind? This is just as he himself promised, saying: "If your sins be as crimson, they shall be as white as snow."[56] That happy sinner declared this when he said: "I shall be cleansed, you will wash me, and I will be made whiter than snow."[57] Leah means "laboring," and Rachel means "the word" or "vision of the beginning." But if we carefully attend to Scripture, we find that Jacob did not serve for a single day from a desire for Leah, but he endured service for all those seven-year periods for Rachel alone,[58] and moreover he tolerated Leah herself in his sight. Now is any person turned to God to suffer labors and hardships and the battles of temptation? Every effort of one seeking God hopes for this and looks for this—to attain rest at some time, and to rest in the joy of the most perfect contemplation as if in the embrace of the beautiful Rachel, so that through the word that he hears he may ascend to see the beginning which he sought.

(33) But it is necessary to apply himself to the labor of various battles before he attains the sweetness of most profound quiet which he desires. First he is oppressed with servitude, so that later he may rightly be raised up to the glory of perfect freedom. He serves for seven years subject to the grace of cleansing, when he guards those seven commandments of the Decalogue that pertain to love of one's neighbor. So, constrained at first by fear, and for that reason bowed down by the yoke of servitude, he at least makes a beginning with the insti-

55. Cf. Gen 29–30.
56. Isa 1.18. Damian's text substitutes *quasi vermiculus* for the Vulg. *ut coccinum.*
57. Ps 50.9.
58. Cf. Gen 29.20, 27.

tutes of the Old Law, to honor his parents, not to commit adultery, not to kill, not to steal, not to bear false witness, not to covet another's wife or his neighbor's goods.[59] Once he has observed these things properly, he is not brought as soon as he had hoped to the pleasures of contemplation, namely, to enjoy the long awaited beauty of Rachel, but instead Leah, who is unexpected, is substituted in the night, because one is enjoined patiently to endure labor in the darkness of human ignorance. Nevertheless, for this he receives many offspring, because he acquires the abundant fruits of spiritual profit through this labor.

(34) He bears with her, then, in order at some time to come to her whom he loves enduringly. Therefore, he is compelled to toil in service another seven years, because assuredly it is necessary to keep yet another seven precepts, but somewhat more freely, not as a servant according to the law but rather as a son-in-law according to the Gospel: namely, to be poor in spirit, to be meek, to mourn, to thirst and hunger after justice, to be compassionate, to have a pure heart, finally, to be a peacemaker.[60] Truly, if it were possible, a person would not want to bear any of labor's troubles, either causing or suffering them, but would want rather to arrive at the delights of the contemplation of beauty at the very beginning of his service, but in fact this does not occur in the land of the dying but in the land of the living, which seems to be the meaning of what is said to Jacob: "It is not the custom in our country," said Laban, "to give the younger in marriage first."[61] Nor is it absurd to call her the elder who is prior in time. Now, in a person's instruction the labor of a good work comes before the rest of contemplation. Once he had completed two seven-year periods, to wit, the one of the Old Law and the other of evangelical grace, he comes at last to the long desired embraces of Rachel, because whoever desires to achieve the joys of divine contemplation must first strive to fulfill the commandments of both Testaments.

(35) But because whoever is chosen is not content with the limit of his perfection, he desires to bear sons for God from a

---

59. Cf. Exod 20.12–17.   60. Cf. Matt 5.3–9.
61. Gen 29.26.

spiritual fecundity; after Jacob had entered into a marriage bond with the two sisters, for the sake of propagating the seed of a more abundant posterity he did not shrink from taking also the maidservants for the purpose of generation, and so that all things may be understood to abound with spiritual mysteries, the very names of the maidservants are made known under mystical symbols.[62] For Bilhah means "of long standing." Clearly, because human language is unable to express with mere words the meaning of a spiritual substance, sometimes wisdom's teaching strives to inform its audience with certain corporeal images. Corporeal images are known from the old life, which was given to the bodily senses, and their usefulness for instruction arises when something is heard concerning the incomprehensible and unchangeable essence of divinity. Certainly Rachel preferred to receive sons from her maidservant than to remain completely barren, because whatever the teaching of wisdom (that is, the grace of contemplation) hides within the hidden places of the mind concerning things invisible, she makes known to her listeners in the forms of things visible through external knowledge, and thus in a certain way she receives sons from a maidservant when she gives birth to spiritual sons for God through that knowledge which is below her.

(36) Zilpah means "open-mouthed." Therefore, this maidservant symbolizes those whose mouth is open in the preaching of the faith contained in the Gospel, but whose heart is not open. Of these people it is written: "This people honors me with their lips, but their heart is far from me."[63] And the apostle said of them: "You steal," he said, "who preach that one ought not to steal."[64] Nevertheless, Leah received sons from this maidservant to be heirs with the others, because the active life has adopted many sons of the kingdom through preachers such as these. Truth says of them: "All that they say to you, do; however, do not do what they do."[65] And the apostle said: "Whether as a pretext or whether in truth Christ be preached, in this also I rejoice and will rejoice."[66]

---

62. Cf. Gen 30.1–9.   63. Matt 15.8
64. Rom 2.21.   65. Matt 23.3.
66. Phil 1.18.

(37) But what we have excerpted from the text of the holy writings thus far is enough already, since it is not our purpose to explicate the Scriptures one after another. But we think that this must be borne in mind from these passages: that just as Jacob accepted all these women with whom he generated sons out of consideration for Rachel alone, so too whoever, established in a cleansing grace, desires to generate fruit for God with a spiritual fecundity must always reach for the grace of contemplation in all that he does.

(38) But what do we say about this, when we see that some who live in Laban's house are heedless of so much sloth or idleness that they neither seek Rachel's beauty nor even seem to exert themselves in labor for Leah? Assuredly these are those who are established in monasteries, but neither pursue the grace of contemplation through a more solitary life—that is, through the perseverance of constant prayer—nor chastise themselves with the stricture of fasts and various labors. Clearly, either they are altogether free from the bonds of marriage or they are content merely with the embraces of the maidservants because either they adopt inactive lives of indolent idleness, or, if they do anything, they do not incline themselves to it in order to bear the fruit of the active or contemplative life but instead only to satisfy the appetite of their own will or desire.

(39) Finally, these are they who, wishing always to be wandering about, rush hither and thither to complete every task whatsoever, and, as they do not know how to be calm, they want to appear to be obedient, and thus they conceal the disease of the vice for which they labor beneath a cloak of virtue they have drawn over themselves. These are they who are not worn out by their labors to be obedient; rather, they resolve to obey their superiors in order not to lose the opportunity for doing this work, so they endure idleness for the work they enjoy, because they consider it a sweet delight to wander about to turn the quiet mill of affairs. For there are some paralytic souls that rejoice to trouble themselves with frequent running about. Now whoever is fettered by the languor of a bodily paralysis is often roused by the violent shaking of attendants, and by this shaking he is also refreshed. These certainly are spiritual paralytics, who either

must be said to be united to the maidservants alone, and this is the reason why their sons in no way reach the right of inheritance, or if they think that they have free women, they are unwilling to unite themselves with the maidservants, so to speak, for the sake of Laban's daughters, but, having reversed the order, they want to be united with the daughters for the sake of the maidservants, because they do not do labor in order to obey, but rather they are obedient in order to do labor. Unlike Jacob, they do not apply the fruit of their works to the active or contemplative life, but rather if they show something of the active life in their effort or say anything about the contemplative life, it is not that they seek the fruits of spiritual profit in them, but only that they chase after the desire of their own will.

(40) Moreover, if I may speak with some irritation, among their number are those who follow the crowd of grammarians, who, having forsaken spiritual studies, desire to learn the absurdities of the earthly art, and who, trivializing the *Rule* of Benedict, take pleasure in applying themselves to the rules of Donatus.[67] Moreover, loathing the practice of ecclesiastical discipline and aspiring toward worldly studies, do these people do anything else but forsake the chaste spouse on the marriage bed of faith to descend to made-up harlots? And, if I may put it this way, seduced by the charms of whores they repudiate the free women, so that once they have broken the marriage contract they may choose the maidservants. They abandon the wives, that is, Laban's daughters, and cross over to lewd concubines, and so rightly they seem old with Bilhah and witty with a prating refinement of speech with Zilpah. But perhaps they object that they labor on the trifles of the external arts for this reason, to profit more fully from divine studies. Certainly Jacob endured the embraces of the concubines at the entreaties of his wives; otherwise, the children they bore, if they were subject to the disgrace of an adulterous birth, would never share in the rights of inheritance with the others. Therefore, let them seek out and consult carefully the authority of the Fathers.

67. Aelius Donatus (fl. 350), a Roman teacher of grammar and rhetoric and author of an *Ars grammatica*, whose name had become virtually synonymous with the art of grammar in the Middle Ages.

(41) If sacred Scripture says that a wife bestows a maidservant on her husband in order to have offspring, then it is permissible for a monk to devote his efforts to these arts. But if Gregory, Jerome, and the other holy Doctors [of the Church] utterly deny this, then they know that they have been deceived by the adulterous love of a mistress, just as without a lawful bond they fight pertinaciously against the marriage contract. For not only are we forbidden to strive after vain teachings of this sort after having accepted this sacred order of living, but we are even required to cut away all the superfluous teachings from among those we learned before. So one learns from the law of Moses that a woman captured in battle and chosen by the victor in marriage should be deprived of any bodily superfluity. "She will shave her hair and pare her nails and she will put off the garment in which she was taken, and sitting in your house she will weep for her father and her mother for one month, and after that you will go into her and sleep with her and she will be your wife."[68] We shave the woman's hair when we cut away from the rational discipline superfluous notions; moreover, we pare the nails when we cut away dead works of superstition from it. In addition, she is commanded to put off the garment in which she was captured, so that she may strip off the outer covering of fables and of fictions of whatever sort she has drawn over herself, to reveal the solid truth of right reason.

(42) Truly, she weeps for her father and mother because our mind considers the authorities of the liberal arts to be dead, and with compassion laments the fact that they perished in error. Moreover, it is the practice of women to be purged each month by an effusion of their blood; therefore we are commanded to go into this woman after a month, so that we may choose as if in marriage the art of any discipline whatsoever, once it has been cleansed of every superstition, in so far as once she has become an Israelite she may enter into marriage with an Israelite as a result, and, being very fertile, she may deliver the offspring of spiritual works.

(43) And certainly all of these things without doubt apply to

68. Deut 21.12–13.

those who received instruction in the arts of liberal studies when they were in worldly service, but is it different for those of us for whom it is not fitting even to speak with guests, in whom Christ himself is addressed and is received, who ought to open our mouth only to ask a question?[69] And how will it be fitting for us who do not dare even to raise a question during the reading of the sacred text when we eat, to burst forth insolently upon the theatrical schools of the grammarians and to produce foolish words with worldly men, as if in the middle of a noisy market? We have said these things against those monks who are entangled in the absurdities of the superficial arts, to show how far their vanity has deviated from the straight line of righteousness.

(44) Beyond this, it is useful that every brother who has abandoned the world with his whole heart unlearn the things he already knows if they prove to be harmful, and consign them to perpetual oblivion, so far as he is able. He should not know how to debate the merits of cooks, he should not know to prefer more luxurious foods to more nutritious foods, nor be so skillful as to bring forth witty or captious words, nor draw upon rhetorical devices for the employment of a strident declaration, nor, finally, to wrest a laugh from anyone with facetious and sarcastic remarks. Let him love fasting, let him choose the bare necessities, let him flee the gaze of people, let him bind himself under a strict rule of silence, let him withdraw from external affairs, let him guard his mouth from idle conversation, let him seek the secret place of his mind, where he may burn with all his efforts to see the face of his Creator, let him seek out tears, let him demand tears from God with daily prayers. Indeed, the moisture of tears purifies the soul of all blemish, and renders fertile the fields of our heart for bringing forth the seeds of virtue. Often the wretched soul loses her foliage and the beauty of her leaves as if under a hoary frost, and, with grace withdrawing from her, the whole soul remains neglected and withered, and appears almost denuded of the beauty of her falling flowers. But as soon as tears burst forth from the gift

69. Cf. *Benedicti regula* 53.23 (CSEL 75.138).

of the most intimate examiner, then this same soul recovers its verdure, is released from the cold of idle sloth, and, just like a tree in spring warmed again by the south wind, she is clothed with the flower of her virtues made to live again.

(45) Moreover, the tears that come from God confidently approach the tribunal of a divine hearing and, procuring immediately what they seek, trust in the certain remission of our sins. Tears serve as mediators of peace in forging an alliance between God and humans, and they are true and very wise teachers in any doubt stemming from human ignorance. For when doubting whether something is pleasing to God or not, we never lay hold of certitude better than when we pray while genuinely weeping. For then our mind will correctly judge what ought to be done, and it will not be necessary to entertain any doubt of this again. In addition, tears wash away all taint of filth from the sinful woman,[70] and bestow upon unclean hands a right to touch not only the Lord's feet but also his head.[71] Tears not only grant that the apostle who denied him will in no way perish after his sin,[72] but even that he will obtain a primacy over the other senators of the heavenly court. Tears not only brought it about that David did not lose his kingdom and his life after having fallen into the deepest abyss of adultery and murder, but instead obtained a promise with an oath that an heir would be born from him, who would possess forever the throne of his kingdom and all the kingdoms of the earth.[73] For his tears, God almighty added fifteen years to the life of Hezekiah, who was about to die, and in addition delivered him and the city of Jerusalem from the hand of the king of the Assyrians.[74] Certainly, divine piety mercifully enabled tears to free Sara the daughter of Raguel from the bond of undeserved reproach,[75] and through an angel chose her to wed a worthy man.[76] With her tears, Esther brought God to free the Israelite

70. Cf. Luke 7.44.
71. Cf. Luke 7.38 and John 12.3 for the feet; Matt 26.7 and Mark 14.3 for the head.
72. Cf. Matt 26.75.   73. Cf. 2 Sam 12.13–22.
74. Cf. 2 Kgs 20.1–6.   75. Cf. Tob 3.15.
76. Cf. Tob 7.13–14.

people from the common danger of death, and turned back against Haman the sentence of hanging he intended, which he had himself prepared.[77] No less did tears enable Judith to cut off the head of Holofernes and to preserve the flower of her most virtuous chastity in the chamber of licentious seduction.[78]

(46) What shall I say about the centurion Cornelius who, by the gift of tears, merited a visit from the apostle and who, as soon as he abandoned the error of the pagans, was transformed in the new life of Christian regeneration?[79] Need I recall Susanna who, as soon as she fled to the protection of tears, was snatched from the hands of those dragging her to her death, when a death sentence was diverted onto the head of the false witnesses, and thus by the spirit of a young boy innocent blood was acquitted?[80] But if I wanted to run through all the gifts of tears, the day would likely conclude before the abundance of examples should be exhausted. For it is these that purify the soul of the stain of sins, and strengthen in prayer the wandering heart. It is these that bring forth joy from sorrow, and when they spring from the eyes of the flesh they raise us up to the hope of supernal blessedness. Now they who have powerful cries in the ears of the Creator cannot be despised in their plea, and he who said, "Hear my prayer, O Lord, and my supplication, give ear to my tears,"[81] often sent forth his cries to God and clearly knew what they could obtain. He who insists that tears do not receive attention from the eyes but are perceived with the ears, plainly indicates that there are voices in tears. Certainly when tears plead in the sight of the tender Judge they are at a loss for nothing, but claim mercy as if it were something due them by right, and confidently rejoice that they have obtained what they sought.

(47) O tears of spiritual delight, better than honey or the honeycomb and sweeter than every nectar! You that refresh minds lifted up to God with the pleasant sweetness of a secret savor and thoroughly water dry and languishing hearts with a draught of heavenly grace. The sweetness and the savors of

---

77. Cf. Esth 14.1–2.   78. Cf. Jdt 9.13.
79. Cf. Acts 10.   80. Cf. Dan 13.22–45.
81. Ps 38.13.

earthly banquets please the palate for those who partake of them, but they do not penetrate the inmost parts, whereas the savor of divine contemplation fills completely, quickens, and sweetens all our inmost parts. Weeping eyes truly terrify the devil, and he so fears the onset of springing tears that he flees them as if from a tempest of winds raging on every side and as if from a hailstorm of violent rain. For just as the full force of a foaming torrent falling upon a river bed washes it clean of all its filth, so too the course of flowing tears banishes the seeds of diabolical cunning and all the deadly plagues of the befouling vices from the mind of the one weeping.

(48) But this water flows out from fire, so whoever desires to overflow with a flood of water must first kindle the fire of divine love in the forge of his mind. We can explain this more easily if we recall an event that is given historical significance in the second book of the Maccabees. Thus Scripture says: "When our fathers were led into Persia," it says, "the priests who then were worshippers of God secretly took the fire from the altar and hid it in a valley where there was a deep, dry pit, and there they kept it safe, so that the place was unknown to all. But when many years had passed, it pleased God that Nehemiah should be sent by the king of Persia. He sent a descendant of those priests that had hidden it, to seek for the fire, and, as they told us, they found no fire but oily water."[82] Of all this, one must pay special attention to the fact that first the fire was hidden in a deep, dry pit in the valley, and afterward it was not fire but oily water that was found by those searching for it. A mind that is sincere and perfect in its intention to seek God is appropriately indicated by the deep, dry pit in the valley, for such a mind certainly is unmoistened by the flowing desires of carnal pleasures, has dug deeply beneath the rubble of earthly concupiscence, and has been established in the vale of true humility. The fire of sacrifice is introduced to this pit when the flame of divine love is conceived in the mind of one of the elect, and the devout intellect is kindled to heavenly desire. But this fire is turned into water because from the fire of divine love the compunction of tears is engendered.

82. 2 Macc 1.19–20. Damian has *nepotem* for the Vulg. *nepotes.*

(49) And one must note that the water that was found there was said to be not exactly pure, but oily. Now what is "oily" water if not the compunction of tears nourished, no doubt, on the rich fat of divine grace? The prophet yearned to be nourished on this rich fat when he said: "Let my soul be filled just as with marrow and rich fat."[83] And another prophet promised this same fatness when he said: "Your soul shall be delighted in fatness."[84] And, again, it was said: "May the Lord be mindful," he said, "of all your sacrifices, and may your whole burnt offering be made fat."[85]

(50) Nor should one overlook the fact that those hiding this fire had indeed hidden it in a safe place; however, they are not said to have extinguished the fire entirely, because the fire of divine love, which we burn on the altar of our heart so that we may offer a sweet sacrifice from the spices of good works at the very beginning of our conversion, must always burn secretly inside us; however, it must never spread itself outside through the flames of vainglory. Therefore, it is made safe once the flames have been stilled, but, so that it will not die out, it is not deprived of the strength of its heat, but later the fire miraculously turns itself into water. Moreover, this water, namely, the compunction of tears, not only purifies us from the contagion of sins, but also commends our good works so that they are pleasing to God. For every sacrifice of good works is rendered sweeter in the sight of the supernal Judge if it is sprinkled with the tears of a contrite mind. Therefore, appropriately, this is added: "And the priest Nehemiah commanded that the sacrifices which were laid on," it says, "be sprinkled with the same water, and both the wood and the things that were laid upon it."[86]

(51) But when we besprinkle the sacrifice of our works with the water of true compunction, then a splendor shines upon our minds and illuminates whatever obscurity, whatever darkness hitherto lay hidden in them. For then a certain ray of the most profound light reveals itself to us, and besprinkles all the

83. Ps 62.6.   84. Isa 55.2.
85. Ps 19.4. Damian adds *Dominus* to the Vulg. text.
86. 2 Macc 1.21.

hidden places of our soul with a new serenity of delightful brightness. This is why when it is said there that "he ordered them to draw [the water] up and to bring it to him, and the priest Nehemiah commanded that the sacrifices which were laid on be sprinkled with the same water, and both the wood and the things that were laid upon it,"[87] then the sequence of the history adds: "And this was done, and the time came when the sun shone out which before was in a cloud, and there was a great fire kindled, so that all wondered."[88]

(52) Earlier we heard that water was found in place of the fire, whereas now it is said, contrariwise, that a great fire was kindled by the sprinkling of the water. Therefore, both water is born of fire, and fire in turn is produced from water. This is because the grace of compunction arises from the fire of divine love, and in turn the heat of heavenly desire is increased again by the compunction of tears. Each depends on the other, and each is responsible for the other, as both the compunction of tears flows from love of God and, in turn, through tears our mind burns more fervently with a love of God. Moreover, no doubt, the mind in which the reciprocal exchange takes place is purged of every stain of its guilt. That is why it goes on to add there, finally: "Nehemiah called this place Nephthar, which means purification."[89] Certainly the faithful soul is our place where sacrifice is offered, where the exchange of water and of fire likewise takes place, as is said. It also may appropriately be called "purification," because at one time it is consumed by the fire of supernal love and at another it is flooded with the tears of a contrite heart,[90] as if washed in the water of a second baptism.

(53) Isaiah looked deeply into these vicissitudes of alternating change and the variations of spiritual alterations when he said: "Your light," he said, "will rise up in darkness, and your darkness will be as noonday, and the Lord will give you rest continually and will fill your soul with brightness, and deliver your bones."[91] Behold the fire hidden in the pit. But hear how

---

87. 2 Macc 1.21.
88. 2 Macc 1.22.
89. 2 Macc 1.36.
90. Ps 50.19.
91. Isa 58.10–11.

this fire is changed into water, for then he adds: "And you will be like a watered garden and like a fountain of water whose waters shall not fail."[92] At length, so that you may know that this water is changed again into fire and that the heat of divine love is aroused even more fervently through the grace of tears, a little further on he adds: "Then you will be delighted in the Lord, and I will lift you up above the high place of the earth."[93]

(54) Moreover, we do not think that something that happened to us should be passed over in silence. For the Lord's day intervened after having written this far, and a responsibility for certain tasks that arose having to do with external affairs prevented us from writing any longer. Then a certain young man named Silvester, who, as I should say in order to give myself due credit, did not transcribe these things from my dictation, but copied the things written down here from writing tablets onto parchments, was so deluded by the great cunning of the wicked enemy that he suddenly burst into tears, and could hardly check the flood of tears day or night, except during the hours of sleep or at mealtime. Moreover, he refused wine altogether and sustained himself on, and was satisfied with, very little food, and also indulged in sleep as much as possible. Meanwhile, the devil suggested he seek out the solitude of a more remote hermitage where he would rarely or even never see another person, and when we offered him an opportunity for complete enclosure he said that in no wise did he want to be completely enclosed, but merely wanted a place to be free and by himself where no one would observe him when he entered or left. All the brothers unanimously objected to this stubbornness, however, and insisted that this was probably a trick and cunning device of the devil. But he was headstrong and obstinate as he professed a faith in luxuriant tears, and remained immovable in his vow, which he had conceived at the suggestion of the wicked spirit. I think that the ancient enemy had stumbled on a suitable instrument for his deception when he placed before his eyes what Silvester himself had written im-

92. Isa 58.11.
93. Isa 58.14. Damian has *altitudinem* for the Vulg. *altitudines.*

mediately above in this little work, where it says that when we
doubt whether something is pleasing to God or not, we never
obtain greater certainty than when we pray while genuinely
shedding tears. He did not pay attention to what was said a little
before this passage, that only those tears which are from God
approach the tribunal of a [divine] hearing, but certainly not
those that are suggested by the tricks of the cunning ambusher.

(55) He also heedlessly overlooked that it said, "genuinely
shedding tears." For he does not shed tears genuinely but falsely, whose false tears are sent by a lying spirit from the outset.
Nor is this unlike what Pope Gregory wrote in his *Moralia*, when
he said: "The hand of compunction examines very subtly those
vices that the ancient enemy hides under the guise of the
virtues. He who genuinely grieves inwardly over his outward actions clearly foresees what things ought not be done. Now if the
power of compunction affects us to the very depths, it immediately causes the sound of every evil suggestion to become silent.
And if the heart genuinely grieves inwardly, the vices cannot
speak against us."[94] See that this eminent doctor, who is in
agreement even with the folly of our own silly opinion, did not
say, "if the heart grieves inwardly," but rather, "if the heart genuinely grieves inwardly." Clearly this implies that there is one
type of grief by which a divinely inspired mind is goaded by remorse, and another type by which it imitates the tears of a contrite heart as if through the mendacity of the ambusher, and it
implies that those other tears that the spirit of wickedness and
error counterfeits are different from those with which the spirit
of truth cleanses the filth and blight from our souls.

(56) Therefore, to return to the order of the narrative, because he was allowed to dwell in another solitary place a short
time ago, he rashly cut himself off and also wandered about to
other places like a vagabond, trusted only in tears, and in no
way was he willing to give his assent to impartial advice, nor did
he believe that one whom compunction flooded each day with
frequent outpourings of tears could be deceived in any way.
What more? Undoubtedly the egg that the viper warmed in the

94. Gregory I, *Moralia in Job* 33.36–37 (CCL 143.157).

little nest of his breast finally hatched out a familiar offspring. For he begged to look at a book for a little while that was very precious to us, and secretly he cut out four quaternions from the middle, and he very precisely cut the bands for binding the codex to the proper size lest we suspect what he did. Then, terrified by a prick of conscience and in order not to be bound in shackles, while standing before the door of the cell he threatened to wound either himself or others with a knife, if anyone should approach him. Then it became perfectly clear that his sort of tears did not come down from heavenly dew, but, without any doubt, had gushed out from the bilge water of hell. We take care to tell you this, my brothers, not to exaggerate the disgrace of the delinquent brother but so that you will always strive to be suspicious and cautious even concerning good works themselves.

(57) It is fitting here to discuss the various offices of the monastery in a concise manner, and particularly to set in order what it is appropriate for those who administer them to observe. In the first place then, O venerable abbot, do what you yourself command, practice what you preach, fulfill what you command; let not your life be at variance with your way of speaking, nor let your deeds appear different from your speech, nor let the authority of the ruler teach one thing and the performance of the religious life display another. In addition, let your movement outside be infrequent, so that you may be able continually to water the seed of the word you have sown, while cultivating it. Do not let your frequent running about show you to be a guest of the monastery, but instead let a long period of fastidious seriousness show you to be a household resident. Let a strict fast commend the person preaching, and do not let the gullet of one who is eating assail the statements of one who is speaking. Certainly the hand teaches sobriety better when it is directed to the mouth with control than when the tongue of a glutton speaks. In addition, in the minds of the disciples it is an especially vivid and efficacious way of preaching when it urges others to the meal, but remains itself in the rigorous observance of the fast while doing so. In this way, apply the rod to offenders in such a way that you check in

yourself the impulse to violent anger under a firm discipline.

(58) Meanwhile, when you reproach, when you threaten, when you strike the guilty with fear, turn your eyes also upon yourself, consider the extent of human weakness, and carefully reflect upon the fact that you yourself could be reproved if a judge were present. Do not wonder if someone subject to you should perhaps transgress by failing to fulfill all the commands you have ordered, since the weakness of the human condition is so great that even your body's own limbs cannot obey you in all things. Moreover, in order to illustrate clearly what we are saying, command your eyes not to let sloth surprise them, command your heart not to admit reason's phantasms, impose chastity on the genitals so that they are not even occasionally aroused by incentives to riotous living, impose sobriety on the gullet so that it is not eager for richer foods, and, finally, command your entire body all at once not to lay itself open to the onslaught of diseases. And when you prove clearly that this requires of you something that you cannot completely achieve, how surprising is it that you are unable to find perfect obedience in all those who differ from you with respect to their rank and behavior? Plainly, if you reflect upon these matters in yourself with intelligent consideration, then you will accept with equanimity the excesses of the brothers' weakness. If perhaps something happens to expand your patrimony, if abundance is perceived to be in store, if the house of God is increased, do not attribute it to your merits or efforts, but ascribe it only to divine favor. Then call to mind the times when you were not in office, and consider that in no way did these things occur because of you.

(59) It follows, therefore, that what you would have been unable to gain without her was not conferred upon you but upon the church of Christ. Do not shudder at the thought of dining at the brothers' table, do not take delight in private banquets, and do not judge those with whom you share the table of the altar unworthy to partake with you of bodily nourishment. Do not then let your absence generate a suspicion of secret gluttony, whereby your good reputation will be burdened with the bane of murmurers and detractors. Nor should you care too

much about how precious that is which fills the privy, but instead be concerned with how fraternal love may grow in Christ through the bond of mutual love.

(60) Do not squander the goods of the monastery, nor wish to procure your own popularity from the things for common use. For if we believe that the sins of those who enrich churches are forgiven, then without any doubt one must believe that those who diminish and destroy them are entangled in the chains of a serious sacrilege, and therefore just as the former are found to be released from the debts of their sins, the latter are liable to punishment for sins. Beware when you are hemmed in by the indulgent attitudes of kinsmen, when you are sweetly buttered by the words of flatterers, lest this preferential treatment or earnest reverence be so flattering to your mind—which God forbid—that the wickedly alluring thought delude you that you are worthy of these when you attain them. The larger the estate entrusted to him, the happier the steward is, but he is proportionally the more wretched when called to render an account, and what he owes when he renders an account will be in proportion to the larger size of the estate on which he prides himself, when he receives it. Plainly, one should fear especially what is said: "The abbot will give an account for all the souls entrusted to him, once he has provided an account for his own soul."[95] Let us contemplate, then, how beneficial it is for the one who comes to his own examination at the Last Judgment, already wearied by the obligation to render accounts for others, to be struck with fear now. But because a teacher has to teach more than he has to learn, let these few words suffice, since one who is appointed to deliver his own may perhaps be loath to listen to another's.

(61) The prior of the monastery, moreover, administers the office of his priorate diligently if he does not disagree with the abbot's desire, if he strengthens the souls of all the brothers in a sincere love for this same abbot, as far as he can. Joseph, the overseer of the master's household, was unwilling to the very end to draw to himself the desire of another man's wife, but

95. *Benedicti regula* 2.33–34 (CSEL 75.27) and 2.38 (CSEL 75.28).

taught her to remain steadfast in the love of her own husband.[96] And Abraham's noble servant, a vigorous man of great humanity, scorned every office so as to provide a wife for his lord in sincere faith; he was forgetful of his toil and long journey, to serve his lord alone, whatever he was to do once he was set on his enterprise.[97] For just as the abbot ought to encourage his sons to the love of Christ by everything that he does, so even the prior, lest some jealousy arise—which God forbid—should strive harmoniously to foster in the brothers a love for their abbot. Certainly he should not show himself to be easy on the faults of offenders, to make the abbot appear cruel, but when the latter is absent he should reprove all wrongful acts so that when later he returns he may rest, just as in the asylum of a tranquil harbor, in the spiritual joy of brothers finding delight.

(62) Let him maintain a strict severity in the censure of transgressors, lest he allow the customary discipline of the rule to grow lukewarm at his house. He should be strict in justice so that the abbot can appear tender in clemency; he should insist on enforcement so that the abbot can pardon something with paternal tenderness. Moses, as a faithful servant, transmitted the commandments of naked justice,[98] whereas Christ as a truly tender lord tempered the severity of the austere law. But Aaron, who revealed himself to a sinful people as somewhat pliant, fashioned idols together with this people for sacrilegious rites.[99] Just as a veil was hung before the ark of the covenant,[100] the prior should be a sort of protective cover for the abbot with respect to practical affairs. Indeed, let him encounter all the dust rising up from the worldly path to which he is always exposed, so that the latter may abide continually, just like the ark of the Lord, in the purity of his splendor. Like an Aaron, the prior is made the abbot's mouthpiece, to speak to the people; the abbot, like a Moses, takes pleasure in divine conversations in all those things that pertain to God. And so with each of them concurring with the other in unity of spirit, let them nourish such offspring for God, if it is possible, whom no pos-

96. Cf. Gen 39.4–9.
97. Cf. Gen 24.1–9.
98. Cf. Exod 24.12; 32.1.
99. Cf. Exod 32.2–6.
100. Cf. Exod 38.26.

terity shall replace in the right to the heavenly inheritance that has been received.

(63) The one who indicates the hours[101] should know, moreover, that no one more than he ought to avoid forgetfulness in the monastery. Now if an hour should be held late or is prevented from being held at its appointed time for the office, undoubtedly it disrupts the entire order for the hours that follow. Therefore, let him not waste time in conversation, nor engage in a long discussion with another, nor, lastly, ask about what is being done by worldly people, but always intent upon the charge committed to him, always careful, and always circumspect, knowing that the spinning globe has no need to rest, let him reflect upon the course of the stars and the passage of time slipping away. Let him establish for himself the practice of reciting the psalms, if he wants to have a way of distinguishing the hours each day, so that when the sun's brightness or the stars' movement can not be perceived owing to the thickness of the cloud cover, he will be able to establish for himself a measure, just like a clock, by the number of psalms he has completed. Truly, the custom that people gather at church when the bells are rung derives from a mystical tradition of the Old Law, with the Lord commanding Moses: "Make yourself two trumpets of beaten silver with which you can call together the multitude when the camp is to be moved, and when you will sound the trumpets all the multitude will gather before you and the door to the tent of the covenant."[102] Just as the Israelite people came together at the tent with the trumpets, so too even now a faithful people hastens to church when it hears the clamor of the bells.

101. The seven canonical "hours," or periods of monastic prayer, established a daily rhythm for the *opus Dei*, or Divine office. The prayers recited at these times consisted principally of Psalms, hymns, and readings. The hours begin with the night office of matins (about 2:00 A.M.), followed at approximately three-hour intervals by lauds, prime, tierce, sext, none, and vespers. As Damian indicates below, one member of the community was appointed to signal when the others should gather together. This demanded at least some ability to measure time by observing the movement of the sun or stars, or by some other device. In an extended metaphor, Damian treats the monks assembled for prayer as an army arrayed to do battle for the Lord against his enemies.

102. Num 10.2–3.

(64) Nor is there a discrepancy when the camp is said to be moved there, since camps are known to be related to a readiness for battle. For this reason it says a little further on: "If you go forth from your land against your enemies who fight against you, you will make a clamor with sounding trumpets and there will be remembrance of you before the Lord your God so that you will be delivered from the hands of your enemies."[103] We march forth to battle as if to the camp, so to speak, when we hurry to church to pray or to recite the psalms. For there the princes of darkness fight against us in a deadly manner, so that they may turn our wandering minds away from the things that flow from our mouths by means of the illusions of phantasms. And truly how beautiful is the appearance of the army, especially at the night hours, when the brothers form a wedge, aroused as if by the clamor of the trumpets, and, inspired to make ready for the divine contest, they go out in unison as if hurrying forward in a well-ordered battle line. Although the wing of boys goes in front, the youth follows just like a squadron of soldiers, whereas last, following upon the footsteps [of the rest], are the old men, namely, the strength of the battle, who guard the rear of the whole army lest anyone fall or the hidden enemy assail it.

(65) Besides this, a lantern is carried in the vanguard of the battle as a very fitting image just as a column of fire is observed to go before the people through the desert. For certainly, as the companies of Christ hurry to eat the manna of heaven, so do the Israelite legions hurry to obtain the land flowing with milk and honey. They hurry to the tent of the covenant with sounding trumpets to eat there banquets of the heavenly Word, and to fulfill the sacrifice of praise to God and vows of good will. Wherefore it is added there, not inappropriately, "If, on festival days and on the first days of the months, when you are having a banquet, you will sound the trumpets over the burnt offerings and over the sacrifices of peace offerings, there shall be for you a remembrance before your God."[104] Let the one who indicates the hours carefully consider from words of this sort, then, how

---

103. Num 10.9. Damian provides *contra hostes* for the Vulg. *ad bellum*.
104. Num 10.10.

watchful, how careful he must always be in the office assigned to him, lest by his carelessness he confound so great a work as the statutes of his order.

(66) Let the lector at the meal reflect with careful consideration upon how clearly, how plainly, and finally how intelligibly he ought to read. At that time he supplies food for souls along with the bodies' refreshment. The apostle says: "Food for the belly and the belly for the foods; but God will destroy both this one and that."[105] Through the one, then, a food that is soon turned to rottenness is offered to the body; through the other are administered divine words, which will not pass away even as the heaven and the earth pass away. Therefore he must read so that as the flesh is refreshed with its own contribution, the soul too is nourished at heavenly banquets.

(67) Therefore, he should not read for the reader but for the listener, nor should he be concerned with idle talk of his own reputation, but rather let him be mindful of another's edification. Neither should he care about what is said of the reader, but about what can be understood from the reading. One must urge upon those who are eating to let sobriety so temper the meal, that the noise of grinding jaws not cause the ears' pathways to cease to listen. Therefore, as a hand observing moderation should pass as a mediator between the mouth and the table, so too, stayed by the bridle of severity, let it check itself, so that the hungry soul is never forced to abstain from divine meals while earthly food is directed through the gullet.

(68) Moreover, the cellarer, since he has been appointed as a sort of father to the monastery, ought to perform the office entrusted to him with such great skill in economic management that he checks the hand as it is opening, and carefully opens it while keeping it in check, to the extent that liberality will be parsimonious in him and parsimony will be liberal. He ought to be especially careful not to mistake niggardliness for parsimony and lavishness for liberality. For often vice cloaks itself in the appearance of virtue, and the more that an evil is

---

105. 1 Cor 6.13. Damian provides *hunc et illam* rather than the Vulg. *hunc et has*.

perceived to be like a good, the more difficult it is to correct. But the good administrator dispenses the things that are necessary for the body in a way that is mindful of the salvation of souls, because he nourishes sobriety while being parsimonious, while by being liberal he prevents the vice of murmuring from arising. For often, as a very wise man said, liberality perishes from liberality;[106] that is, when something is lavished carelessly on those who do not need it, then later what ought to be given to those who truly need it will be gone.

(69) What is superfluous, then, ought to be denied to us, so that there will be something left over from which charity can be distributed to strangers. Nehemiah, in order to receive at the feast at his own table those who came to him from among the Gentiles round about him, thought it shameful to spare his own flocks, and thus he added to the funds for necessities from his own, in order to extend the performance of charity even to strangers.[107] Tobias, although he toiled in such poverty that his wife undertook paid employment as a weaver,[108] divided the little he had to provide at least some comfort to his brethren who were fellow-captives. And though a foreigner, he did not allow compassion to be foreign to him, and, though poor in possessions, he did not lose the riches of the most splendid charity. When Abigail removed a portion from a magnificent banquet, she averted from her husband's throat the sword of David, who was hastening to avenge an insult, and thus she did well to remove, like a thief, food from her own use, and certainly saved a life by ministering to strangers.[109] Moreover, Paul instructs that on the first day of the week there be put aside whatever shall please each person, so that it can be sent to the holy ones in need in Jerusalem by the grace of the Corinthians.[110] And thus we ought to administer the funds for the daily provisions for our own brethren in such a way as to remind ourselves to provide aid to outsiders in need when the opportunity arises. Therefore, let him be a steward of the Church who does not

---

106. Cf. Jerome, *Letter* 58 *(ad Paulinum)*, CSEL 54.537.
107. Cf. 2 Esd 5.14–19.   108. Cf. Tob 2.19.
109. Cf. 1 Sam 25.18, 36–39.   110. 1 Cor 16.1–3.

distinguish among persons, but who considers weaknesses, who
does not seek favor, but supports another's weakness, in order
to distribute equal portions in a fair manner to the needy; and
let the measured stewardship of his administration identify
those whom various types of weakness set apart. Thus every
seed-bed for scandals is rooted out, if for each individual member there is provided not what the will seeks but what necessity
requires.

(70) Again, because we embrace the whole body of this holy
monastery as if in the outstretched arms of brotherly love, we
think it is valid to distinguish the different age-groups, and to
tailor garments, so to speak, appropriate for their admonition
to the individual members. Therefore, in order to begin with
the beginners, you have to learn, O boys, that your age is now a
very impressionable one, and just as you are still of tender age
while your limbs are small, so too you are wavering among different types of customs. The further you move from the
branches of the Pythagorean letter,[111] the more easily you may
be directed to the right, or turned aside to the proclivities of
the left side. But if in the hand of a potter the clay suffers the
marring of some defect, unless it is immediately corrected, it
cannot be restored and it will become like stone afterward. If
by some accident a twig growing up from the first root twists itself to the side, it never is made straight again; if it remains
slanted in the same way considerably longer, it is considered
food for the devouring flames because it is perceived to be
worthless as a spear shaft.

(71) Therefore take care lest some vice burn you up at the
same time with your body's growth, and lest the knot of any depravity harden in you, but be instead vessels made in honor,
not in reproach,[112] and prepared for every good work in the

111. Presumably, the letter "Y," whose branches correspond to the elements,
their qualities, the seasons, and the different ages. Damian suggests, then, that
as young men travel through these correspondences, their behavior or *mores* are
shaped. On the Pythagorean letter, cf. Hubert Silvestre, "Nouveaux témoignages
médiévaux de la 'Littera Pythagorae,'" *Le moyen âge* 79 (1973): 201–7; and idem,
"Pour le dossier de l'Y pythagoricien. Nouveaux témoignages," *Le moyen âge* 84
(1978): 201–9.

112. Cf. Rom 9.21.

house of the Lord. Clearly, if you wish to thrive with the uprightness of adults, and to abound in the virtues without the irksomeness of toil—which is impossible for others—take up in some manner the arms of sobriety and fight against the burning allurements of the flesh with all your strength. With God standing by your side, assure yourselves of certain victory at the very beginning of your military service and, carrying the banner of the Cross, boldly begin the struggle unallied with hostile spirits. Trample upon pride, let anger be curbed, let envy be crushed, hold the tongue to the severity of silence, extinguish the gullet's appetite by ruminating on the Scriptures, let not your tongue utter some detracting remark, and let your ear censure it by not listening. Solomon said: "Have nothing to do with detractors, seeing that their destruction will come suddenly and who knows the ruin of both?"[113] The ruin, that is, of both the one who detracts and of the one who pays attention to the one detracting, and in truth, nevertheless, the one by whom a brother's sin must be corrected ought not conceal it, but neither should he utter some detracting remark.

(72) Sometimes, surely, this is the more easily caught in boys, the more they have no idea of practicing it or putting up with it. Clearly, Joseph accused his brothers of the very worst crime to his father,[114] and although on account of this he bore their hatred, later he obtained lordship over them. Jonathan and Ahimaaz, stationed by the fountain Enrogel, lay hidden and sent a message to king David to flee quickly from Absalom,[115] and so Abiathar and Zadok did through their sons what they were unable to do themselves. Indeed, very often a fault is uncovered through the young men that may be profitably amended by the elders. Now that you are almost grown up, however, do not wrongly debate the merits of your superiors who are perhaps still living, and, paying attention not to the path on which they may increase but in whose place they serve, humbly be obedient to them in Christ. For, as the apostle said, "We had fathers of the flesh as instructors, and we revered

---

113. Prov 24.21–22. Damian's text has the additional noun *colloquium*, as well as *veniet* in place of the Vulg. *consurget*, and *utrorumque* rather than *utriusque*.
114. Cf. Gen 37.2.   115. 2 Sam 17.17–22.

them; how much more shall we obey the Father of spirits, and live?"[116] Samuel learned from Eli what to answer to the Lord, who was calling him, and because he was humbly obedient to the priest, despite the latter's unworthiness, he soon received an oracle of divine revelation.[117] A wicked spirit vexed proud Saul, and yet David did not refuse to serve him by plucking his harp.[118]

(73) In order for you to be able to extinguish the flames of desire, turn aside from things that excite the gullet just as if these were a tinder of tow, naphtha, pitch, and faggots. For in the fiery furnace a fourth one appeared among the three chaste boys who will afford the consolation of his Spirit to you just like a wind bearing dew.[119] Therefore, put aside the toys of a nursing baby in all things, and with the nature of a free man dedicate to the Lord the novitiate of your military service. Follow after him as a leader in the struggles against temptations, seek him out as a guardian in the peacetime of prosperity. Therefore, girded round with the unconquerable spears of the virtues, say unanimously to Christ your champion: "Judge, O Lord, those who wrong me, overthrow those who fight against me, take hold of arms and shield, and rise up to help me."[120] When he has brought you "to perfect manhood, to the measure of the age of fullness,"[121] he will make you the victors by his own power. He will enable you to trample upon the necks of your enemies with triumphant feet. Read also the letter we sent to our nephew, Marinus.[122]

(74) You growing adolescents, however, even you pubescent youths, have a greater need for the weightiest aids of exhortation because you endure the harsher struggles of the flesh's fire. To be sure, every hostile impulse attacks you in a direct assault; upon you all the power of war presses. Hailstorms thick with every kind of dart assail you and, once the iniquitous spir-

---

116. Heb 12.9.   117. 1 Sam 3.9–10.
118. 1 Sam 16.23, 18.10.
119. Cf. Dan 3.49–51, 92; cf. *Letter* 27.3 (FOTC, MC 1.248).
120. Ps 34.1–2.
121. Eph 4.13.
122. Cf. *Letter* 132 (FOTC, MC 6.57–72).

its have been gathered against you, then the most violent storms assail you with the vices of the flesh. Wars rage, they rage in your bones, and the furnace of your body spews out balls of fire just like restless Vesuvius or smoking Aetna.[123] For this reason, it is necessary that the more sharply you are attacked at the watch-station of your tutelage, the more strongly you should press on. Therefore, it is imperative that those who continually brandish spears be vulnerable to spears, and those who are eager to inflict a wound, suffer wounds. For either one must put to flight, or one must flee; either one must force to flee or, on the contrary, expose one's back. This battle is of the type that whoever does not drive out is himself driven out, and he who does not gloriously achieve a victory will be shamefully vanquished. There is always a danger, when the enemy's army is surrounded, that a troop of dissident citizens will form an alliance with the enemy and, while the battle-array is drawn up to engage in battle, the entrance to the camps will be opened by mutinous citizens. Indeed, the vices that are within us unite with the tempters in tempting us, and their hostile forces render service to the iniquitous spirits.

(75) For this reason, beloved, take up the weapons of sobriety, humility, patience, obedience, chastity, and love, and of all the virtues, and fight not for your fields and cities, not for your wives and children, but for your very souls, which outlive every bond of friendship. Above all, for your youth to come to know its power, you must fast and pray, inasmuch as fasting will subdue the flesh's strength and prayer will lift the soul to God. Nevertheless, be aware that because some fast indiscriminately, they fail to enjoy the fruit of the fast. For whatever they abstain from on one day, they make up for on another day, satisfying themselves as they please. And thus it happens that the fast day contends against the next day, and when yesterday's or today's meal is barely digested, the sumptuousness of tomorrow's preparation will be recommended to an empty stomach, and when something richer and different from the common fare is sought, all the secrets of the apothecaries are abused, not with-

123. Cf. Isidore, *Etymologies* 14.3.46.

out inconvenience for the servants.[124] Therefore he fasts well who is content with the common fare on the day he eats, that is, if he does not vary from the type of foods and does not exceed as well the quantity of those eating every day. By no means should you forsake obedience, which is the golden path to heaven, by placing too much importance on fasts.

(76) Let me describe now something which I did not learn secondhand, but which I saw with my own eyes. There was actually a brother in Pomposa named Raimbald, namely, the brother of the most reverend Peter, who now discharges the office of abbot at Vicenza. He was accustomed to tame his own adolescence with frequent fasts, and in many respects provided a model, as it were, for the initial signs of a celebrated ability. He was given the responsibility of ministering to a certain German hermit established near the church, who led a very difficult life after his eyes had been plucked out and his right hand cut off. However, it was a rule of the monastery that none of the cloistered monks should speak when going outside of it. Sometimes, however, when Raimbald was in chapter, he complained bitterly that he could not instruct untutored boys by signs to

124. Damian's complaint here seems to be that when individuals fast without proper direction, they may succumb to an eating disorder akin to the binge-and-purge cycle of anorexia/bulimia. In addition, it appears that when some monks consumed richer foods, they sought to purge themselves—perhaps because they had eaten what was not permitted under their rule?—with herbs or medicaments, creating a mess to be cleaned up by the monastery's servants. Not only monks but secular clergy as well fasted for long periods. In *Letter* 168.5 Damian recalls the poor example of Albuinus, the bishop of Paris, who had fasted for seven months. When a boar was taken in the hunt, he decided to put off his fast and ordered his cooks to prepare the pork in an elegant fashion for him. He satisfied his appetite with the rich food, but within a week he died, appropriately punished. To hermits, Damian recommended fasting four days each week—including Saturday—and five days each week during the Lenten season. See his *Letter* 137.4–6 (FOTC, MC 6.91–92). A strict fast meant subsisting on bread, water, and salt. For further discussion of the monastic diet and fasting, see also *Letter* 160.3–4 in this volume. Fasting for Damian was not only a means to subdue the flesh, but also a symbol of the hermit's harsher religious discipline. Carolyn Walker Bynum has noted, "The food asceticism of the eleventh-century Italian hermits, for example, imitated and equaled that of the early monks of Syria, and propagandists such as Peter Damian spread their fame." *Holy Feast and Holy Fast: The Religious Significance of Food to Medieval Women* (Berkeley, Los Angeles, London: University of California Press, 1987), 42.

wash clothes for the servant of God and especially what foods to prepare for him, finally asserting and threatening that unless he broke silence he could not obey his orders at all. In response, the holy man, that is, the abbot Guido, vehemently insisted that silence not be broken, and remained firm in the judgment of his authority, until, after many things had passed, it came to this, that he ordered Raimbald to cease from ministering to him and stay quiet. But O, swift severity of divine retribution! Barely half an hour had passed and Raimbald protested tearfully that he had been struck in the throat by a malady sent by a hand from above. What more? After the third day, if I recall correctly, he died, once he had made satisfaction and received the blessing of the holy father.

(77) We have told you this story concerning our household, beloved, so that you will remember that holy obedience must never be neglected for the sake of any work of piety or religion. In addition, be careful in the wars against your temptations; on every side be vigilant and circumspect, so that the hour of temptation may pass and so that what is suggested in thought actually remain unconsummated in act. For often, in the battles of worldly people there occurs in an instant what can not be corrected later in any length of time. But, by contrast, one who is careful to avoid the blow of a single wound, in a very brief moment wins the increase of a long life. You know that we say that often one falls suddenly into the gulf of sin, for which he is necessarily compelled to weep all his life. We must therefore be shrewdly attentive in every moment of temptation in order that temptation never achieve its goal, for if a wicked deed is put off for but a brief moment, it is avoided, and when the quick blow is warded off, so to speak, then afterward life is preserved safe for a long time.

(78) Truly, those who have only recently converted to the order of religion must be admonished to take up the battles against the gullet first, so that when the belly is forced to yield to the laws of sobriety, then, as a consequence, the flame of desire will be tempered even in those parts that are beneath the belly. Let the tongue be restrained not only from idle speech but even for the most part from chatter with the brothers, so

that as a vain wordiness wearies it less with the vicissitudes of circumlocutions, it may apply itself more freely to prayer or divine praise. Let the eye wear out the floor with uninterrupted gazes, let the mind be raised to heaven on an engine of burning desire. Let each substance consider its origin, both so that the flesh not doubt that it is the dust that it beholds, and so that the soul, raised up to that which it lost, yearn for it with an eager and unflagging desire. May your diminished need make you inclined to tattered and rough clothing, and may the cold commend to you cheap and despised garments. Sleep that has been long deferred and quickly granted admittance will soften a hard bed. Indeed, one who thinks only of the length of time for the rest granted to him disparages the bed's softness, but one who intensely desires to spend watchful nights in prayers with Macarius[125] does not yearn with Sardanapalus[126] to float on a feather bed. Let him keep away from public places, and flee from the sight of men. Search for unfrequented places, and enter into the secret places of remote retreats. Furtive prayers bring down a power from heaven and carry off forgiveness, as often in the darkness they are flooded with a light of heaven. Do not respond in an insolent voice to insults that have been offered, but either let the respondent's modesty sweeten the taunter's bitterness, or, if this cannot be done easily, at least let the severity of silence restrain the tongue of one who is angry so that a quarrel does not break out in a deadly manner. For certainly a ship under sail is often sunk by raging winds, but if the sail-yard is lowered, necessarily all the force of the winds is soon poured out against her in vain. The arrow of reproach does not find its mark when the mind of the one reviled, as if it were laid low, commits itself to humility. The novice should often attempt great things, so that the lesser may be rendered easy by comparison.

(79) What I really want to say is this. In this struggle one of-

125. Macarius the Egyptian, a famous fourth-century monk, a disciple of St. Anthony, and founder of a semi-eremitic community in the desert.

126. The last king of the Assyrians, on whom see Pauly-Wissowa, RE 2/1:2436–75. He is also identified as Assurbanipal. For another reference to him, see also Damian's *Letter* 140.5 and n. 5 (FOTC, MC 6.105).

ten drinks muddied or tepid water, so that, having rejected a desire for wine, one will judge water that is merely clear or cold to suffice. Often a bran-loaf is served, so that when one develops an appetite for ordinary bread he will not seek a wheat bread. After cushioned couches, a mat does not suffice, although he will be able to satisfy himself with straw if previously he has worn out the bare floor with his flanks. Let one who is nauseated by olive oil after meat, live on salted vegetables for a time, so that a sober liquid will taste sweet in his throat. A person who takes pleasure in riding on horseback[127] should gather himself up within the narrow confines of his cell, and then later he will imagine the cloister of the monastery to be a public marketplace. To a person who loathes the softness of rams' wool for a robe, after sable or martin, if he has put on a monk's cowl, it makes no difference whether he is kept warm by domestic or imported pelts.[128] Indeed on the mountain Moses abstained from all food or drink for double a forty-day period, so that he would be content with the simple food of manna and would not desire to sit over the fleshpots with the other Israelites.[129] The sons of the prophets did not refuse to cut up bitter apples in the pot, so that they would not shrink from any little vegetables.[130] When Daniel was forced to live between the savage, open jaws of the lions, he learned at last not to fear the snares of wicked people.[131] When Nebuchadnezzar endured the madness of a brute beast, when he wandered through the thick woods and pastures like a wild animal, he was changed so that he would not take pride in the dignity of the royal power.[132] When David was cast down from the loftiness of the royal throne by his own son, he learned not to revenge himself on the strange man Shimei.[133] After Isaiah had gone barefoot and naked for three years, one has to believe that then he did not demand to be clothed with soft or unnecessary garments.[134]

---

127. For the use of horses and mules for personal transport at Fonte Avellana, see *Letter* 37 (FOTC, MC 2.71–72).

128. Cf. *Letter* 97.14 (FOTC, MC 5.77–78).

129. Cf. Exod 16; 24.18.

130. Cf. 2 Kgs 4.39–41.

131. Cf. Dan 6.16–24.

132. Cf. Dan 4.22–25.

133. Cf. 2 Sam 15.13–17; 16.5–10.

134. Cf. Isa 20.3.

(80) Therefore, anyone who wants to make the effort of any task easy for himself, must boldly go on to attempt even higher things, so that roughness will smooth out roughness and, if I may put it so, so that nettles may be thought bearable compared to thorns and prickly brambles. We do not say this so that someone would not have to begin with the lesser things, but rather so that when more difficult ones are attempted, the lesser ones may be made smooth in comparison. Let also the novice who enters a narrow passage when attempting very difficult things, take pains to return immediately to the broad way when he has begun to be burdened beyond his strength. If a needle is driven violently into hard things, unless it is drawn out carefully, necessarily it will break when forced. If, however, a shoemaker drives it in and draws it out again in the way cobblers are accustomed to do, it will easily penetrate any solid substance that had blocked it. It is the same way when, at the beginning of our religious life, first we exert ourselves, then we relax for a while, then we vehemently pursue hard, harsh ways, and then we relax, sparing ourselves, until little by little the path opens so that everything that had blocked it may be cleverly passed by.

(81) I should not overlook you old holy men, moreover, for whom it is necessary to become even more cautious in battle, the more you perceive that the end of the fighting is already near at hand for you. Whence it follows that if you lose now, you cannot recover the tokens of a victory that has been lost from another battle. Now, then, let the fervent mind be kindled to act courageously, and let old age conceive a youthful strength to subdue completely the savageness of the vices. Now indeed you place your feet on the threshold of the city, in so far as now you are approaching the repose of blessed rest through the middle doors.[135]

(82) Abandon idleness, then, cast aside sloth, and do not let the memory of a labor completed perhaps over a long period of time draw back you whom the offer of a reward summons to a hardship that is now before your eyes. The more deeply the

135. Perhaps a reference to the royal portal of a medieval church.

gold miner digs out the veins of the earth, the more robustly and the more fervently does he gird himself up for completing the work that remains. For the work that is already done does not weaken him as much as the hope of a treasure already close at hand encourages him in the effort of digging up the soil. One who is hurrying as a groomsman to the marriage feast, has no reason to be eager for breakfast. For behold, the bullocks and the fattened animals of the Gospel have been killed, and all things have been prepared, and moreover the voice of the herald intones: "Come," he says, "to the wedding."[136] Why then does one who is coming to feast on wedding dishes want to taste the delicacies beforehand? Why does he want to belch before sitting at the table? Why should one who is hurrying to the foods of angels content himself with the husks of swine? Why should he whom the height and the perfect blessedness of heavenly glory await not restrain himself now from the hungry fulfillment of all his desires? Why should he who will gaze forever in unmediated contemplation upon the very Word, through whom all things are made,[137] not hold back his tongue now from common talk and worthless prattle? Why should he who is attempting to reach the court of the eternal emperor and of the heavenly senators not distance himself now from human presence in favor of the discipline's severity? Why should he who must put on the robe of immortality shudder at being covered with rough garments?

(83) Therefore, do not be reluctant to abstain from all the delights of the world, so that we may deserve to overflow with the abundance of all the delights of heaven, so that our mind not cleave to created things but instead yearn for the Creator's embrace. For whoever comes from far away to approach the threshold of the princely court would be convicted of madness if he were so intent upon the buildings that he did not eagerly desire to see the king's face; and do not let the weakness of a worn-out body discourage you from the hope of acting valiantly, because if the Spirit is in the heart, then he will guide powers

136. Matt 22.4.
137. Cf. John 1.3.

to the inmost parts of the limbs. Therefore Caleb, still vigorous with youthful strength because he had zealously fulfilled the commandments of God, said: "Today I am eighty-five years old, as strong as I was at that time when I was sent to investigate; the strength of that time continues in me until this day, to fight as well as to march."[138] Namely, that is, in resisting the vices as well as in increasing in good works by means of the path of religion. And in Deuteronomy it says: "Moses was one hundred twenty years old when he died; his eye was not dimmed, neither were his teeth loosened."[139] This is the reason he said to Asher in blessing: "His shoe shall be iron and brass, and your old age shall be just as the days of your youth."[140]

(84) Therefore, beloved, do not cast aside the weapons of fasts or vigils to the extent that is permitted, as if the vices already extinguished, and do not indulge in tempting delights as if you were already safe when you are still running in the race. Old men are well acquainted with fasting, and although weakness may often desire foods, yet the innate inclination of nature concurs with the fast and with sobriety. Barzillai the Gileadite was invited to rest: "Come," said King David, "rest securely with me in Jerusalem."[141] But he appealed to the dullness of old age and excused himself from the pleasure of royal banquets: "Are my senses quick to discern the sweet and the bitter, or can food and drink delight your servant, or can I hear any more the voice of singing men or women?"[142] From this one can determine how much at peace, how clearly well-mannered was that old man. For how would he who looks down upon the dishes of that royal table to which he had been invited not be content with poverty, if it should befall him, as a familiar thing? How would he who disdains to listen to the strange sounds of melodies with his chaste ears take delight in drawing out idle chatter or words intended to evoke laughter? And he who was unwilling to find delight there where sometimes the instruments of the psalms are strummed, how could

---

138. Josh 14.10–11.   139. Deut 34.7.
140. Deut 33.25.   141. 2 Sam 19.33.
142. 2 Sam 19.35. Damian has *vel cantricum* (s. v. *cantrix*) for the Vulg. *atque cantatricum* (s. v. *cantatrix*).

he rest where the shows and the dancing of stage-players echo?

(85) There are some old people—and this ought not be passed over—who even after they have come to the order of the religious life are so occupied with fabled events that they even cause harm to themselves and they appear to their listeners to be delirious. First they weave the fragments of past deeds, then they narrate the victories or edicts of ancient kings, and in this way they pass the entire day in the vain recitation of old wives' tales. And thus it happens that ridiculous, vain, and superstitious chronicles are recited from memory by a tongue consecrated to God, which they do not use for salvific prayers, and those who sate the tongue on baleful feasts of fables do not even hold the belly in check under the due constraint of moderation, because verbosity is always inimical to the fast.

(86) Finally, we have an old man in the monastery of Sitria, named Mainard, who, when I admonished him to become a monk while he was still wearing a military uniform, became animated with a sort of quarrelsome response, as he had always been verbose and snappish. "Look," he said, "on a daily basis my maidservants wait upon me assiduously on all sides and keep me warm, and yet I am barely able to survive; so how would I be able to take hold of the path of the spiritual life, when I am barely able to keep my footing, in any event, without any weight of the discipline?" A little after this he became a monk, although I do not know what pressed him to do so. Although certainly already old and ill, he began with such fervor that it seemed a miracle to the old and the mature, that is, to the men of sound counsel, whereas to the deceitful and lascivious youths of the monastery he became an object of derision. And those who actually were tearing at him with slanders and gnawing away at him with biting words could never so turn him aside from the rigor of his rule that he did not complete four psalters each day, and in addition he spent four days of each week, in summertime and wintertime, without any food or water. And moreover he still observed this from ancient custom, so that he dedicated each month in such a way that for the first week of each month he would not eat anything at all, unless it was the Lord's day or Thursday. He has already been wearing

the habit of holy religion here in the monastery of the brothers for twelve years, if I am not mistaken.

(87) There is also another enclosed within the walls of a cell, namely, Leo of Prezia,[143] whom we recall we have mentioned briefly in other little writings we have dictated, a man so very old that he remembers the deaths of those born some time after his birth, and he is considered old by those with whom he has grown old in his lifetime. He never drinks wine, except perhaps on two or three very special feast days of the year, even in the feebleness of such a worn-out and trembling body. He never eats before the ninth hour except on the Lord's day, and he will not accept more than one portion on the two days of the week when he lives more indulgently, as it were. The order of his prayers is arranged in such a way that every day, whether in summer or in winter, he completes one psalter with its canticles and litanies before the night office of the Church, and in addition he sings a second psalter from dawn's twilight to the sixth hour with the nine readings for the departed, and concludes yet a third psalter with the *Gloria* at the end of the day when evening is approaching.

(88) Moreover, he has this gift which I have been unable to find in any other man no matter how perfect, that no thought ever intrudes itself upon him when he is reciting the psalms, and such great purity of heart flourishes in him that without any occasion for resisting him, the mind thinks nothing whatsoever out of harmony with his lips while reciting the psalms. And it is also especially remarkable that he never hungers, never thirsts, and the weariness of sloth never weighs down his eyes. In addition, although he is unable to recognize a person's face owing to the foggy vision of old age, he reads and recognizes letters and, while reading the psalter, he runs through it twice every day.

(89) It is also astonishing that when he is confined within the cell, where surely the light is rather dim, he distinguishes the word of Scripture letter by letter; however, once he has gone out where there is a better opportunity for seeing, he

143. For Leo of Prezia, see also *Letter* 28, n. 2 (FOTC, MC 1.255–56).

does not perceive the outlines of the letters. Already he tolerates no struggles of the flesh, and he does not toil even for a
moment with a wandering mind, just as he often admitted to
me after carefully questioning him. Therefore, already crucified to this world, he barely perceives the things that are human, but, wholly unleavened and wholly sincere, he lives, as I
declare, like an angel.[144]

(90) See, beloved, I have offered you only two examples, although many are available, one from the common life and the
other from the solitary life.[145] Surely, from these one clearly
gathers that where the zeal of a fervent spirit has been kindled,
old age does not grow indolent in devotion to a good work, but
just as a tenacious spirit lifts up[146] a serpent to run, supporting
itself not on feet but on its ribs, so divine love moves aged limbs
onwards through the contest of spiritual warfare. For we who
"have not here a lasting city, but seek one that is yet to come,"[147]
ought not hope for rest in any period of life here; the just must
toil on the high sea of this world, where the reprobate take
their rest. The raven and the dove sent forth from the ark symbolize this difference very well.[148] The raven, perching on dead
bodies, did not return to the confines of the ark, whereas the
dove did return because she found no place where she might
rest her foot. Here, then, where wicked men content themselves with carnal pleasures, holy men are unable to find any
place where they can rest the foot of their desire. It is for this
reason that one who is discovered to have sinned is required,
under the commandments of the law, to suffer forty stripes.[149]
To be sure, the number forty comprises symbolically the entire
period of time during which holy Church, spread to the four
corners of the world, lives under the ten commandments.
Therefore, we who have committed offenses submit to this
number forty if we are chastised in this period with stripes of repentance. Therefore any sinner, whether he is old or young,
ought to be bruised in these times so that at the time of judg-

---

144. Cf. 1 Cor 5.7; Gal 6.4.
145. That is, from the cenobitic and eremitic models.
146. Cf. Heb 12.12.   147. Heb 13.14.
148. Gen 8.6–9.   149. Deut 25.3.

ment he can be found purged. For there no punishment will be able to afflict those whom the discipline of perfect penitence has struck here, regardless of their age or rank.

(91) Now then, beloved brethren, I speak to all of you together, I beseech you all in the name of Christ, at which every knee shall bend.[150] Remain steadfast in fraternal love, join forces unanimously in the devotion of mutual love against the snares of the ancient enemy. Let the whole frame of your holy way of living raise itself on the foundations of love and let the entire edifice that you are constructing from the living stones[151] of the virtues be strengthened with the mortar of sincere love. In fact, the divine voice commanded that the ark, which contained eight souls during the deluges of the flood, be lined with pitch both inside and out.[152] To wit, holy Church, which struggles toward the glory of the resurrection, is also lined within and without with pitch, so that outside she is caressed in fraternal sweetness and within she will be united in the truth of mutual love. For whoever loves inwardly, but outwardly is at variance with the brothers owing to the unsuitable harshness of his practices, has pitch, to be sure, on the inside but does not have it on the outside. Whoever presents himself as kindly, but does not conserve the reality of friendship in the hidden depth of the heart, feigns friendship on the surface but lies damnably wide open on the inside, although outwardly he is held together by the appearance of pitch that has been smeared on. Neither of them shall be snatched from the shipwreck of the flood, because neither is fortified by the double pitch of love, as was commanded by divine inspiration.

(92) One who presents himself outwardly as worthy of love and conserves inwardly a loving nature, who displays the fruit of kindness outwardly with the branches of the Word, inwardly establishes a deep root because he loves from the heart; here actually he is lined with pitch both within and without because he is joined to his neighbors by the double mortar of love. Besides this, because it was commanded earlier that the ark be

150. Phil 2.10.   151. 1 Pet 2.5.
152. Cf. Gen 6.14.

made of smooth wood, and then later that it be lined with pitch, we described above how much your wood must be smoothed and polished by the mattock of penance and discipline; now we will persuade you with a compelling, logical argument to apply pitch to the framed structure. For as long as people's manners are harsh and uncouth, the mortar of love is applied to them in vain, seeing that they quickly fly apart from one another when an evenly applied bond of polished manners is not observed among them.

(93) Be smoothed, then, by the discipline of spiritual exercise, be covered with pitch by means of the harmony of brotherly love. This bond can be perfectly fitted only when the ark is finished in a cubit,[153] that is, when one is set over the many in place of Christ. To be sure, unity makes many things fit themselves to one another, so that the wills of different people concur in a union of love and with the unanimity of a shared spirit.

(94) Therefore, beloved, if you want to be fitted one to another in the love of Christ, obey him who is set over you in place of Christ more attentively and with a humble heart. Let there be no prattling Shem among you, who denounced the nakedness of his father as shameful,[154] who published abroad the indecency of his father's sin. For in the midst of his two brothers he was not counted among the first fruits of the Israelites, nor did he deserve a place in the fullness of the nations.[155] Let no one be there who, after having despised the shepherd, seeks a hireling, who listens to the voices of strangers,[156] who beats the hammers of discord in a furnace of hatred, who divides the kingdom of Israel by sowing seeds of schism. "We have no part in David," he says, "nor inheritance in the son of Jesse."[157] Clearly, so long as bees make honey together, they abide by one leader. Cranes also come together at a call in a straight line, so much so that they do not confuse the order by following one of the letters on either side.[158] Once Rome was

---

153. Cf. Gen 6.16. 154. Cf. Gen 9.22.
155. Cf. Gen 9.25–27. 156. Cf. John 10.5.
157. 2 Sam 20.1.

158. The allusion here is of course to the fact that the flight of the birds seems to imitate a letter, usually the letter "V." Isidore, *Etymologies* 12.7.14,

founded, it could not have two brothers as king at the same time, and this is why it dedicated to parricide the first walls being raised up. In the womb of Rebecca, who conceived them, Jacob and Esau, although they wore no clothes except the maternal womb, joined in battle as if they were already clad in armor.[159]

(95) Therefore the rector should embrace and cherish the brothers as if they were his sons, and let them defer to him as sons defer to a father. You surely know this from the speech to Domitius: "Why should I treat you as a leader, when you do not treat me as a senator?"[160] Not that the spiritual disciples ought to be reproached with this, but so that the weaker brothers might have no occasion for grumbling. Therefore, he should love all to be loved rightly by all. In this way then the shepherd and the sheep, the general and the body of soldiers, should be united in one spirit for the exercise of the virtues, so that love, which is God,[161] may hold among them the chief place for undivided unity. See, my beloved fathers and lords, I check the point of my pen from its eagerness in running to you because I am not unaware that what is written is crude and uncultivated, and so that what rightly is despised because it is unseasoned by salt may at least be recommended for its brevity. Therefore I beg you who sometimes eat lupines after sea-delicacies not to scorn to look at this little leaf of parchment after the sacred volumes. Let the name of the Lord be blessed.

---

describes this ordered flight of cranes as well, and it becomes a commonplace example of animal intelligence throughout the Middle Ages. See, for example, Albertus Magnus, *De animalibus* 1.1.4.58 and 23.1.24.113(49). For translation and explanation, see *Albertus Magnus* On Animals: *A Medieval Summa Zoologica*, trans. Kenneth F. Kitchell and Irven M. Resnick (2 vols.; Baltimore: Johns Hopkins University Press, 1999), 1:67, n. 90, and 2:1626, n. 353.

159. Cf. Gen 25.22–23.
160. Quoted from Jerome's *Letter* 52.7 (CSEL 54.427).
161. 1 John 4.8, 16.

LETTER 154

Peter Damian to the Duke and Margrave Godfrey of Tuscany; he reproaches him, because he continues to support Cadalus, the antipope Honorius II. His support for an enemy of the Roman Church, Damian contends, marks him as an enemy of God as well as a defender of Antichrist.

(Lent 1068)

 O THE MOST excellent duke and margrave, lord Godfrey,[1] the monk Peter the sinner sends a reprimand of fervent zeal.

(2) A new and previously unheard rumor concerning you has repeatedly reached us, which has brought us a grief of no small sorrow, has struck the viscera with trembling, has restrained our lips from the customary praise of your glory, and has pierced a broken heart as if with the most profound pain's sharpest prick. Namely, that you have been in communication with Cadalus,[2] whom, as you clearly are aware, the universal Church vomited forth not long ago like a deadly venom, and cut off as a truly rotted limb from its own trunk, plunged into the depths of a hellish pit, and stopped up the vent-hole as if he were human excrement that has been buried in the pits of a latrine, lest he stink up people's nostrils otherwise. Laborers in the field, merchants in the marketplace, and soldiers cry out in public that your wisdom has communicated with such a man as this.

(3) Oh, alas, most eminent man, where were the copious streams of tears then which you had been accustomed to shed like a torrent from the most fervent love of a tender breast, and

---

1. Damian's *Letters* 67–68 were sent to the same recipient; see FOTC, MC 3.70–87.

2. Cf. *Letters* 88–89 (FOTC, MC 3.309–69).

with which you, kindled with the love of the Holy Spirit, did not cease to bedew faces made wet with tears? How much have the fruits of alms been diminished, with which the bounty of your very pious, generous clemency not only refreshed the needs of the poor throughout the continuing period of the Lenten fast, but, following the example of our Redeemer, even washed their feet, and did not blush to fix kisses upon them? Therefore you ought to fear what is said about that man through Solomon: "He who had money and put it into a bag with a hole in it."[3] Surely, whatever is deposited through the orifice's opening into a bag with a hole in it necessarily falls out through the exit of the breach. And what benefit is there if at first a small purse expands from the weight of the money, and then, as soon as it puffs out, it is emptied through a careless loss?

(4) And, indeed, you have fought manfully against this Antichrist, and you, together with your most serene and most illustrious wife, have often opposed his sacrilegious and perverse endeavors. Now, however, I do not know who has reined in the constancy of your religious life from this intention, and so loosened the rigor of honorable severity, while suggesting pernicious things, and persuaded you to bury, as it were, the work already begun. Thus, even Solomon said: "he that is loose and dissolute is the brother of one who wastes his own works."[4] This is because one who does not strictly follow through on good works, once they have been initiated, imitates with negligent slackening the hand of one who destroys them.

(5) Tell me, most splendid lord, if someone should attempt to bring violence to your very chaste and honorable marriage bed, would your kinsman, would a servant, dare to join with him in friendship? Which of them would presume to be united with him in a compact of friendship? If, then, a person dare not enter into an alliance with his lord's adversary, then why is your excellency unafraid to communicate with him who has presumed to violate the bride of Christ, namely, holy Church, as if

---

3. Hag 1.6. Here Damian has *qui pecuniam habuit* for the Vulg. *qui mercedes congregavit*, whereas at *Letter* 39.7 (FOTC, MC 2.103) he follows the Vulg. Also, note that he incorrectly attributes this statement to Solomon.

4. Prov 18.9. Damian omits *in opere suo* from the Vulg.

by a rape of obscene deception? He is convicted of being an enemy of God, who associates in friendship with [God's] enemy. This is the reason why Jehoram, a destructive and impious man, even though he was king of Israel, was mindful of Elisha, saying: "'Why has the Lord gathered together these three kings, to deliver them into the hand of Moab?' And Elisha replied to him: 'As the Lord of hosts lives, in whose sight I stand, if I did not reverence the face of Jehoshaphat, king of Judah, I would not have listened to you nor looked on you.'"[5] This is the reason one reads that Jehu, son of Hanani, spoke as a prophet to this same Jehoshaphat, because he gave aid to Ahab: "Do you offer aid to the ungodly and are you joined in friendship to those who hate? And therefore you deserved indeed the wrath of the Lord, but good works are found in you, because you have taken away the groves out of the land of Judah, and you have prepared your heart to seek the Lord the God of your fathers."[6] This is the reason that Ahab, because he allowed King Benhadad of Syria, whom he had bruised in battle, to escape unharmed, heard what was fitting from the prophet's mouth: "Because," he said, "you have let go out of your hand a man worthy of death, your life will be for his life, and your people for his people."[7] This is the reason why Saul, even more unfaithful, lost his kingdom, because he did not take vengeance on Agag, king of Amalek, as was appropriate.[8]

(6) What if God almighty should enter a complaint against you about his injury, and should place this complaint before you with a proper argument? Saying, I have raised you up above all the princes of your realm, I have made you illustrious and eminent to the ends of the Roman empire. I have bestowed upon you many more riches in foreign parts than you have inherited by paternal right, and I permitted none, shall I say, to take precedence over you, nor even to be your equal, except for the commander of the royal empire. If this is not

5. 2 Kgs 3.13–14.
6. 2 Chr 19.2–3. Damian omits *Dominum* from the Vulg., following "those who hate."
7. 1 Kgs 20.42.
8. 1 Sam 15.9.

enough, add that I have bestowed on you the quality of a passionate heart, and eloquence in speaking, as well as forces for making war, and I have placed the stiff necks of many enemies beneath your feet. I have conferred all these things on you along with the many endowments of other virtues, and have you decided to receive in communion my adversary who had been cast away from me, cut off, actually, from my members, condemned by the unanimous judgment of my priests?[9] If, I say, God himself should press these charges against you, eminent man, what could one offer in defense as an excuse? What refuge for evasion would the subtlety of your wisdom find?

(7) Pay careful attention, distinguished and exalted man, to these and other things like them that can be raised in objection against you, wash away with the tears of a worthy penance the sin of the offense you have admitted, sever the bond of lethal friendship, confess publicly to all that you have sinned, and turn back swiftly to the grace of the apostolic see, whose noble and illustrious son you are. When you drive away what is praised by the devil's members, and correct yourself voluntarily with the lamentations of repentance, you will acquire not only forgiveness from God, along with King David, but grace as well. Let your excellency have mercy upon my lips, most splendid lord, and draw the conclusion that they have not spoken out against you, but in their own defense, and consider what I have said not as kindling for malice or hatred but instead as the cautery of a medicinal cure.

9. For the synodal condemnations of Cadalus, see *Letter* 88.3 (FOTC, MC 3.309–10).

LETTER 155

Peter Damian to the Roman prefect Cencius. He recommends that he had better attend to his office and responsibility for administering justice, which he has neglected in order to pursue forms of personal piety and devotion. He reminds him that it is the ruler's role to establish justice, and that the administration of justice in the world is a form of prayer.

(ca. 1068)

O THE LORD prefect Cencius,[1] the monk P<eter> the sinner sends greetings in the Lord.

(2) Beloved, it is especially terrifying if you who administer an office of such great dignity should lay yourself open sometimes to the sloth of idleness. I hear that many complaints are made against you by those who have cases, because they do not have the influence to obtain the decree of a legal judgment from you. Hear, then, what a wise man should say: "A wise judge will judge his people, and the government of a prudent man will be steady for the land. As the judge of the people is himself, so also are his ministers, and what manner of man the ruler of a city is, such also are they who dwell in it."[2]

(3) It is clearly understood from these words that if you will guard justice and will, as a result of this, be just, then not only will the ministers be just but also your subjects in the urban populace. Therefore take care, lest out of devotion to your own prayer and for your own convenience you neglect the governance of such an innumerable population entrusted to you, and disregard the general well-being of the common people, which expects justice from you. For it is written: "He that keeps

---

1. Damian also addressed *Letters* 135 and 145 to Cencius; see FOTC, MC 6.77–83, 150–54.
2. Sir 10.1–2. Damian adds *terrae* following the Vulg. *sensati.*

the law multiplies prayer and it is a wholesome sacrifice to take heed of the commandments."[3] Therefore what is it to do justice, other than to pray? For elsewhere it is written: "Justice exalts a nation."[4] And the psalmist says: "Blessed are they who keep judgment and do justice at all times."[5]

(4) I clearly recall that it was the most excellent duke Godfrey[6] who told me what I write now. My uncle, he said, also named Godfrey,[7] a very powerful man, was especially intent upon doing justice and held the government and force of legal decrees over the peoples subject to him, so that indeed sometimes when a crowd beyond number of the common people was gathered before him, the duke himself would exclaim, in a lofty voice: "Let one who wants to have a judgment present his case in our midst." And when the one charged with the responsibility for proclaiming these words said them three times, and no one from among the entire people responded, then he knew that all were satisfied and every lawsuit was properly ordered and laid to rest. Then, happy, he mounted his horse, and he left the people not quarreling, but finding enjoyment in mutual peace with gladness.

(5) After his death, there was a certain man carried off in the spirit who was conducted to hell in a dream, and witnessed the various torments of punishments. He saw abbot Richard of Verdun[8] among them, as if he were erecting lofty, turreted war-machines, and looking anxious and troubled, just as if he were constructing fortified ramparts for the camp. The abbot suffered from this fault while he lived: that he foolishly expended almost all the attention of his household management on constructing buildings, and he ruined several church properties in frivolous activities of this sort. Therefore what he did in life, he

---

3. Sir 35.1–2. Damian has *orationem* for the Vulg. *oblationem.*
4. Prov 14.34.
5. Ps 105.3.
6. For Duke Godfrey of Tuscany, see also Damian's *Letters* 67–68 (FOTC, MC 3.70–87) and 154.
7. Godfrey, Duke of lower Lotharingia (d. ca. 1023). See Reindel, *Briefe* 4, p. 72, n. 5.
8. That is, Richard (970–1046), abbot of the Benedictine abbey of Saint-Vanne de Verdun.

was enduring as a punishment. In the same way, the one who perceived these things in a dream, as he observed with curiosity many things on this side and on that, saw my uncle, who was mentioned above, presiding on a golden judgment seat. Two angels, to be sure, seemed to assist him, and attempted to temper the heat on his face, waving fans with their hands, according to the custom of ministers. And when the one who saw these things inquired who he might be, he received this answer: Justice. Assuredly, he who did justice while he lived deserved the very name Justice after death.

(6) You, then, beloved, exercise the office of administration entrusted to you diligently, so that you imagine yourself just like a laborer in a vineyard entrusted to you, and if you expect a coin of proper remuneration, you will not be listless in the work's effort. Let the severity of legal decrees, then, check those whom the integrity of a good reputation does not restrain from the excesses of injustice, and let them know the power of the law, whom depravity's violence convicts of transgressing the limit of rectitude, so that when the rights of each person are protected by those who are subject to you, then also the proper wages of your own stewardship will be guarded for you before God.

LETTER 156

Peter Damian to the archdeacon Hildebrand and to Cardinal Stephen. Hildebrand, later Pope Gregory VII, is often mentioned in Damian's *Letters* in a friendly, although formal, manner. It may have been Hildebrand who earlier had advised Pope Stephen IX to name Damian Cardinal-Bishop of Ostia in 1057. Since Damian accepted the episcopacy with reluctance, Damian also sometimes refers to Hildebrand with mild reproof as his "friendly opponent" or "holy Satan."[1] In this letter, Damian asks Hildebrand and Cardinal Stephen to ensure the return of a book stolen from him by Pope Alexander II. He also uses the occasion to attack the anti-Pope Cadalus (Honorius II).[2]

(January 1069)

 O HIS LORD HILDEBRAND and our dear sweet brother Stephen, indomitable defenders of the Roman Church, the monk Peter the sinner sends his service.

(2) I entrust to God almighty and to you, who are his members, a complaint concerning our lord pope,[3] who distresses my heart with such overwhelming sorrow and provokes the soul of this already aged elder to bitterness. For he took away our book, which, with a great deal of work, I had plucked from the poverty of a destitute, feeble intellect, and embraced, as if an only child, with the arms of a kinsman's delight, and you should know how valuable the work is that he took away.[4] As he

---

1. Cf. *Letter* 122.3 (FOTC, MC 6.10); and 149.18, where Damian deprecates Hildebrand as a "reed of support" (FOTC, MC 6.180). *Letter* 160 in this volume is also addressed to Hildebrand.

2. Cf. Damian's *Letter* 154.

3. Pope Alexander II, to whom *Letters* 84 and 96 are also addressed; see FOTC, MC 3.247–49 and 5.51–67.

4. The title of the work in question is uncertain. Some scholars have suggested that Damian was referring to his *Liber gratissimus;* others have argued for the

knew that he could not get this from me in any other way, he handed it over to the lord abbot of the Holy Redeemer[5] in my presence, ordering him to transcribe it. But at night he took it away without my knowledge and stuffed it into his book chests. And, surely, this is the character of his priestly cleanliness, or rather this is the proof of his papal purity. And when I complain about these things he laughs, and he caresses my head with sweetness as if with an oil of playful refinement. His mouth bursts forth with laughter while his hand boxes my ear; he butters me up with words while he attacks me with objects—in other words, he treats a priest like a stage actor.[6] In Proverbs, Solomon says to one much like him: "As he is guilty who shoots arrows and lances unto death, so is the man who hurts his friend deceitfully, and when he is taken says: I did it in jest."[7]

(3) In addition, Roman history reports that stage-actors used to call Tiberius Caesar, as he was named Claudius Tiberius Nero, Caldius Biberius Mero,[8] because very often he guzzled a great quantity of wine. Perhaps I too—because I do not know how to dance but only how to write—should sometimes write what is fitting not for a priest but for a stage-actor. For I could easily spice up my lord's name with a droll witticism, if the preeminence of so great a rank did not prevent me from doing so. Indeed, "Alexander" means "lifting the straits of darkness," just as one finds in the interpretations of Hebrew names.[9] What else is designated by the "straits of darkness" than the many tribulations of toil and misfortune, which the frenzied Cadaline madness and rage brought upon us? Clearly, Cadalus stirred up the straits of darkness that Pope Alexander lifted—according to his

---

Liber gomorrhianus (or excerpts from these). See Reindel, *Briefe* 4, p. 75, n. 4, for bibliography.

5. It has been suggested that the monastery of San Salvatore di Monte Acuto in the diocese of Perugia is likely meant. See Reindel, *Briefe* 4, p. 75, n. 5, for bibliography.

6. For other references to stage actors, cf. *Letter* 138.4 (FOTC, MC 6.98), 153.84, and *Letter* 156, *passim*.

7. Prov 26.18–19.

8. This nickname for the Emperor Tiberius, with a pun on the verb *bibere* (to drink), is found in Suetonius, *De vita caesarum* 3.42, and in Paul the Deacon's *Historia Romana* 7.10.121.

9. Jerome, *Nom. hebr.* 78.17.

name's etymology—because when the light of the apostolic see went forth to extinguish the sulfurous smoke of Mt. Etna's desire, if I may put it so, he forced us all to endure the straits of darkness. For this reason, not only our lord pope but even all of us can be called an Alexander, compared to Cadalus, because when he imposed upon us straits of darkness we, who become participants with him in the work, deservedly are granted the name as well. But although he bears the name "to lift," "to fall" expresses the other,[10] and by this conflict between one who rises and one who falls, we are compelled to recall the one that John reports. He said: "And there was a battle in heaven, Michael and his angels fought with the dragon."[11] A little later, this is added concerning the battle: "And that great dragon was cast onto the earth, that old serpent, who is called the devil and Satan."[12] Following his example, Cadalus has fallen from heaven into hell, when he rushed from the summit of the apostolic see, which he hoped for, into the abyss of anathema.

(4) Moreover, never does one read that a pontiff of this name presided over the apostolic see, except perhaps only that distinguished martyr, established in fifth place after blessed Peter on his throne, whom we know was pierced through in all his members.[13] And, since I am forced to joke, this name appropriates all types of torments for itself in the apostolic see, and does not depart from ancient custom, as it possesses tribulation as an inheritance. Rather, according to the meaning of this name, the whole world is made an Alexandria[14] when the whole universal church, established throughout the world, groans under various straits of afflictions. It lies open on this side and on that to violations by rapacious men, it is rent by injuries, it is oppressed by a bundle of misfortunes, it is straitened daily as its possessions are taken away. And when it suffers the evasions

10. "To fall": *cadere*. On the etymology of the name Cadalus, see Damian's *Letter* 88.13 (FOTC, MC 3.315–16).

11. Rev 12.7.

12. Rev 12.9.

13. Pope Alexander I (107?–116? A.D.).

14. According to Damian, "Alexandria" derives its name from Alexander and enjoys the same etymology. See his *Sermo* 50.16, in *Sancti Petri Damiani sermones*, ed. G. Lucchesi, CCCM 57 (1983).

and tumult of ones speaking perverse things, it is blackened in some way with the soot of torches, saying through Solomon: "I am black but beautiful, O daughters of Jerusalem;[15] do not look at me because I am dark, since the sun has altered my color."[16]

(5) But when our aforementioned lord hears these words, perhaps he will reply to them as he is accustomed to do: You speak harshly, and how have I deserved it? What grave injustice have I done to you? This was not unlike what the sons of Dan said to Micah, from whom they had stolen all that he possessed. They said, "What do you want? Why do you cry out?"[17] He answered them: "You have taken away from me my gods which I made, and the priest, and all that I have, and you say: 'What does it concern you?'"[18] But since, just as the wise man says: "A tale out of time is like music in mourning,"[19] although I may be a stage-actor, still it is no pleasure for the lips to laugh when the heart is forced to grieve, nor does it delight him to pluck a harp, who is upset by the loss of a book that has been taken away. Let him return the book, then, if he wants to hold on to the bookmaker, and let him not lose the same pen's poor author on account of a brief series of worthless passages. So many expenditures of effort, so many dangers of death, deserve this, although we are driven to sing in the mournful voice of the prophet: "Since for your sake we suffer death all the day long, we are counted as sheep to the slaughter."[20]

(6) Clearly, just as the Gospel enumerates eight beatitudes,[21] so in his *Laws* Cicero describes eight types of punishments, no less.[22] And since just as these beatitudes exist for us in the understanding, would that the individual types of punishments we enumerate here were realized in act according to Cicero's order, to wit: condemnation, chains, stripes, retaliation in kind, ignominy, exile, death, slavery. Since, then, we have endured almost all of these in the service of the apostolic see, I ask, is it

---

15. Song 1.4.　　　　　　　　　16. Song 1.5.
17. Judg 18.23.　　　　　　　　18. Judg 18.24.
19. Sir 22.6.
20. Ps 43.22; Rom 8.36. Damian has *extimati* for the Vulg. *aestimati*.
21. Matt 5.3–10.
22. Cicero, *De legibus, frag.*, quoted in Augustine, *De civitate Dei* 21.11.1 (CCL 48; see also FOTC 24.368).

right that now we should pay the principal interest for an injury
to this same see for a debt of punishment already discharged,
as it were, although we do not seem to have any share at all in
the Gospel's beatitudes for service to this same pope? We do
have the first and the last, that is, we overflow with the riches of
these beatitudes—namely, poverty and persecution. Indeed,
the Romans want an Alexander, but the coppersmith, that is,
the one the apostle reproves,[23] and not one who follows the way
of life of the apostles and the apostolic pontiffs. They do not
want an Alexander displaying the evangelical wealth of the ecclesiastical table, but rather one weighing out money of a de-
basing avarice.[24] They reject the successor to Peter, and they
embrace that foster-son of Simon[25] who offers money for the
power of buying the Spirit. Accordingly, our lord, since he does
not lack his own to offer to us, should not in any event take
away what is ours. Indeed, the apostolic judgment is: "The children ought not to lay up for their parents, but the parents for
the children."[26] But, anticipating that, with shameless lips we
request penance from you, beloved, because we overstep our
bounds by our accusations when we speak against so great a father. In a lawsuit between the servant and the master there
ought to be both satisfaction from the offender and punishment for the one lashing out.

23. 2 Tim 4.14–15.
24. Cf. Acts 8.9–24.
25. Not Simon Peter, but Simon the magician (cf. Acts 8.18–24), from
whom the crime of simony—the purchase of ecclesiastical office—received its
name.
26. 2 Cor 12.14.

LETTER 157

Peter Damian to Bishop Mainard of Gubbio. He requires him to bring order to the affairs of his church, which has suffered harm during his episcopacy, and calls upon him personally to lead an exemplary life. He criticizes him for having mortgaged goods belonging to the church, and exhorts him to condemn and despise the world's riches.

(Lent 1069 or 1071)

ECAUSE I KNOW, brother, that you are not lacking in wisdom, I apply the discipline of correction without fear and free from care. For in Proverbs, Solomon says: "A reproof avails more with a wise man, than a hundred stripes with a fool."[1] And again: "If you rebuke a wise man, he will understand the discipline."[2] Again, he says: "The ear that hears the reproofs of life will abide in the midst of the wise,"[3] and then immediately after he adds: "He that rejects the discipline, despises his own soul, but he who yields to reproofs, possesses understanding."[4] I am repeating in writing what I have often admonished you face-to-face, and I am binding the motion of fleeting eloquence in a written form just as if to a safe anchor.

(2) Restore to your church, venerable brother, the estates that have been bestowed extravagantly on secular men, recover the jewels of various kinds that wickedly have been mortgaged, and at least let the most notable or the best of these be restored, which, because they have been removed during the period of your prelacy, cause us to sigh grievously. Also correct yourself in your practices, and be everywhere on your guard and everywhere utterly circumspect; compose yourself in priest-

1. Prov 17.10.
2. Prov 19.25.
3. Prov 15.31.
4. Prov 15.32.

ly gravity and integrity, and do not be pleased to overflow with an abundance of false riches that may be presented to you, nor should you seek to find joy in the reputation of the cathedral over which you preside. For often God almighty blocks off to a reprobate mind—may it be far from you!—which he observes has set out on a journey among the dangerous rocks of its desires, every possibility for the enterprise it has begun. And just as often he prevents the one who already presides from rejoicing when he wishes to rejoice; so too he restrains one aspiring to rule lest he ascend to the summit of the rank he desires.

(3) John of Marsica,[5] previously an archpriest of the church and now a religious monk in the monastery of Monte Cassino, informed me yesterday of the story which I narrate now. Alberic,[6] he said, brooded over possession of the title of the episcopal office of my church. This man who, like a pimp, clung to an obscene little harlot, falsely claimed to be celibate, when he feared the approaching arrival of the august Otto.[7] He removed the harlot therefore from his presence and fraudulently arranged for her to be clothed as a nun under the sacred veil; nevertheless, after the emperor's departure, he returned to the ignominy of his earlier foulness and, in addition, at the height of his shameful infamy, he produced a son with this same victim of an infernal brothel. As soon as he was pretty well grown up and had matured with the passage of years, the father placed him[8] in the episcopal dignity, in his own place.

(4) But when he recalled the long habit of ruling, and he blushed with shame that he did not receive the praise or reverence to which he had been accustomed earlier, he obtained advice offered from the deepest bile of a diabolical breast. Therefore, having first spoken with certain unwholesome monks, and then with some laymen who know nothing of God, finally he entered into a mutual agreement with the stipulation that the wretched purchaser would pay the price of one hundred

---

5. For literature treating John of Marsica, his entry to Monte Cassino, and the dating of this letter, see Reindel, *Briefe* 4, pp. 80–81, n. 4.

6. Bishop Alberic of Marsica.

7. Otto I, who was in Marsica in 964 and again in 970.

8. Guinisius, Bishop after 994 A.D.

pounds of the coin of Pavia. And thus it was guaranteed that
they would deliver the monastery of Monte Cassino to him
from the abbot[9] who ruled at that time, once he had been
blinded, and so he would obtain [this monastery] at last without any obstacle to oppose him, propped up with their aid. And
the first-born sons of Satan added this to the conspiratorial
pact: that he should send at least a part of the predetermined
price with his servants, and he would make no decision concerning the rest until he should behold the abbot's eyes placed
in his own hands.

(5) What else? Once he had procured, with some difficulty,
womanly jewels thick with gold, from wherever he could, he
sent sixty pounds of coin with his accomplices to the town[10] of
blessed Germanus, and he would tell them how and with whom
he vomited forth the snake-like poison that the wretched disciple had drunk up from the devil's dregs. Once the execrable secret had been communicated to them and they were instructed, those coming to the city actually were sent to a crypt of
this same city and they were concealed there for a period of several days, whereas Satan's retinue violently seized the abbot,
plucked out his eyes from their sockets, and secretly and swiftly
sent them wrapped in a small linen cloth to those who lay hidden in the crypt. Just as if they had embraced eagerly a long-
awaited treasure, they immediately became excited and began
to return to their own homes with haste. Once they had already
completed a very long distance, when only the last part of the
journey remained, and they would perceive their rewards just
like masters of an already secured pledge, suddenly a certain
stranger came upon them, and having been asked for any news,
he answered them that Alberic, who previously had been bishop, had died. Exceedingly astonished and terribly downcast,
they were unable to believe it. At last, knowing it for a certainty,
carefully they learned, further, the number of days for which he
had lain ill, and they clearly understood that he had died miserably at the very hour when the light had departed from the
abbot.

9. Manso, abbot after 985.
10. San Germano.

(6) See how one who desired to live sweetly and delightfully departed by such a bitter end, and how from that very moment of time when he hoped he would ascend the highest peak, as it were, he who had caused blindness was himself, like one truly blind, seized by something unforeseen and was suddenly plunged into hell. This prophecy is appropriately suitable for him: "While I was yet but beginning, he cut me off."[11] Moreover, his son, namely, the apostle of Antichrist, whom the father had drawn to the summit of ecclesiastical rank, endured many bitter experiences of misfortune and strife as long as he lived, until finally he went to his rest[12] pierced through on every side by his own savage blades. It is fitting that such an end to life should occur for those who aspired to the summit of the sacred order against God's will, and thereafter this life's sweetness, which they had imagined in the mind, turned into bitterness, and the prosperity which had favored them through a false appearance, turned for them into calamity. This passage of Isaiah's rightly suits them: "We hoped for peace, and there is no good; we sought goods, and behold trouble."[13] And this one of the psalmist's: "When they were lifted up, you have cast them down."[14]

(7) By contrast may you, venerable brother, condemn whatever delights and mistakenly agreeable things there are in this world, despise the artificial charm of worldly glory and an abundance of transitory things, and propose for yourself some difficult paths, following the rough footsteps of the Redeemer, so that passing through the difficult ones you may reach the pleasant ones, and as if passing through rough brambles you may bring your journey to a delightful end.

11. Isa 38.12.
12. 14 November 996.
13. Jer 14.19. Damian has *quaesivimus bona* for the Vulg. *et tempus curationis*, and has erroneously identified the source of the quotation.
14. Ps 72.18.

LETTER 158

Peter Damian to his nephew, Damianus, the recipient of other letters from his uncle and frequently the subject of his concern.[1] He warns him about the danger of excessive or uncontrolled ascetic practices, while praising his zeal, and invites him to return from the cloister to the superior practices of religious life found in the hermitage. He concludes with an extended allegory on the significance of the poles and axes of the Cross.

(Lent 1069)

O HIS NEPHEW Damianus, the monk Peter the sinner sends the affection of paternal love.

(2) If the God who led his people from Pharaoh's workhouse had ceased to be their guide in the desert, Israel never would have been able to reach the promised land. It needed a guide for the journey who was the author of their going forth. Therefore [God] had said to Abraham: "Come into the land which I will show to you."[2] Because he does not say, "go," but instead says, "come," he promises to be a participant in the future journey. And what is actually added next, "into the land which I shall show you," clearly reveals that he who challenged him to go forth from the land of his birth would be his guide until the goal of his journey had been achieved.

(3) I have rejoiced greatly that this is not unlike what had begun to befall you, as I learned of some of the distinctions of your novitiate's fervent zeal from a report of a completely reli-

---

1. Peter Damian had an older brother named Damianus, who became a monk in later life and to whom he addressed *Letter* 138 (FOTC, MC 6.97–101). He also had a nephew, Damianus, whom he identifies as his sister's son (cf. *Letter* 166.3). Peter Damian addressed his *Letter* 123 to this nephew, who is also mentioned at the end of *Letter* 122; see FOTC, MC 6.11, 12–20.

2. Gen 12.1.

able man, brother Ubaldus.[3] Among other things, he said that at a time when he was shivering from the very harsh winter's cold in those Alps,[4] so that the accumulation of snow covered the tops of whatever shelters or houses exist there, you, after having cast off your clothes, secretly buried yourself naked in the depths of the snowy drifts, and there this brother found you almost half-dead. And when he reproached you very severely, as was appropriate, you are said to have replied to him: "The flesh attempts to slay me, but I will slay it instead." And afterwards, you were found not under the open sky but under some building—I do not know which—similarly covered in snow. In this event, although the correction of the rule ought not be neglected, I prefer nevertheless that a person's excessive fervor exceed the measure of discretion than that a torpor of cowardly idleness restrain base minds.

(4) For it is easier to drain off the reflux from a vessel that has overflowed than to fill one which is empty. It requires far more effort to graft onto a trunk branches it does not have than to cut off those that are superfluous to the tree. A horse which requires reins to restrain its impatience for a race is worth more than one which reveals, by the listlessness of its natural torpor, that its flanks must be pricked with spurs. Indeed, a horse that is agile and swift when he prances, whirling about like a bird, is easily held in check after the bridle has gradually been relaxed, when he is whipped and struck; but one that is still not spurred on to the speed of a horse's natural agility reveals himself to be just like an ass, on account of the listlessness of a genuine torpor.

(5) Therefore, although it would certainly be wrong to exceed the limit of discretion, it is better for you to be reproached for excessive ardor than to be known for the foul disease of idleness. I do not want, then, this flame of praiseworthy zeal to abate in you; nonetheless, when it is necessary, I want

3. For other references to Ubaldus/Herbaldus, see also *Letters* 67.13 and 119.86 (FOTC, MC 3.75, 5.385).

4. "Alps" would also include the Apennines, which join with the Ligurian Alps in northwest Italy.

the power of your prior and the discipline to check this aberration of indiscretion, with you left unharmed. For through this zeal that is said to live in you, I have understood that that spirit which admonishes you to go forth from your home like Abraham has not abandoned you, but, having become a guide for your journey, has not ceased to go before you.[5]

(6) Nevertheless, I suffered it badly, because I knew that you had entered the monastery of the blessed Bartholomew[6] to learn the modes of ecclesiastical chants. When I heard this, it certainly seemed to me that the tender lamb had jumped out of the sheepfold and rushed to the cruel jaws of the predatory wolf. But even then, and when brother Ubaldus brought this message to me concerning you, which was not what I wished for, Peter, the abbot of the monastery, distinguished by the genuineness of his religious way of life, approached and recalled to mind with much affection that there flourishes in the city of Salerno a building decorated with the title of blessed Benedict. He is the one who told me that a hidden wolf, hungry for men, attacked a little boy from the family of our monastery, snatched him up, and went off. After this the mother, pierced with grief, said, crying aloud: "I adjure you, you beast, through the blessed Benedict, whose servant he is, not to ravage my son further but to release him with haste." After the wolf heard this, he immediately dropped the one he carried from his open mouth, sprang unexpectedly upon another boy, and, cutting off the trunk of the corpse, he suddenly spurned it, and once he seized the severed head, the excited wolf carried it off to his den.

(7) I too, then, who fear that you have been seized by the teeth of the invisible wolf, trust in the deliverance of our same holy father, Benedict, whose servant you were made. For why would you have descended from the hermitage to a monastery unless the artful ambusher dragged you out by the bite of his pernicious cunning? Nevertheless, I do not want to pursue this first sin any longer, which, as I believe, did not arise from light-minded inconstancy on your part, but proceeded from the unadvised caution of the ones giving orders, especially since the

5. Cf. Gen 12.1.
6. I.e., Camporeggiano.

already mentioned Ubaldus told me that in the end, unwillingly and only when forced to do so, you would barely consent to
this command.

(8) Return to the hermitage, then, beloved son, with all due
speed, lest as monastic laxity seduces your youthfulness, at
some time the severity of the hermitage would become hateful—may God forbid—through having forgotten its practice.
Immovably plant the trophy of your cross there, hang yourself
there together with Christ, so that, as the apostle says: "being
rooted and founded in charity, you may be able to comprehend, with all the saints, what is the breadth, and length, and
height, and depth."[7]

(9) This is without any doubt the cross of the Redeemer. All
of Christian religion is depicted in this sign of celestial victory,
the whole perfection of the spiritual virtues is designated in the
character of this life-sustaining sign. For since the entire divine
law consists in these three virtues, namely, faith, and hope,
together with charity, and the multitude of all the virtues proceeds from them, faith, which is the foundation of Christian religion, is symbolized by that part of the Cross which is fixed to
the ground. The entire fabric of a good work rests upon this
foundation, and the entire frame of the spiritual virtues is sup-
ported on it, so that it can stand. Thus the apostle said to the
disciples: "For you stand in faith."[8] Hope is understood by
the highest point on the vertical shaft, which stands out above
the others, by which our soul is challenged to seize the heavens.
Truly, the breadth of twin charity is indicated by that wood
which, placed in the middle, is stretched to two arms, one on
each side.

(10) Without any doubt, the number of the four cardinal
virtues is expressed by the sign of this same life-giving Cross;
from these the harvest of all the virtues is germinated as if from
seeds, to wit, justice, fortitude, wisdom, and temperance. By the
highest point on the shaft,[9] which gazes upon heaven, justice is
symbolized, just as one may gather from the words of the Re-

7. Eph 3.17–18. Damian has *altitudo* for the Vulg. *sublimitas.*
8. 1 Cor 16.13. Damian has *statis* for the Vulg. *state.*
9. "Shaft": lit., "horn," "wing," or "extremity" *(cornu).*

deemer himself. Because, although he had first said, "The Holy
Spirit will convict the world of sin, and of justice, and of judgment,"[10] a little later he added: "And of justice, because I go to
the Father and you will see me no longer."[11] And a wise man
said: "Justice exalts the nations,"[12] no doubt, to heaven. The
lower part of the Cross, which supports the upper structure, indicates fortitude, which bears burdens and misfortunes of every
sort with equanimity. The right arm of the Cross actually expresses wisdom, with which we cast down the darts thrown by
the wicked spirit, as if blocking them with the right hand, and
once we have pierced him with the lance of a fervent spirit we
carry back the spoils of victory, strongly overthrowing him,
guarded by divine protection. Temperance, not improperly, is
indicated by the left side of the shaft. For there is less strength
in the left hand than in the right. Therefore, we attract
strength, in a certain manner, by the tempering of our virtue
when we live modestly and temperately, when often we soften
the rigor and judgment of justice with the skill of a teacher's
discernment.

(11) What shall I say, but that the law of the Old Testament,
at the very beginning of its own promulgation, already was
redolent of the mystery of the Cross, when namely just as the
latter was framed of wooden beams, so no less is the former
known to have been inscribed by the finger of God on twin
tablets. And because the number ten is expressed by the letter
"X," which represents the sign of the Cross, and it is certain,
moreover, that the law was given through the decalogue, it is
evident that the clarity of evangelical grace, while shining
throughout the world, later revealed that the law also contained in itself the mysteries of the salvific Cross, although in a
hidden way.[13] Thus it is said through Zechariah: "In that day,
that which is upon the bridle of the horse will be called holy to
the Lord."[14] The holy Gospel is the bridle of the horse, which

10. John 16.8. Damian has *Spiritus sanctus* for the Vulg. *Paracletus.*
11. John 16.10.
12. Prov 14.34.
13. Cf. Peter Damian, *Sermo* 18.8, in *Sancti Petri Damiani sermones*, ed. G. Lucchesi, CCCM 57 (1983).
14. Zech 14.20. Damian adds *vocabitur* to the Vulg.

certainly reins in the appetite of carnal desire as if with a horse's reins. The Cross, then, is upon this bridle because whatever is commanded through evangelical precepts is undoubtedly related to the Cross, as the Lord himself proclaims: "Whoever will come after me," he says, "let him deny himself and take up his cross daily and follow me."[15] To be sure, this cross is rightly called "holy to the Lord," because the world, which until then had been profaned, is blessed by it. But since we have written at greater length elsewhere about the holy and precious Cross,[16] lest perhaps the same thing happen to be repeated here, we decide that the things treated here in haste in an epistolary summary suffice.

(12) Paint this sign of your life, dearest son, as if on your forehead; also imprint it no less on the threshold to your heart, so that when the avenging angel perceives this he will not delay to pass over without causing you injury.[17] Let these phylacteries hang before your eyes without cease, let these marks brand your body on every side, just as the apostle testified concerning himself: "I," he said, "bear the marks of Jesus in my body."[18] Break the body with fasts, abstain from your own desires, submit yourself in very prompt devotion to the command of another's order, let the modest judgment of silence check the impudent remarks of an insolent tongue, let the charms of droll speech not break out, let the rigor of severe continence tear out the illicit motions of the carnal passions, so that for you who die now with Christ of your free will, the heavier his Cross is observed to be in your religious life, the more fully the glory of his resurrection will accrue to you.

15. Luke 9.23.
16. See Reindel, *Briefe* 4, p. 89, n. 23, for bibliography.
17. Cf. Exod 12.29.
18. Gal 6.17.

LETTER 159

Peter Damian to the Abbot Desiderius of Monte Cassino. He discusses why in artistic representations Peter is depicted on the left side, and Paul on the right side of Christ. His solution suggests that it is because Peter symbolizes the active life, whereas Paul symbolizes the life of contemplation.

(1069, after Lent)

O LORD ABBOT Desiderius of the holy way of life and to the religious community, the monk Peter the sinner offers service in the Lord.

(2) As I learned that lord Martin[1] is undertaking a journey to you, I immediately ordered a scribe to come in next. But seeing that I spent the entire Lenten cycle with you in close familiarity, venerable father, whatever things seemed necessary to discuss we discussed face-to-face, and since we intimated very often what things had to be communicated or treated, I do not understand how anything new could be written to you, when I consider that very often we were able to communicate to one another whatever was necessary in conversation. What then should I do? Now that I have begun to speak, shall I become stupidly quiet for lack of material?

(3) But when I observe the scribe's hand armed with a pen and poised for writing according to his practice, a fresh topic presents itself to me, for which my mind may be eagerly roused to discussion. Indeed, from the very right hand of the scribe there suddenly occurred to me precisely what you yourself had demanded from me in a question regarding order, which you have often posed: namely, why is it that in copies of pictures throughout all the provinces bordering on Rome Peter, who is

1. Martin, a monk of Monte Cassino, later named Bishop of Aquino (d. ca. 1073).

the first [of the apostles], is placed on the left, whereas his fellow apostle Paul is placed on the right, when according to common opinion the proper order demands that Peter, who is the first member of the apostolic senate, by right should occupy the right side of the Lord, whereas Paul, who is junior, should occupy the left? But it is terribly difficult for us to imagine that such a long-standing and pious practice devoted to God, should have allowed so distinguished and celebrated an order of the apostolic arrangement without consideration and inadvisedly. Neither may one believe that the emperor Constantine, or rather Pope Silvester, and the many princes and priests after them who were vigilant and intelligent concerning the correction of ecclesiastical discipline, would allow this order of such great princes to be neglected, if they thought it was in some way deserving of correction. Lest, therefore, the order of this sacred history appear disordered, let us briefly make clear to your holiness what seems to us to be the case.

(4) Who doubts that Paul clearly came from the tribe of Benjamin? Moreover, in the Hebrew language Benjamin is called, in Latin, the "son of the right hand."[2] Why is it remarkable, then, if the one who draws the name "of the right hand" from paternal right is placed on the right? For in truth, so that the old history be seen to accord clearly with blessed Paul, Scripture says, not without reason, that "when Rachel's soul was departing, for pain and death were now at hand, she called the name of her son Benoni, that is, the son of my pain. But his father called him Benjamin, that is, the son of the right hand."[3] For through Rachel, who is called a "ewe" or "the first to see,"[4] the Church is indicated, not undeservedly. For assuredly she both lives innocently like a ewe and burns in her inmost soul, through a devotion to contemplation, to see the appearance of her Redeemer.[5] It was he who said to the Jews demanding to

2. Cf. Jerome, *Nom. hebr.* 3.24; 16.17; 74.1; 76.24; 80.14.

3. Gen 35.18. Damian adds *Rachel* to the Vulg.

4. Cf. Jerome, *Nom. hebr.* 9.25; 63.1; Gregory the Great, *Moralia in Job* 30.25.72, ed. M. Adriaen, CCL 143b (1981).

5. For Rachel as a symbol of the contemplative life, see *Letter* 50.4, n. 5, FOTC, MC 2.291.

know about him: "I am the beginning, who also speak to you."[6]
The mother Rachel died therefore as Benjamin was born, while
as Saul approached the light of regeneration, he cruelly assailed the Church with persecutions. For just as Luke said in
the Acts of the Apostles: "Saul made havoc of the church; entering houses, and dragging away men and women, he delivered them to prison."[7] Rachel called him appropriately, then,
"Benoni, that is, the son of my pain," whom Jacob named "Benjamin, that is, the son of the right hand,"[8] because Paul, who
was the pain of Mother Church, who slew her by attacking her
in some manner as she was born, is called the son of the right
hand by God the Father when divine power, as if through his
strong right hand, contended against the Gentiles through
him, violently hurled back verbal darts, endured the salubrious
wounds of the heart, and triumphed through him with glory
once the enemies had been conquered and laid low. This is
the reason that this same Paul said to the Galatians: "When it
pleased him, who separated me from my mother's womb and
called me by his grace, to reveal his Son in me that I might
preach him among the Gentiles, at that time I did not find
peace in flesh and blood."[9]

(5) Paul, then, is called not undeservedly the son of the
right hand, through whom every multitude of the nations,
which has to be placed on the right hand of God, is gathered
up to the sacraments of the faith.[10] Indeed, he is girded with
the Word of God, which is the sword of the Spirit,[11] and today
until the end of time it contends against the madness of all of
the vices and the iniquitous spirits, and cuts off the stiff necks
of those who resist God with gleaming swords of heavenly eloquence, just like Christ's lightning hand. Correctly, then, Paul,
who did not hesitate to exercise the power of God's right hand,
obtains the dignity of the right side next to the Redeemer. Now,
does he not confess that in some manner he is the right hand
of God fighting against the devil when he says: "I therefore so

---

6. John 8.25. Damian adds *Ego* to the Vulg.
7. Acts 8.3.   8. Gen 35.18.
9. Gal 1.15–16.   10. Cf. Matt 25.31–33.
11. Cf. Eph 6.17.

run, not as at an uncertainty; I so fight, not as one beating the air"?[12]

(6) He comes to that side because Paul ascended, taken up to the third heaven,[13] where he heard secret words unsuited for speaking to people. Moreover, who is ignorant of the fact that the earthly life signifies the left side of God, whereas the heavenly life signifies the right, just as the bride says in the Song of Songs: "His left hand is under my head, and his right will embrace me"?[14] Now, the left is said to be under the head because the present life, which is undoubtedly the "head" of thoughts, is trod under the mind as something despised among any of the elect. But the right side the bride of God is said to embrace, because when a faithful and holy soul is kindled to its burning desire by the fire of the Creator, it is warmed on every side just as if with certain divine embraces. Therefore, the one who, when still surrounded by the frailty of the flesh, is known to have ascended to a heavenly life, is properly called the son of the right hand. God almighty always stretched out this son of the right hand, as if he were his own right hand, across the entire breadth of the world, and through that hand he gathered up the adoptive peoples to the unity of faith.

(7) The perfect farmer turned this right hand to the threshing floor of his church, winnowed with it the spiritual grains, in order to introduce cleansed kernels of mystical corn to heavenly granaries. God stretched his right hand hither and thither at a great distance when Paul traversed the entire surface of the earth to gather up the nations in the mystery of faith. Indeed, as much as he burned with a powerful love, so much did he turn himself about, wandering from place to place. He wanted to pass to some places from others because the goad of love itself, which filled him, drove him on. For, situated far away from the Romans, he wrote: "I make a commemoration of you always in my prayers, beseeching that somehow by God's will I may at last have a successful journey to come to see you. For I long to see you."[15] Held at Ephesus, he wrote to the Corinthians: "See

---

12. 1 Cor 9.26.
13. 2 Cor 12.2–4.
14. Song 2.6.
15. Rom 1.9–11.

now a third time I am ready to come to you."[16] And delaying again at Ephesus, he spoke to the Galatians, saying: "I would willingly be present with you now and change my voice."[17] Also, when he was locked up in the custody of a prison in Rome, because he was not permitted to go by himself to the Philippians, he promised to dispatch a disciple, saying: "I hope in the Lord Jesus to send Timothy to you shortly, that I also may be of good comfort, when I know the things concerning you."[18] In addition, when he was bound in chains and held at Ephesus, he wrote to the Colossians: "For though I am absent in body, yet in spirit I am with you."[19]

(8) See how much the apostolic heart boiled over from a fire of brotherly love, how much he was driven to exert himself by a desire for the salvation of the nations. Held in one place in the body, he was led to another in the spirit, and he extended to those who were absent from him the affection of fatherly love, which he applied to those who were present to him. He displayed works for those in his presence, and expressed solemn promises to his audience. For those with whom he was, he was effectively present; nevertheless, he was not absent from those with whom he was not. We recognize his love better if we consider also his words to the Corinthians. For he said: "Now I will come to you after I have passed through Macedonia, for I will pass through Macedonia, and perhaps I shall abide or even spend the winter with you."[20] Why is it that he was divided so anxiously among so many places, unless because he was constrained by a single love directed toward all? For love, which is wont to unite those that are divided, forced Paul's one heart to be divided among many. This heart, nevertheless, the more ardently it collected itself in God, the more widely it extended itself through holy desires.

(9) Therefore, while preaching, Paul wanted to say everything at once; while loving, he wanted to see everyone together because, still remaining in the flesh, he wanted to live for all, and, passing from the flesh, he wanted to benefit all by the sac-

---

16. 2 Cor 12.14.   17. Gal 4.20.
18. Phil 2.19.   19. Col 2.5.
20. 1 Cor 16.5–6.

rifice of faith. Nor is it remarkable if the eminent preacher burned more ardently in brotherly love, if the riches of true love abounded in him beyond all other mortals, when the Fountain of life, which called him a vessel of election,[21] determined that he would flow into him more abundantly, and deigned to refresh him in an incomparable fashion at the streams of his mysteries. This is the reason that he says: "Do you seek a proof of Christ, who speaks in me?"[22]

(10) Clearly, by a privilege of singular grace the Savior of the world bestowed on blessed Paul that which he asked of no mortals after the mystery of his Incarnation. For once the blessed and divine humanity of the Redeemer was lifted up to the court of paternal majesty, so that he would no longer be present among people in a corporeal manner but would instead preside over the powers of heaven, he effectively instructed [Paul], not through a teacher, but he instructed him in a special way by himself, and he ascribed to himself the mysteries of all of his acts, so that not only would he in no way require the teaching of his predecessors, but would surpass them besides in the depth of all heavenly wisdom. Thus even the first of the apostles, Peter, admired his wisdom, saying: "And also our dear brother Paul, according to the wisdom given to him, has written to you, as also in all his epistles, speaking in them of these things, in which there are certain things hard to understand, which the unlearned and unstable distort."[23]

(11) Moreover, to the fact that he had no human teacher at all for learning the mysteries of evangelical doctrine but had God instead as a special instructor, he himself attests when he speaks in this way at the beginning of his epistle to the Galatians, saying: "Paul an apostle, not of men, neither by man, but by Jesus Christ, and God the Father, who raised him from the dead."[24] For the Fountain of eternal life, who poured out the streams of his wisdom among the other apostles over long periods of time, plunged himself whole, all at once, just like a huge torrent, into the vessel of his election. And a little later: "For I

21. Cf. Acts 9.15.   22. 2 Cor 13.3.
23. 2 Pet 3.15–16.   24. Gal 1.1.

make it known to you, brethren, that the Gospel which was preached by me is not according to man, for neither did I receive it of man, nor did I learn it, but by the revelation of our Lord Jesus Christ."[25] What, then, the Lord, while still mortal, taught Peter through many proofs, he revealed as a whole, all at once, to the blessed Paul after he was already constituted in the glory of paternal majesty, just as if any teacher when he is in private life would teach disciples but afterward, once he has ascended to obtain the scepters of the royal empire, chooses from among many to instruct the most distinguished one, after having removed the one who is the most noble from the body of companions.

(12) In order, though, to return to the discussion with which we began, when the blessed Peter is placed on the right side, the primacy of the one who was chosen from among the other apostles is honored. But when Paul occupies a place on this same right side, he hints at the mystery of a mystical symbol in Benjamin, whose son he is, although let this also not be wanting in mystery that blessed Peter holds the left side of the Lord. Through him, indeed, the active life is signified. And just as the contemplative life is expressed by the right side, so too the active life is expressed by the left. Moreover, that Peter symbolizes the present, that is, active life, is especially demonstrated by this: just as very often the evangelical history attests that Peter loved the Lord more than all his fellow disciples, and the Lord assigned not to Peter, but to John instead, the prerogative of his special love,[26] John designates the contemplative life, but the active life, as was already mentioned, is designated by Peter. Because in this life all the saints love God more, according to Peter's example, and are, as it were, loved less, as they sustain labor's harsh burdens on account of him, nevertheless, they do not achieve the sweetness of his embrace still enclosed in mortal flesh. Those, however, who are already with God, love him less in some sense, but are loved more, as they experience no buffeting winds of toil on his behalf, and nevertheless they en-

---

25. Gal 1.11–12. Damian adds *Domini nostri* to the Vulg.
26. Cf. John 21.15.

joy the pleasures of his most intimate familiarity. It is not re-markable, then, if blessed Peter is sometimes seen to occupy the left side, who, from the authority of the Scriptures, contains a symbol of the active life.

(13) Whereas there appears in blessed Paul the one who is distinguished, because, although all the apostles obtain their own chairs[27] among the regions of the earth apportioned to them, he, while he holds none in a special sense, seems to pre-side in some way over all in general. Clearly, because he estab-lished the universal church over the entire surface of the world, just as he spread the seed of faith among all, he is worthy even to hold the right of presiding over all. Now, he said to the Corinthians: "By the grace of God I am what I am, and his grace has not been void in me, but I have labored more abun-dantly than all of them; yet not I, but the grace of God with me."[28] Moreover, to the Romans he said: "I give glory to God in Christ Jesus for the obedience of the Gentiles by word and deed, by the power of signs and wonders, in the power of the Holy Spirit, so that from Jerusalem round about as far as Il-lyricum I shall minister by the Gospel of Christ. And I have so preached this Gospel not where Christ was named, lest I should build on another's foundation, but as it is written: They to whom he was not spoken of shall see, and they that have not heard shall understand."[29] This is the reason, then, why Paul may not hold any specific chair, because if we dare to entrust the lesser to the highest, he seems by an unbroken right to pre-side over all the churches of the other apostles, according to a likeness to Christ.

(14) Moreover, as far as the common interpretation is con-cerned, since the Lord suffered in Jerusalem, not the Roman

27. Chairs: Lat. *cathedrae*, referring to the bishop's throne or chair in his church, i.e., cathedral. Although the other apostles were understood to have founded a particular church—as Peter was according to tradition the first bish-op of Rome—Damian suggests here that Paul is not the founder of any particu-lar church but served instead as an apostle to all peoples everywhere.

28. 1 Cor 15.10.

29. Rom 15.17–21, quoting Isa 52.15. Damian has *evangelio* for the Vulg. *evangelium*, and has omitted the passage *Non enim audeo aliquid loqui eorum, quae per me non effecit Christus* at Rom 15.18.

but the Jerusalemite church instead ought to be in charge over all the churches. But since according to the authority of the canons the Roman church should hold the first place, the Alexandrian the second, the Antiochene third, Constantinopolitan fourth, and Jerusalemite the fifth, it follows that the Lord, the Savior, does not preside over any single chair by a special right, but rather the one shepherd presides over all generally. It is clear therefore that the order of the churches is disposed according to the privilege of Peter, not according to the incomparable excellence of the Redeemer. Since all the apostles obtain this authority according to their measure through the grace of a gift that has been bestowed on them, Christ possesses the whole through the authority of a natural majesty. Paul, properly speaking, enjoyed a certain likeness to Christ, in so far as he presided over not one church but over all. Not without reason, then, does blessed Paul obtain the right side in pictures, when the weightier accumulation of fruits would in no way demand it, but only the mystery of a symbolic understanding.

(15) The mind yearns to write still more on this theme, but the letter-carrier who speeds to hurry to you, as he wishes to fly rather than to run, does not permit me to have even brief moments for writing [further]. May divine compassion instruct you, beloved, that your holy brotherhood not cease to pray for me.

LETTER 160

Peter Damian to Alberic, the Deacon of Monte Cassino, and to the Cardinal Archdeacon Hildebrand. Damian takes occasion to compose this letter from a conversation he has had with the addressee over the meaning and observance of Lent. Finding mystico-allegorical significance beyond the literal interpretation of Numbers 33.1–38, he explains the passage of the Hebrew people through forty-two rest stops as so many stages of the people of God on the way to perfection. He also finds this number paralleled in the forty-two generations from which Christ descended. In *MSS Vaticanus Urbinus latinus* 503 and *Monte Cassino* 359 this letter is addressed to Hildebrand; but in *MS Vaticanus latinus* 4930, which contains the *Collectanea in vetus testamentum,* the various excerpts are always addressed to Alberic. It is possible, and even likely, that the same letter was sent to both of them, but the familiar style of the introduction seems foreign to Damian's usual formality and reserve in addressing Hildebrand.[1]

(1069, after Lent)

O MY MOST reverend brother, Hildebrand, the monk Peter the sinner sends the affection of his intimate love.

(2) Venerable brother, what you and I were recently discussing as we talked together would not, I think, be useless or superfluous if I should put it into writing. For on that occasion I told you, if you have not forgotten, that I was acquainted with a servant of God who, besides the Lenten periods that were established by the Fathers and were prescribed throughout the year for a limited time, privately observed other fasts by which he overcame the enticements of carnal lust and mortified the

---

1. For a discussion of this problem, see O. J. Blum, "Alberic of Monte Cassino and a Letter of St. Peter Damian to Hildebrand," *Studi Gregoriani* 5 (1956): 291–98.

sexual desires that burned within him. At times for forty days he abstained from fish; at others he refrained from eating fruit or even vegetables, whichever was more convenient for him. Now and then, in season, he ate cherries, melons, figs, or grapes, or anything that he found delicious. But as soon as his appetite tempted him to eat, he at once applied restraint, lest these foods become an addiction. And since what one avidly desires and has already tasted is longed for all the more, he promptly applied the curb of abstinence to his eating, not indeed despising foods "which God created to be enjoyed with thanksgiving by believers," nor unaware "that all of what God created is good, and that nothing is to be rejected when it is taken with thanksgiving."[2]

(3) When at first he began to eat anything at all, even though his repast was more a penance than a source of pleasure to him, so that by abstinence his desire to overindulge was broken and the fires of lust were extinguished, he did not, of course, despise God's creation. And by so doing he received a greater reward, because his abstinence from things of little account was not done openly to make him famous or outstanding, but rather like something secret that remains unknown. And if one of the brothers were to ask him why he did not take this or that food, he would promptly reply that he knew that this item was dangerous to his health. But in saying this, he was speaking of the infirmities of his soul, while the other thought that his remarks applied to some bodily affliction. And so, it was his custom always to abstain from these particular foods for a period of forty days.

(4) You yourself also recently told me that you totally abstained from using onions or chives because you were especially fond of these pungent foods. Indeed, with regard to these items that are of small concern, abstinence is more difficult and brings little renown. As you are aware, it is easier for one to give up meat than salt, more difficult to turn down fruit than dishes sprinkled with fragrant spices. Admittedly, it was fruit, and not spices, that occasioned the expulsion of our first par-

2. 1 Tim 4.3–4.

ents from paradise,[3] for the fault was in procuring not what can be more expensive, but what can be more eagerly desired. Yet abstaining from richer things is found to be more praiseworthy, while denying oneself cheaper things is thought to be less worthy of mention. And so it happens, that what is less esteemed in public may be held in greater respect in private, as the celebrated preacher says: "Though our troubles are slight and short-lived, their outcome in us is eternal glory, which outweighs them by far."[4]

(5) Nevertheless, it seems to me that the servant of God of whom I was speaking, was inspired by the Holy Spirit to be ready at all times to spend forty days after forty days experiencing all sorts of trials in his continuing abstinence, and never seemed to depart from the sacred number he had set for himself. For this was the number of days during which the heavens opened causing the flood,[5] when God's holiness renewed the face of the earth after the sins of the wicked had been washed away. By practicing self-denial for this period of time, Moses was rewarded by receiving the commandments of the Law written by the finger of God,[6] and also through this number of days and nights of self-denial Elijah, with untiring step, came to Horeb, the mountain of God.[7] A still greater honor was accorded this number when the Lord himself fasted for forty days in the desert,[8] and later saw fit to lie in the grave for the same number of hours.[9] After the resurrection he also remained with the disciples for forty days[10] until he ascended in triumph to be seated beside his Father in majesty.

(6) But that this brother was so pleasantly sustained by the mystery of this sacred number, that within its limits he was always able to bear the vicissitudes of salutary abstinence, was undoubtedly the result of the inspiration of the divine Spirit, for while constantly walking within the bounds of the number forty, he could say with the Israelites that he hastened from Egypt to his homeland. In fact, it was in keeping with this num-

---

3. Cf. Gen 3.3–24.
5. Cf. Gen 7.12.
7. Cf. 1 Kgs 19.8.
9. Cf. Luke 24.21.

4. 2 Cor 4.17.
6. Cf. Exod 24.18.
8. Cf. Matt 4.2.
10. Cf. Acts 1.3.

ber that the people of Israel entered the promised land.[11] Oh,
how great is the depth of this sublime mystery, that according
to its norms God became man, and as a result, man returned to
his Creator. For as you know, during the exodus of the children
of Israel from Egypt there were forty-two rest stops, and the
coming of our Lord and Savior into the world progressed similarly through forty-two generations, which Matthew the evangelist enumerates when he says: "There were thus fourteen generations in all from Abraham to David, fourteen from David
until the deportation to Babylon, and fourteen from the deportation to Babylon until the Messiah."[12] It was, therefore, in
keeping with this very number that the Lord descended into
the depths of this Egypt [of ours], and the people of Israel went
up into the promised land. He descended, I say, that the people might ascend. He assumed the form of a slave,[13] that they
might go free from the prison of slavery. And Moses took notice of this point, when he said: "The children of Israel were
brought up out of Egypt by his great strength."[14] For what is the
strength of God's chosen ones if not Christ, who is the power of
God?[15] Therefore, whoever ascends, ascends with him who
came down to us, not out of necessity, but because he deigned
to do so, that we might have no doubt of the truth of that
saying of the apostle: "He who descended is no other than he
who ascended above all heavens, so that he might fill the universe."[16]

(7) But while the aforesaid brother was the occasion of my
discussion of this subject, I do not consider it useless to spend a
little more time on it, especially since some people who are ignorant of God's plan argue that it is frivolous and superfluous
to read the account of these rest stops in the church. For they
are of the opinion that knowing or reading about this matter
serves no useful purpose whatsoever, thinking that Old Testament history narrates only what has happened, and that this
event has now passed away with age, and that today it should
have no further interest for us. But if we carefully consider the

11. Cf. Num 14.33; Deut 29.5.   12. Matt 1.17.
13. Cf. Phil 2.7.   14. Deut 4.37.
15. Cf. 1 Cor 1.24.   16. Eph 4.10.

words of sacred Scripture, it becomes as clear as day how insane it is to say such a thing. For the historical report states: "These are all the stages [in the journey] of the children of Israel, when they were led by Moses and Aaron in their hosts out of Egypt." And then it added: "And Moses recorded their starting points stage by stage as the Lord commanded him."[17]

(8) Did you notice that Moses wrote these things at the command of the Lord? And who would dare say, and, what is more, rashly presume to speak such nonsense by stating that what was written on orders from the Lord, conveyed nothing useful or bestowed nothing that would benefit our salvation? I will therefore undertake the task, my brother, if it is not too burdensome for you, of explaining briefly, and with attention only to the main points, the figurative sense of these stations, and will note in a few words what I am able to learn by investigating the writings of the Fathers,[18] so that any querulous person might gather merely from tasting the crumbs that fall to the floor how overflowing is the table, filled with dishes of delicious food.

(9) It should be remarked, however, that all this discussion, and whatever is said to have happened in the past, is totally fulfilled for us through the mystery that underlies our spiritual understanding. For whatever then occurred visibly, is adapted to our needs by allegorical interpretation, as this age long past is made to serve us at the present time. As the apostle says, these events "that happened to them were symbolic."[19] We too come forth from the ordeal of Egyptian servitude, and strive to enter the promised land by many stages, that is, by varied advancement in virtue. But since with the sole exception of the tribe of Levi, almost all the fathers left their bones lying in the wilderness, and only their children reached the land [of promise], it is to our benefit that the man we once were should die, and that our new nature, "which was of God's creating,"[20] should grow strong and reach the land of the living.

17. Num 33.1–2.
18. This reference would include the works of Jerome and of Pseudo-Ambrose cited in later notes.
19. 1 Cor 10.11.
20. Eph 4.24. See also Col 3.9–10 and 2 Cor 5.17.

(10) That the tribe of Levi did not perish in the wilderness along with all the others, can be easily deduced from this, that after the total number of all the Israelites, aged twenty years and upwards, had been counted and recorded by Moses, it was stated outright: "The Levites were not listed with them by their fathers' families."[21] For the Lord said to Moses: "You shall not record the total number of the Levites or make a detailed list of them among the children of Israel."[22] But later on Scripture says: "These were the detailed lists prepared by Moses and Eleazar the priest when they numbered the children of Israel. Among them there was not a single one whom Moses and Aaron had previously recorded in the wilderness of Sinai."[23] Indeed, the Lord had foretold that all of them would die in the desert. Surely, by this passage from history it is clearly shown that while the others had fallen in the desert, the tribe of Levi reached the promised land safe and sound. And so, whoever is able to enroll among the ranks of priests and Levites, and has no interest in acquiring his hereditary portion on earth, along with all other men, but like the tribe of Levi, is content to possess the Lord alone, will certainly not die in the wilderness of this world, but will win the right to enter the promised land alive and well.

(11) Therefore, he who would realize the promises made to his ancestors, together with the tribe of Levi should turn his back on the rights to his earthly inheritance. For whoever abases himself to attain earthly goods, who promises himself that he will live a long and happy life here below, where the Passover should be celebrated entirely in haste and in bitterness of spirit, by confidently saying to himself: "Man, you have plenty of good things laid by, enough for many years: take life easy, eat, drink, and enjoy yourself,"[24] will certainly deserve to hear these words: "You fool, this very night you must surrender your life; the things that you have accumulated—who will get them now?"[25] Such a man, therefore, will be killed, not during the day, but at night, just like the firstborn of the Egyptians.[26] For

---

21. Num 1.47.
23. Num 26.63–64.
25. Luke 12.20.

22. Num 1.49.
24. Luke 12.19.
26. Cf. Exod 12.29.

he who has not despised Egypt, but has offered his services to the potentates of this dark world,[27] will that very night surrender his life, because he has hated the light, and did not pursue the truth of justice. But since I am digressing to explain extraneous matters, as if I were forgetful of the purpose with which I began, let us now return in something like a recovery of our rights, to the rest stops of the Israelites in which, as I promised, we shall spend a little time.

(12) And so, as was said above, in forty-two stages the children of Israel came to the beginning of the distribution of their inheritance.[28] The beginning of this distribution occurred when the Reubenites, the Gadites, and the half tribe of Manasseh were given the land of Gilead as their possession.[29] Moreover, just as they went up through forty-two stages, so too our Savior descended through the same number of ancestors into the Egypt of this world. But if we already understand how great was the mystery this number contains, namely, that of man's ascent and of God's descent, let us now begin to ascend by considering the mystery by which Christ came down to us, and build for ourselves that first resting place which he has most recently occupied. For if someone comes to us by way of various lands, and upon his return would lead us through the same regions, we should begin our journey where he ended, and end it where he began.

(13) Now, the first generation of Christ began with Abraham, and the last, like the final stage, ended in the Virgin. And since Abraham may be said to mean "sublime father,"[30] we begin this journey with the Virgin giving birth, so that by passing through the various stages that followed, we may at length arrive at the Father on high. Hence, the virgin birth is the starting point for us who wish to leave the land of Egypt, since we who believe that the Word of God made flesh came into this world, find our rest in him alone after abandoning all perishable and transitory things, and establish in him the quiet abode we hoped for. After that, if we are still striving to make progress and rise through each individual stage of faith and virtue, we

27. Cf. Eph 6.12.   28. Cf. Num 33.54.
29. Cf. Josh 17.6.   30. Cf. Jerome, *Nom. hebr.* 2.28.

must rest a while until these virtues can become habitual. And then it will be observed that we are not passing through the desert of the spiritual life, but we will be judged to be making rest stations or even dwelling in them to make progress in virtue. For he who begins to do good, but does not have the purpose to persevere, is just in a hurry to move on; but he who continues to live a holy life in the place he has now reached, seems there to build his resting site. And we should note that since traveling and lodging, and therefore a journey and a resting place, are totally opposed to one another, and have nothing in common, still Scripture confirms that both converged in reference to the host of the Israelites, so that as they moved through the wilderness, they were said both to be on a journey and to have observed rest stops. This applies also to us who struggle to enter the land of the living, in that we must remain true to the vows we have made in our profession, and always progress by constantly improving our way of life and increasing the harvest of our virtues.

I. First of all, the Israelites left Rameses (Ramesse).[31] Rameses, as some have thought, in our language means "violent agitation or the movement of a moth."[32] In this we are given to understand that everything in this world is subject to agitation and disturbance, and is found to be liable to corruption, which is signified by the moth. It is clear that in temporal matters the soul should not take comfort, but should abandon them without delay. Others, however, have thought that Rameses might be interpreted as "commotion or thunder."[33] This, too, can easily be adapted to our purpose, because as we were shaken by the trumpet blast when the Gospel was preached, we left the Egypt of this world, incited by thunder from on high. Now, [the

31. Modern place names, with Vulgate variants in parentheses, are employed here.

32. Cf. Jerome, *Letter* 78.3 (CSEL 55.53). This letter of Jerome, *Letter* 78, or *Liber exegeticus ad Fabiolam* (CSEL 55.49–87), is the principal source for this letter of Damian. In pre-Maurist editions of Jerome's letters, *Letter* 78 is numbered *Letter* 127. This and all subsequent stages of the Exodus have their source in Num 33.3–48, which summarizes the account of Exod 12.35–17.2.

33. Cf. Jerome, *Nom. hebr.* 14.20, where the meaning "thunder" is given. See also Jerome, *Letter* 78.4 (CSEL 55.54).

Israelites] left on the fifteenth day of the first month, that is, at the full moon at the beginning of spring. And we too should hurry to depart the darkness of Egypt when we are illumined by the rays of the light from above, when the flowers of good will burst forth within us, when all things are revived, and finally, when the fields of our hearts grow warm under the heat of the heavenly sun.

II. The second camp was made at Succoth (Soccoth). And Succoth is said to mean "tents."[34] And thus, the first advance of the soul occurs when it avoids earthly disturbances, and, like pilgrims and strangers, does not build a home, but erects an exile's tent, lamenting with the prophet: "Hard is my lot, that my exile is prolonged."[35]

III. And then they came to Etham or, as the Septuagint has it, to Buthan, which is on the edge of the wilderness. Etham is the same as "strength."[36] Therefore, those who live in this world as pilgrims for God, who recognize that they are strangers and exiles, must realize that the weaker they are in things pertaining to this world, the stronger they are in practicing humility and patience. Buthan, however, has the meaning "valley,"[37] which in no way contradicts the interpretation given above. For it is necessary that anyone who is on his way to the land of the living stand firm in the valley of humility and patience, and endure the attack of temptations.

IV. And then they moved on to "Pi-hahiroth (Phihahiroth), which lies facing Baalzephon (Beelsephon), and encamped before Migdol (Magdalum)."[38] Pi-hahirot is said to mean "the mouth of the noble,"[39] by which is indicated the teaching of learned men. For one who is living in the valley of suffering, the more severely he is afflicted by the scourges of persecution and temptations of the flesh, the greater is his need for help

34. Cf. Jerome, *Nom. hebr.* 14.29.

35. Ps 119.5.

36. Cf. Jerome, *Letter* 78.5 (CSEL 55.55.).

37. Damian is here using some source other than Jerome.

38. Num 33.7.

39. Cf. Jerome, *Letter* 78.6 (CSEL 55.55); F. Vigouroux, *Dictionnaire de la Bible* 5, 253–58. But Vigouroux's scientific discussion of Egyptian and Jewish place names is of little help in tracing the symbolic interpretations given by Damian.

from "the mouth of the noble," that is, from the advice of the holy doctors. But if Os Irath is used instead of Pi-hahiroth, as another translation has it,[40] one should be aware that Irath is translated by the word "village."[41] Therefore one comes to the mouth, that is, to one's first entrance into the village, which symbolizes the beginning of a new way of life. And so, they come not to the city, but to the village, for it is required that all beginners first confine themselves to living on the outskirts of the city, and should not immediately presume to reach the heights of senatorial perfection. And hence, it is well put that Pi-hahiroth "lies facing Baalsephon."[42] Now Baalsephon can be translated as "the ascent of the lookout or tower,"[43] since one mounts from small beginnings to that which is greater. For this station was not on the heights, but faced the heights, because any novice, even though he now yearns for the contemplative life, cannot aspire as yet to reach the heights of perfect contemplation. Wherefore, it is then aptly stated: "And they encamped before Migdol."[44] Migdol has the meaning "magnificence."[45] When one has newly come to the service of God, it is already his purpose to scale the heights and view the magnificent scene, but he is as yet unable to do so. For even though he is now fed and nourished by the hope of practicing contemplation and of reaching perfection, he does not yet enjoy the brilliance of perfect purity and heavenly grace. But if Baalsephon is translated "the lord of the north wind,"[46] as some have said, what else could this "lord of the north wind" mean but the ancient enemy who rules over frigid hearts that are alienated from the love of God? And so, we camp before him, that is,

40. Os Irath (Os Eroth) is used in Pseudo-Ambrose, *De XLII mansionibus filiorum Israel* (PL 17.16D). The author of this work depends on Jerome, and uses Origen's homily on the book of Numbers in the translation of Rufinus. For a brief modern discussion of the Exodus, see J. E. Huesman, "Desert Journey of the Israelites," *NCE* 4, 793–97.

41. Cf. Jerome, *Letter* 78.6 (CSEL 55.55), where, as the author says, some have badly translated *hiroth* as "villas."

42. Cf. Num 33.7.

43. Cf. Jerome, *Nom. hebr.* 16.27; *Letter* 78.6 (CSEL 55.56).

44. Num 33.7.

45. Cf. Jerome, *Nom. hebr.* 54.26.

46. Cf. Jerome, *Letter* 78.6 (CSEL 55.56).

against him, when we fight against him in implacable combat.

V. After passing through the Red Sea they came to Marah (Mara), which is interpreted to mean "bitterness."[47] Good order dictates that those who travel to the land flowing with honey, should drink the bitterness of exertion and temptation in the desert of this world, and after experiencing the harshness of our present disciplined life, come to the sweetness of an interior reward. Hence the apostle says: "Discipline, no doubt, is never pleasant; at the time it seems painful, but in the end it yields for those who have been trained by it the peaceful harvest of a just life."[48] For those who are enrolled in the forces of spiritual combat, bitter wine is at times mixed with sweet, and sweet wine with bitter, so that thus they may experience the human condition, what they must endure as a result of their own weakness, and what they should hope for from the power of God. And this is exactly what was said to this people: "I humbled you and fed you on manna in the desert which your fathers did not know, until you might discern what was in your heart."[49]

VI. Then the text says that they "left Marah and came to Elim,"[50] where there were twelve springs of water and seventy palm trees. You will note that after the bitterness of temptation they came to a most pleasant place of sweet fruit and flowing water. And thus, after struggling with temptations they were brought to the palm trees, and through parched and arid lands that caused intolerable thirst, they came to an abundant supply of living water. Truly, almighty God, the physician of souls, manages everything in an ordered way, as follows: just as honey is infused with color, joy is mixed with sadness and sadness with joy, so that when the soul is struck down by illness, it may never take pride in its well-being, and when at length it is restored, it will not succumb to adversity. Elim, moreover, may be translated as "the rams,"[51] the leaders of the sheep that follow them. But who are the leaders of the human flock, that is, of the Christian people, if not the holy apostles? For they are the twelve springs

47. Cf. Jerome, *Nom. hebr.* 14.8.   48. Heb 12.11.
49. Cf. Deut 8.3, 16–17.   50. Num 33.9.
51. Cf. Jerome, *Nom. hebr.* 13.4; *Letter* 78.8 (CSEL 55.57).

that irrigate our parched souls with the waters of heavenly teaching. And since our Savior chose not only these twelve apostles, but also seventy other men, the text states that at this camp there were not only twelve springs, but also seventy palm trees. Indeed, they are called apostles as we know from the words of blessed Paul. For when treating of the Savior's resurrection, he said: "He appeared to Cephas and after that to the eleven, and then to all the apostles."[52] From these words it is obvious that besides the twelve, the other disciples are aptly called apostles.

VII. After they left Elim, the Israelites encamped by the Red Sea. Note that they did not again enter the waters, but camped near them, so that they could only view the sea and its tempestuous waves from afar, but in no way had to fear its movement or violence. We also, after a flood of temptations, after fearsome shipwrecks amid the roaring waves, often look back at the evils we encountered, so that now, as we stand safely on the shore, we can give proper thanks to the God who rescued us.

VIII. Then, moving away from the Red Sea, they encamped in the wilderness of Sin. Sin may be translated as "bush" or "temptation."[53] For now the hope of good fortune begins to smile on the knight of Christ, and hold forth the promise that he will hear God speaking to him. As we know, the Lord appeared to Moses from the bush[54] and ordered him to bring his commands to the children of Israel. And so, the sign of the mercy you hoped for is given to you in the very place where the Israelites first encountered God. But it is not unimportant that Sin also has the meaning "temptation." It frequently happens that temptation intervenes in visions, since at times the evil spirit "transforms himself into an angel of light."[55] And thus, one must be careful to discern the kinds of visions that appear. This is similar to the experience of Joshua when he beheld an angel. He had little doubt that at times temptations were involved in visions of this kind, and promptly inquired of him who stood before him: "Are you for us or for our enemies?"[56]

52. 1 Cor 15.5–6.
53. Cf. Jerome, *Nom. hebr.* 14.30.
54. Cf. Exod 3.2–6.
55. 2 Cor 11.14.
56. Josh 5.13.

And it was the apostle [whom we alluded to above] who enumerated the ability to distinguish true spirits from false among
the gifts of the Holy Spirit.[57] It is said that Sin may also mean
"hatred,"[58] and this too is not without spiritual significance,
since anyone who arrives at the vision of God, or at intimate
communication with him, immediately fosters a hatred for this
world.

IX. But then they moved on and came to Dophka (Depthca),
or as another version has it, Raphaca.[59] Now Dophkah has the
meaning, "knocking."[60] And after we came to the Church, signified by the bush mentioned above, where man is found worthy
to converse with God, where we behold a vision of angels, then
we begin to ask, seek, and knock at the secret recesses of the
heavenly kingdom, as the Lord commanded and promised
when he said: "Knock and it shall be opened to you."[61] But if
one prefers to use Raphaca, which means "health,"[62] this name
is easily adapted to the soul that has been ill for a long time, but
now, as a gift from the holy Church, is freed from the bonds of
its sickness. For this is the soul to which these words were addressed: "Bless the Lord, my soul; all that is within me, bless his
holy name."[63] Which Lord, you ask? "He who heals all your diseases," he says, "and rescues your life from death."[64] Indeed,
vices are the disease of the soul, while criminal sins are the cause
of its death.[65] "And when sin is full-grown it breeds death."[66]

X. And then they encamped at Alush (Alus). Alush may be
translated as "hardships" or "yeast."[67] And certainly, hardships

57. Cf. 1 Cor 12.10.

58. Cf. Jerome, *Letter* 78.10 (CSEL 55.59).

59. Cf. Jerome, *Letter* 78.11 (CSEL 55.60).

60. Cf. Jerome, *Letter* 78.11 (CSEL 55.60).

61. Luke 11.9.

62. Cf. Jerome, *Letter* 78.11 (CSEL 55.60), where the name Pephca, or the
LXX word Raphaca, occurs, with the meaning "cure."

63. Ps 102.1.

64. Ps 102.3–4.

65. Damian uses the term *peccata criminalia* also in *Letter* 17.3 (FOTC, MC
1.146–47), where he describes them as the effects of the seven principal vices.
They are the equivalent of the more modern term "mortal sins." See Reindel,
Briefe 1, p. 156, n. 4.

66. Jas 1.15.

67. Cf. Jerome, *Nom. hebr.* 16.7, where the meaning "yeast" is given. But

follow upon [a return to] good health, since the holy soul should desire good health only for the purpose of bearing hardships and affliction for God's sake. Peter's mother-in-law, in fact, recovered from her fever that she might eagerly serve the Lord,[68] and Paul was healed by Ananias, that later he might undergo constant hardship and fatigue.[69] This is why Ananias heard these words spoken in reference to [Paul]: "I myself will show him all that he must go through for my name's sake."[70] Alush is also said to mean "yeast," and this too has a significant interpretation for us. The reference here is to that yeast which a woman took and mixed with three measures of flour until it was all leavened, that is, the holy Gospel.[71] While [the Israelites] were in this wilderness, the people complained, and they received manna and quail. And since both the yeast and the manna symbolized the holy Gospel, in a marvelous way these came together at the tenth encampment, so that the bread of the Gospel would seem to follow from the decalogue of the Law that went before.

XI. After that they came to Raphidim. We may translate Raphidim as "praise of judgment."[72] And certainly it is quite proper that hardship should precede praise, and that praise should originate from hardship. And indeed, we are speaking of the praise of not just anything, but obviously of the judgment that results from rational discernment, and not of the praise that springs from vanity and pride. For, "a man gifted with the Spirit can judge the worth of everything, but is not himself subject to judgment by his fellow men."[73] Other interpretations of these names can be found, but if I were to use all of them that are supplied on this subject, my remarks could not be kept within the confines of a letter, but would become an enormous and weighty volume. And so I am succinctly skim-

"hardship" appears as the translation in Ps.-Ambrose, *De XLII mansionibus* (PL 17.21C).

68. Cf. Mark 1.30–31; Matt 8.14–15.
69. Cf. Acts 9.17–18.
70. Acts 9.16.
71. Cf. Luke 13.21.
72. Cf. Ps.-Ambrose, *De XLII mansionibus* (PL 17.22C).
73. 1 Cor 2.15.

ming through the encampments of the Israelites, not to inspect all the secrets of their households but simply to show by their place names the exteriors of the walls.

XII. And then they came to the wilderness of Sinai. There can be no doubt that Sin, of which I spoke above, and Sinai are one and the same desert. Sin refers to the level area, while Sinai is a mountain that rises in the same wilderness, on which the Lord promulgated the precepts of the Law, and where Moses built the Tabernacle.[74] And this was certainly quite proper, so that after the soul of man was first endowed with sound reason, and therefore praiseworthy judgment, it then constructed within itself a Tabernacle dedicated to God, where by speaking with the Creator he might learn those excellent mysteries of his heavenly commands.

XIII. And after that they came to the graves of lust,[75] in all of which we perceive a marvelous ordering of events. For since the blessed soul is a tabernacle for its Creator, when, by riveting its attention on the precepts of God's law, it begins to meditate on heavenly things, the ardor of burning vice is extinguished, and all desire for carnal pleasure is put to rest, so that our flesh no longer strives against the spirit, and the spirit does not fight against the flesh.[76]

XIV. From there they moved on to Hazeroth (Aseroth), which may be translated as "the courts of perfection" or "blessedness."[77] And how wonderful is the orderliness of this mystery, how fitting the progression of spiritual growth, so that after burying the lusts of the flesh, you at once arrive at the court of perfection and the reward of blessedness. Happy the soul no longer driven by carnal vices, since it will soon enter the blessedness of the reward that is in store for it.

XV. After that they came to Rithmah (Rethma) or Paran (Pharam).[78] Rithmah, it seems to me, may be rendered as "highest vision,"[79] while Paran has the meaning "visible mouth."[80] In

---

74. Cf. Exod 24.13; Exod 26.1–37.

75. Cf. Num 11.34 and 33.16; see also Jerome, *Letter* 78.15 (CSEL 55.64).

76. Cf. Gal 5.17.   77. Cf. Jerome, *Nom. hebr.* 15.19.

78. For Pharam, see Num 13.1.   79. Cf. Jerome, *Nom. hebr.* 20.5.

80. Such an interpretation does not appear in the sources used for this letter.

all of this, what other interpretation suggests itself, but that any holy soul after its carnal desires have been buried, is brought to the "court of perfection," with its reward of "blessedness" assured, and then comes to the highest vision of God, where it beholds his visible mouth, that is, the sight of God, before its very eyes? For as the apostle says: "Now we see only puzzling reflections in a mirror, but then we shall see face to face. My knowledge now is partial; then it will be whole, like God's knowledge of me."[81] Yet, since none of the saints who are still in this flesh can have all of this fully, in all its reality, they now possess it as the object of their hope. And indeed, their hope is now most steadfast, because they have as a pledge the Holy Spirit[82] who strengthens them in their difficulties along the way. And so, that other interpretation, by which Rithmah is said to mean "sound" or "juniper,"[83] should not be thought out of place. For it is said that the wood of this tree remains burning for a long period of time, so that if the embers are covered with ashes, they will continue to glow up to a year.[84] And since, as we read, the Holy Spirit is well aware of what men say,[85] and was sent down upon the apostles in the form of fire,[86] this interpretation, according to which Rithmah means "juniper" or "sound," seems most apt when applied to the Holy Spirit.

XVI. And then they departed and encamped at Rimmonparez (Remon Phares), which in Latin has the meaning of "cutting away on high."[87] For when the mind of a soul that returns to God is expanded, it is then endowed with perfect understanding, by which it is able by means of knowledge from on high to cut away earthly concerns from those of heaven, and to separate base and transitory things from those that endure forever. But if Rimmon-parez is taken to mean the "division of the pomegranate," which is found elsewhere,[88] this would undoubtedly symbolize the holy Church, which, as it were, covers many

---

81. 1 Cor 13.12.
82. Cf. 2 Cor 1.22, 5.5; Eph 1.14.
83. Cf. Jerome, *Nom. hebr.* 20.5.
84. Cf. Isidore, *Etymologies* 17.7.35.
85. Cf. Wis 1.7.
86. Cf. Acts 2.3.
87. Cf. Jerome, *Nom. hebr.* 20.6.
88. Cf. Jerome, *Letter* 78.18 (CSEL 55.67).

seeds in one skin, while gathering a vast crowd of believers within the inseparable unity of the Catholic faith.

XVII. Then they moved on to Libnah (Lebna), which may be translated as "whitening."[89] We are not unaware that at times the word "whitewash" is used for crime, as is said in reference to tombs covered with whitewash or to a whitewashed wall,[90] but here we must think of that whitening of which Isaiah said: "Though your sins are as scarlet, they will become white as snow; though they are dyed crimson, they will become white as wool."[91] And in the Psalm: "They will be whitened with snow on Zalmon."[92] And in the Apocalypse it is said that Jesus' hair was like white wool.[93] Accordingly, whitening here is properly understood as proceeding from the brightness of the true light, and as coming down from the brilliance of the highest vision. But as some would have it, Libnah should be translated as "brick,"[94] in the manufacture of which the people of Israel were forced to toil in Egypt. By this we should understand that after being at lofty heights they again came to those made of brick, and that also we at times are forced by necessity to descend from the heights to the depths so long as we travel as pilgrims in the wilderness of this world, and to move from spiritual concerns to the affairs of this world.

XVIII. After that they came to Rissah (Resa), which is translated as "bridles,"[95] and that, quite aptly. For if upon reaching the summit of perfection we descend to a sordid world, we must be bridled by the bonds of discipline and the reins of penance, lest we wander to the edge of steep precipices, and so that we may quickly return to the purity of the cleanliness to which we were accustomed. Rissah may also be interpreted as "visible or praiseworthy temptation."[96] For even though the soul of every just man is now making progress toward higher goals, it is still brought down to baser things by temptation, so

---

89. Cf. Ps.-Ambrose, *De XLII mansionibus* (PL 17.27B).
90. Cf. Matt 23.27; Acts 23.3.   91. Isa 1.18.
92. Ps 67.15.   93. Cf. Rev 1.14.
94. Cf. Jerome, *Letter* 78.19 (CSEL 55.68).
95. Cf. Jerome, *Nom. hebr.* 20.7.
96. Cf. Ps.-Ambrose, *De XLII mansionibus* (PL 17.27D).

that surging pride does not cause him to boast of his virtues. Indeed, temptation is the goad that is useful in guarding humility. Hence the apostle says: "And so, to keep me from being unduly elated by the magnificence of such revelations, I was given a thorn for my flesh which came as Satan's messenger to bruise me."[97] Therefore, this temptation is visible because it is obvious, praiseworthy because it is salutary.

XIX. From there they came to Kehelathah (Ceelata) , which is understood to mean "the Church,"[98] so that those who are unstable and are rushing headlong for the rocky cliffs of vice, are drawn back to the Church by the curbs of sacred Scripture. Another translation uses the word Machelat, which has the meaning "domination of the rod,"[99] which seems to express a twofold power. Clearly, it is important that the soul be dominant in exerting authority over the flesh that is tempted, so that when the latter undergoes conflict, the former, as it were, wields the threatening rod over it as it employs rigorous discipline to frighten it.

XX. Leaving that encampment, they arrived at Mount Shapher (Sepher or Sephar), which is called "the blast of the trumpet."[100] The trumpet blast is the signal for combat, for the horse of God "scents the battle" and when he "hears the horn, he cries, 'Aha.'"[101] And if the knight of Christ feels himself hemmed in by temptation from attacking vices, he at once snatches up the weapons of virtue, proceeds to the encounter, and without hesitation engages in battle, lest, weakened by sloth and indifference, he be easily cut down by the enemy. Then he will be able to sound the glorious trumpet, that is, also incite others to enter the spiritual combat.

XXI. And then [in Numbers] it is reported that they journeyed on and came to Haradah (Arada), or, as stated elsewhere, to Caradath, which in our language means "suitable effect,"[102] so that when one has now become a preacher, he can

---

97. 2 Cor 12.7.
98. Cf. Jerome, *Letter* 78.21 (CSEL 55.69).
99. This interpretation is not found in the sources here cited.
100. Cf. Ps.-Ambrose, *De XLII mansionibus* (PL 17.28B).
101. Job 39.25.
102. Cf. Ps.-Ambrose, *De XLII mansionibus* (PL 17.28D).

properly say with the apostle: "It is he who has made us suitable to dispense his new covenant."[103]

XXII. Then, moving on, they came to Makheloth (Maceloth), which may be translated as "from the beginning."[104] For whoever strives to reach the heights of perfection, beholds the beginning of all things as he turns the total desire of his inner self to God. And when the heart is constantly directed to its Maker, it does not withdraw from the beginning of all things. But if, as some have thought, Makheloth should be translated as "assembly,"[105] then it has the meaning "church," in which all the faithful come together. And so, the canticle has it: "How good it is and how pleasant for brothers to live together in unity."[106]

XXIII. The next encampment was at Tahat (Taaht), or, as we read elsewhere, Caath, that is, "suffering" or "strengthening."[107] For whoever wishes to enter the land of the living by undergoing the hardships of this present life, must be strengthened by suffering to endure the dangers of the world. But if Tahat is translated by the word "anxiety,"[108] as some have maintained, let this be said to everyone engaged in combat, even if perhaps with God's grace he is victorious: "Put away your pride and be on your guard."[109]

XXIV. Again taking to the road, they came to Tarah (Thare), which in Greek means "amazement," but in our language is rendered "contemplation."[110] It follows, therefore, that whoever is first tried by suffering, at length arrives at the grace of contemplation, and whoever in the beginning is afflicted by trouble, is later lifted up to the joys of intimate vision. But if by Tarah we are to understand "cunning" or "malice,"[111] as some think, this would seem to be an apt reference to the rectors of

103. 2 Cor 3.6.
104. Cf. Ps.-Ambrose, *De XLII mansionibus* (PL 17.29A).
105. Cf. Jerome, *Letter* 78.24 (CSEL 55.70).
106. Ps 132.1.
107. Cf. Ps.-Ambrose, *De XLII mansionibus* (PL 17.29B), giving the meanings "longsuffering" or "tolerance," which are similar.
108. Cf. Jerome, *Letter* 78.25 (CSEL 55.70).
109. Rom 11.20.
110. Cf. Ps.-Ambrose, *De XLII mansionibus* (PL 17.29D).
111. These meanings are not found in the sources here cited.

churches, who should fear for those who listen to them as they suffer the hardships of temptation. We, however, should guard against the cunning and malice of him to whom these words apply: "Our enemy the devil, like a roaring lion, prowls round looking for someone to devour."[112]

XXV. They then moved on to Mithcah (Methca), or, as we read elsewhere, Maathica, which may be said to mean "new death."[113] Never do we so perfectly avoid the cunning of the devil as when we die with Christ,[114] by which we are made insensible to the assaults of this sly enemy. Contemplation begets this new death, which makes the world dead for us, and us dead to the world.[115] But if Mithcah is translated as "sweetness,"[116] as some would have it, why should we be surprised if after contemplation we come to sweetness, since contemplation itself is nothing else but an ineffable and boundless sweetness?

XXVI. After that they arrived at Hashmonah (Esmona), which has the meaning "making haste."[117] For after reaching the sweetness of contemplation, we will not brook any delay. Oh, how painful was the delay that he experienced, who said: "Why did you not rend the heavens and come down, and make the mountains melt before you?"[118] How grievous was the waiting for him who said: "What I should like is to depart and be with Christ; that is better by far."[119] But if one were to use the word Senna, which means "bones,"[120] this would refer to the strength of our perseverance. And this is necessary for one who loves Christ, that he does not become impatient because of the excess of his love.

XXVII. From there they then moved on to Moseroth, which is thought to mean "excluding."[121] Indeed, the soul that has ar-

112. 1 Pet 5.8.
113. Cf. Ps.-Ambrose, De XLII mansionibus (PL 17.30A).
114. Cf. Rom 6.3–8.
115. Cf. Gal 6.14.
116. Cf. Jerome, Letter 78.27 (CSEL 55.71).
117. Cf. Jerome, Letter 78.28 (CSEL 55.72). But see also Ps.-Ambrose, De XLII mansionibus (PL 17.30D), who uses the word "acceleration."
118. Isa 64.1.
119. Phil 1.23.
120. Our sources here do not give this meaning.
121. Cf. Jerome, Nom. hebr. 19.12.

rived at perfect love of its bridegroom, excludes from itself the temptations of the cunning seducer. Hence the apostle says: "Leave no loophole for the devil."[122] But if, as some have thought, Moseroth should be translated as "chains,"[123] an entirely rational and proper understanding emerges. For any holy soul that is united in love with the heavenly spouse, must be indissolubly bound to him by diligent meditation on the Scriptures, as if he were fettered with chains. And of such chains Isaiah says to Christ: "Men of stature shall come to you and be your slaves, and shall march behind you in chains."[124]

XXVIII. And so now they deservedly came to Benejaakan (Banaeain), which is understood to mean "springs" or "filtering,"[125] that is, where the soul drinks and filters the sources of the divine Scriptures, or rather, carefully investigates and meditates on them. He filters them, I say, when he observes this advice of the Gospel: "That not a letter, not a stroke, will disappear from the Law until all [that it stands for] is achieved."[126] But if Benejaakan is translated to mean "the children of necessity or of a gnashing sound"[127] as some have said, this would indicate that whoever is learned and fully trained in the word of God, must influence others to follow him, and thus to beget children, and hence, as they face the threat of weeping and of gnashing teeth, he forces them, as it were, to be converted to God. Such men, then, are the children of necessity or of gnashing, of whom the prophet sings: "Bring to the Lord, you children of God: bring to the Lord the offspring of rams."[128]

XXIX. After that they went up Hor-haggidgad (Mount Gadgad), which is translated to mean "announcer" or "one who is armed" or "mutilation."[129] For we must undoubtedly remind those to whom we announce the word of God, that they should arm themselves with the weapons of virtue and destroy the rear-

122. Eph 4.27.
123. Cf. Jerome *Letter* 78.29 (CSEL 55.72).
124. Isa 45.14.
125. Cf. Ps.-Ambrose, *De XLII* mansionibus (PL 17.32C).
126. Matt 5.18.
127. Cf. Jerome, *Letter* 78.30 (CSEL 55.73).
128. Ps 28.1.
129. Cf. Jerome, *Letter* 78.31 (CSEL 55.74).

guard of our invisible enemies with spiritual swords. But when we do not take pains to teach them to fight bravely, we must join them in their flight into the mountains. But if Gadgad is to be read "temptations,"[130] as some have thought, this would imply that those who push on to the heavenly homeland cannot be rid of temptations. And often temptation is intermingled with virtues, so that a greater reward may be gained by the industrious knight of Christ.

XXX. And since we pass through the evils of temptation to the good things with which we are rewarded, it aptly follows that after further travel [the Israelites] came to Jotbathah (Getebatha), or, as we find elsewhere, Jabatha, which is translated by the word "goodness" or "the good."[131] Therefore, after experiencing temptations, we arrive at the good, which undoubtedly is Christ.

XXXI. Then they traveled on to Ebronah (Ebrona), which is called "the passage."[132] All things must be bypassed by the soul, and you must fix your mind's attention on him alone with whom you will be able to live without end.

XXXII. After that they encamped at Ezion-geber (Asiongaber), which may be translated as "wisdom of man."[133] For after we have immersed ourselves in Christ, after placing our heart's total trust in him, we must never again become children depending on our senses, imitating the apostle who says: "But when I became a man, I was finished with childish things."[134] And again: "Do not become children in your outlook."[135]

XXXIII. But since he who applies himself to knowledge, prepares himself for sorrow, they again went into the wilderness of Sin, that is, of Kadesh (Cades). As I said above, Sin is interpreted to mean "temptation." For just as one frequently uses the hammer to beat a golden or silver vessel, as one often applies the file here and there in polishing it, that the vessel may be-

130. Cf. Ps.-Ambrose, *De XLII mansionibus* (PL 17.33A).
131. Cf. Jerome, *Letter* 78.32 (CSEL 55.74).
132. Cf. Jerome, *Letter* 78.33 (CSEL 55.74–74).
133. Cf. Ps.-Ambrose, *De XLII mansionibus* (PL 17.34A).
134. 1 Cor 13.11.
135. 1 Cor 14.20.

come more bright, thus repeated temptation removes rust from the soul of him who perseveres and does not lose heart. "As the work of a potter is tested in the furnace, so upright men are tried by affliction."[136] And since Kadesh is said to mean "holy fruit-bearing,"[137] you will notice that holy fruitfulness emerges from the furrows made by temptation.

XXXIV. Leaving Kadesh, they encamped on Mount Hor on the frontier of Edom. Hor has the meaning "of the mountain."[138] For whoever does not fall when he is tempted, but bears fruit because of the temptation, will victoriously scale the mountain, which is Christ. He is a mountain of many peaks, a massive mountain,[139] of whom Isaiah says: "In the days to come the mountain of the Lord's house shall be set over all other mountains, lifted high above the hills. All the nations shall come streaming to it."[140] This mountain is called "of the mountain," because where Christ is, there undoubtedly we find the Christian. "Where I am," he said, "my servant will also be."[141]

XXXV. And then they came to Zalmonah (Salmona), which may be said to mean "shadow of the part."[142] And rightly so, for after we have climbed the mountain which is Christ, we flee from the heat of vice, and sit under the protection of its shadow. And indeed Jeremiah says of this shadow: "The breath of our mouth, Christ the Lord, is taken in our sins, to whom we said: 'Under your shadow we shall live among the Gentiles.'"[143] And the angel said to Mary: "The power of the Most High shall overshadow you."[144] Elsewhere we find that Zalmonah has the meaning "little image,"[145] which certainly is not out of place at this point, since there the brazen serpent was erected, symbolizing the image of the crucified Savior.[146]

XXXVI. They then moved on to Punon (Phinon), which is

---

136. Sir 27.6.

137. Not found in the sources here cited.

138. Cf. Jerome, *Letter* 78.36 (CSEL 55.77), where he gives the meaning "mountain."

139. Cf. Ps 67.16.   140. Isa 2.2.

141. John 12.26.   142. Cf. Jerome, *Nom. hebr.* 21.1.

143. Lam 4.20.   144. Luke 1.35.

145. Cf. Jerome, *Letter* 78.37 (CSEL 55.79).

146. Cf. Num 21.8–9; John 3.14–15.

translated to mean "mouth" or "little mouth."[147] The word "mouth" is used, for as soon as we come to know the mysteries of Christ's passion, we proclaim with our lips what we believe in our heart, as it is written: "I have believed, therefore have I spoken."[148] And the apostle says: "For the faith that leads to justice is in the heart, but the confession that leads to salvation is upon the lips."[149] The term "little mouth" is used, because as soon as we are unable to understand the profound mysteries of man's redemption, we place our finger to our lips, leaving to our betters the exalted truth of Christ's divinity, while we reflect only upon his cross. As the apostle says: "I resolved that while I was with you I would think of nothing but Jesus Christ—Christ nailed to the cross."[150]

XXXVII. After this encampment they went on to Oboth, which is well translated as "magicians" or "soothsayers."[151] From this we should understand that after we perceive God's image by our mind, and after we accept the faith that we profess on our lips, heretics rise up against us, preaching poisonous and perfidious error like soothsayers and magicians, spewing forth their vicious chants and incantations.

XXXVIII. Thence they passed on to Iye-abarim (Gebarim) on the border of Moab. Gebarim has the meaning "heaps of stones that cross over."[152] These, indeed, are living and holy stones not only from which the heavenly Jerusalem is built, but also with which the present Church is adorned as with shining pearls. They are rightly called "crossing over," because with the mind they tread on all that is worldly and transitory, and hasten to cross over to heavenly things. But if we were to read Gai instead of Gebarim, as another version has it, this does not stray from the interpretation "crossing over." Now Gai may be translated as "boundless empty space."[153] For Abraham said to the rich man: "There is a vast empty space fixed between us."[154]

147. Cf. Jerome, *Letter* 78.37 (CSEL 55.79).
148. Ps 115.10.　　　　　　　　149. Rom 10.10.
150. 1 Cor 2.2.
151. Cf. Jerome, *Letter* 78.38 (CSEL 55.79).
152. Cf. ibid.
153. This interpretation is not found in Jerome or in Ps.-Ambrose.
154. Luke 16.26.

And so, the saints always wished to "cross over" to him, that, like blessed Lazarus, they might joyfully take their rest in his company.

XXXIX. And then quite appropriately they moved on, leaving the emptiness of the soothsayers and magicians, that is, the utter darkness of the crafty heretics, and soon came to Dibongad (Dibongad), which is said to mean "the beehive of temptations."[155] Bees carry honey in their mouths, but pierce with their stings; and so too heretics openly offer charming compliments with their words, but, as it were, hide the stings of error behind their backs. At first, they pour sweetness from their mouths, but afterwards spread the error of barbed falsehood. Hence the prophet complained in these words: "They surround me like bees, and attack me as fire attacks brushwood."[156]

XL. From there they journeyed to Almon-diblathaim (Helmondeblathaim), which may be rendered as "contempt of the palate," that is, "of figs," or "contempt of reproach."[157] Now the fig is a delicious fruit, from which we need to understand that those who are now approaching heavenly gifts should despise all the allurements of carnal pleasure. But if one should accept the meaning "contempt of reproach," by this we should undoubtedly understand that if we are disparaged by the insults of heretics or other accursed people, we must not be disturbed. From this, in fact, we derive both kinds of benefit, so that we are neither affected by the derision of disgraceful contempt, nor weakened by any pleasure derived from earthly delights, and thus may be able to say with the prophet: "To you both dark and light are one."[158]

XLI. And then they moved on to the mountains of Abarim east of Nebo (Nabo). Abarim has the meaning "passage," Nabo "departure,"[159] where having passed through all the encamp-

---

155. Cf. Ps.-Ambrose, *De XLII mansionibus* (PL 17.38B).
156. Ps 117.12.
157. Cf. Jerome, *Letter* 78.41 (CSEL 55.82–83); Ps.-Ambrose, *De XLII mansionibus* (PL 17.38C).
158. Ps 138.12.
159. Cf. Jerome, *Nom. hebr.* 16.5 and 50.19.

ments of the journey, so to speak, the soul will have progressed through all the virtues. Since now it has scaled the heights of perfection, in intention it soon passes from this age and departs. Even though, in fact, it still seems to linger in this world, living in the flesh, but not according to the flesh,[160] it has already left the world. Just as it was said of Enoch: "He was seen no more, because God had taken him away,"[161] so too whoever is perfect in holiness, is already dead to the world, passes out of the world, and dwells in the region of virtue.

XLII. The last encampment was in the lowlands of Moab by the Jordan near Jericho.[162] We force ourselves to undertake this long journey, and with such difficulty and effort struggle through the vast wilderness of this world, that [by all of this] we may reach the Jordan, that is, come to the inexhaustible fullness of heavenly wisdom. Along its banks we pitch our pilgrim tent, and hurry to cleanse ourselves in its waters, washing away all the filth of Egypt, that thus purified we may enter the promised land, and might be as the bride in the Song of Songs, of whom it was said: "Her eyes are like doves beside brooks of water, bathed in milk as they sit where it is drawn."[163] And we should note that this journey ends not in the mountains, but in the lowlands, because the more highly the saints are endowed with perfection, the more deeply they are grounded in humility. Note also that they encamped near Jericho, for they fight implacably against the world, which is symbolized by this city. To them it was said: "If you belonged to the world, the world would love its own; but because you do not belong to the world, for that reason the world hates you."[164]

(14) Venerable brother, I have briefly hurried through the encampments of the Israelites for you, but have left for your leisure time, of which you have more than I, the consideration of more profound mysteries. I have given you the opportunity for further investigation and understanding, but have not provided you with full knowledge on the subject. In fact, I have only opened the doors of these same camps, but now it is up to

160. Cf. Rom 8.1, 4.
162. Cf. Num 33.48.
164. John 15.19.

161. Gen 5.24.
163. Song 5.12.

you to enter and to explore their mysteries, like hidden talents of heavenly treasure. But it was enough for me to have only reached the point where a foolish man, ignorant of what he is saying or of what he affirms, may no longer spread the nonsense that these matters are absolutely useless, but may have no doubt that all of them are replete with mystical secrets of spiritual allegory. And so, after passing through so many camping sites, after so many hardships on this long journey, since Moses and Aaron are now dead, that is, since the ancient priesthood and the Law have passed away, we have now entered the promised land of the Gospel with Joshua as our leader. I am speaking of the land flowing with milk and honey, that is, the land that is watered by the mysteries of Christ's humanity and divinity. Here there remains nothing else to do but to construct a temple to the Lord in the Jerusalem of our hearts, resplendent with the beauty of virtues, as if with the varied brilliance of gold and silver and every precious stone. In the court of this temple let us erect two columns on either side, following the example of Solomon, setting chainwork at the capitals of the columns.[165] For as Scripture attests: "He erected one pillar on the right and one on the left," and then continues: "The one on the right he named Jachin," that is, "firmness,"[166] "and the one on the left Boaz (Booz)," meaning, "in strength."[167]

(15) What should we understand by the column standing on the right, and called "firmness," if not the love of God? And what of that to the left, called "in strength," if not the love of neighbor? It is one thing to speak of firmness, that is, of strength itself, and another to say "in strength," for to love God himself is quite different from loving one's neighbor in God. To be sure, in loving one's neighbor a certain limit is assigned; but we are urged to love God without any limitation. Hence, in the court of the temple we erect a column that is named "firmness," when with steadfastness and constancy and with all our strength we love God in the Church as it now exists, which is the court of the Church in heaven. And as John the Evangelist

165. Cf. 2 Chr 3.16.
166. This symbolic meaning is not in the sources.
167. Cf. 2 Chr 3.17.

tells us, God is love itself.[168] And of God the prophet sings: "You are my God and my strength."[169] We place the column that is called "in strength" on the left side of the court, when we love our neighbor in God, just as we love ourselves. Here we should note that Scripture continues: "He made also, as it were, chain-work in the inner shrine [of the temple] and placed it on the capitals of the pillars."[170] We also put chainwork on the heads of the columns in the shrine of our mind, by which we connect both columns, one to the other, since we cannot truly love God without loving our neighbor, nor our neighbor without loving God.

(16) You too, venerable brother, with divine assistance can build a noble temple to God, since you have taken from the Egyptians vessels of gold and silver and precious vestments. One, indeed, takes treasure from the Egyptians with which to build a tabernacle to God, if he reads the poets and philosophers, using them astutely to penetrate the mysteries of heavenly wisdom.[171] May he who was able to rebuild the fallen temple of his body in three days, deign to erect this tabernacle in our heart.

168. Cf. 1 John 4.8.
169. Ps 42.2.
170. 2 Chr 3.16.
171. Here Damian reflects the traditional patristic interpretation of the "spoliation of the Egyptians," and perhaps reveals his true attitude toward secular learning, elsewhere in his letters diluted by ascetical concerns. This remark, and his reference to the leisure time of his correspondent at the beginning of his peroration, would seem to indicate that Alberic, the Monte Cassino rhetorician, was the recipient of this letter, rather than Hildebrand, the industrious "business manager" of the Holy See.

LETTER 161

Peter Damian to the monks of Monte Cassino. He exhorts them to return to the practice of public flagellation on Fridays, which they had abandoned at the command of Cardinal Stephen of St. Chrysogonus. Damian argues that because of his pride in offering this bad advice, the otherwise worthy cardinal and his brother had suddenly died on the feast of St. Scholastica, 10 February 1069. In this he sees the hand of God, which should convince the monks that this pious practice is not to be mocked, especially since it imitates the passion of Christ and propitiously anticipates the punishment that will be meted out to us by the heavenly judge.

(May to June 1069)

o THE HOLY MONKS living in the heavenly school of Monte Cassino, the monk Peter the sinner offers his service.

(2) That the religious observance of Friday, my dear friends, to which your holy resolve has devoted both the abstemiousness of salutary fasting and the discipline of apostolic scourging, has attracted large numbers of people to follow your wholesome example, and has caused them to bring forth vigorous offspring like new olive shoots planted by God, is witnessed not only by the monasteries that rejoice to walk in your footsteps, that is, those of their teachers, but also by a multitude of towns and villages that in common throw themselves joyfully into this same praiseworthy practice. Indeed, it has come to this: that those who have eagerly committed themselves to this pious regimen, feel that they are jeopardizing their own salvation unless they promptly take up these observances. They are never in doubt that, while punishing themselves by bodily abstinence from food on the day dedicated to the Cross, they truly take part in the passion of the Redeemer, and fully believe that they shall

enjoy the glory of the Lord's resurrection, since like Christ hanging on the cross, they too crucify their bodily desires on the gibbet of self-denial. So it was that the apostle said: "If we suffer with him, we shall reign with him; if we died with him, we shall live with him."[1] And again: "If we have become incorporate with him in a death like his, we shall also be one in a resurrection like his."[2] And a little further on: "But if we thus died with Christ, we believe that we shall also come to life with him."[3]

(3) But we should know that since the enemy of the human race is unable to snatch away the total sacrifice from the hands of those who offer it, like some rapacious harpy he will try to carry off at least some part of it. This is why it is written, that when Abraham was offering a sacrifice of various animals to God, "birds of prey swooped down on the carcasses, and Abraham scared them away."[4] Birds of prey swoop down on the carcasses we immolate, when powers of the air pounce on the sacrifice of our tormented bodies, that they might snatch either the whole offering from the hands of those who undertake this atonement, or, having carried off some part of it, they congratulate themselves over the spoils of a victory.

(4) And so, the evil spirit, the author of primeval pride, uses the lips of certain men, like instruments that do his bidding, to rattle you, when he says: "We must not totally condemn wasting the body by fasting, but it is most shameful and unseemly to bare one's limbs before the eyes of our brothers who are looking on." Now from whom do such words originate, if not from him who caused the parents of our race to be ashamed of their nakedness?[5] Before the serpent had spoken, Scripture reports: "They were both naked, Adam and his wife, but they had no feeling of shame toward one another."[6] But after the cunning and crafty dragon had poured his venomous advice into their ears, it was promptly stated: "And when they discovered that they were naked, they stitched fig leaves together and made themselves loincloths."[7]

---

1. 2 Tim 2.11–12.   2. Rom 6.5.
3. Rom 6.8.   4. Gen 15.11.
5. Cf. Gen 3.1–11.   6. Gen 2.25.
7. Gen 3.7.

(5) I shall make bold to say, my dear brothers, that anyone who is ashamed to remove his clothes that he might suffer with Christ, has undoubtedly listened to the word of the serpent. And because he was embarrassed by his nakedness, like our first parents he hides himself, so to speak, from the sight of God: "I heard your voice in the garden," he says, "and I was afraid because I was naked, and I hid myself."[8] And undoubtedly, anyone who refuses to bear the ignominy heaped on Christ, is cut off from the vision of God, since the apostle says, "Let us then go to him outside the camp, bearing the stigma that he bore."[9]

(6) Therefore, a humble brother will join Paul in going outside the camp, and is not ashamed to bear the Savior's disgrace. But he who is proud and arrogant, and with our first parents searches for a hiding place that he might avoid the sight of God who sees all things, is certainly one of those to whom it is said: "Out of my sight, all of you, you and your wicked ways; I do not know you."[10] I do not know, he says, because I did not see you since you were avoiding me, that is, I condemned your presumptuous pride.

(7) Moreover, since at the start of this salutary practice each one of you took the discipline while naked, and had no fear of undergoing the shame of nakedness, who was it that later bewitched you and taught you to be ashamed of the suffering of Christ, which is the glory of the world and the salvation of men? Far be it from me, my lords, to be so presumptuous as to throw up to you the apostle's words to the Galatians: "Can it be that you are so stupid? You started with the spiritual; do you now look to the carnal to make you perfect?"[11] Yet I will boldly say to you what he said in reproaching the Corinthians: "How gladly you bear with fools, being yourselves so wise! If a man tyrannizes over you, exploits you, gets you in his clutches, puts on airs, and hits you in the face, you put up with it."[12] Who will doubt that all this has reference to those who teach false doctrine? And besides, as God said to Adam: "Who told you that

---

8. Gen 3.10.   9. Heb 13.13.
10. Luke 13.27.   11. Gal 3.3.
12. 2 Cor 11.19–20.

you were naked? Have you eaten from the tree from which I forbade you to eat?"[13] And so, deservedly one might severely censure you, and say: "Who influenced you to fear bearing the humiliation of Christ's cross, unless you listened to someone giving you bad advice?"

(8) And thus it was that when I anxiously asked you to explain the cause of all this, you simply replied that Cardinal Stephen of blessed memory insultingly jeered at this practice, and while holding it in contempt and despising it as something shameful, utterly forbade you ever again to engage in it. Nor should we be surprised, since the apostle says: "This doctrine of the cross is sheer folly to those on their way to ruin, but to us who are on the way to salvation it is the power of God."[14] Now it seems clear to me that by the grace of Christ Sir Stephen displayed many virtues, but some were saying that, impelled by the eagerness of youth, he suffered from the disease of pride. And perhaps it happened by the just decision of almighty God, that because of the sin incurred by this advice, he met death unexpectedly. Just a short time after he spoke with you over this matter, he took some medicine. But on the feast of the blessed virgin Scholastica, while still strong and in good health, he rose for Matins, and on that very day, first he and then his younger brother died suddenly, and were both buried on the following day.

(9) One might well believe that this all happened at the disposition of divine providence, and that this venerable brother incurred the judgment of an unexpected death occurring on the very feast day of this virgin, against whose monastery he had spoken such unguarded and arrogant words. We may hope that, because of this fault, his soul did not suffer harm, and that only his flesh, by its sudden collapse, was subjected to the punishment of death that was over in a moment. For it often happens that mercy is so intermingled with divine justice, that in this life the sinner receives the just deserts of his crime, so that later he may escape the punishment of eternal damnation.

13. Gen 3.11.
14. 1 Cor 1.18.

Here, indeed, he undergoes the penalty of an affliction that will run its course, so that there he may avoid the retribution that will never end.

(10) At this point, let me recall the story that the illustrious Peter de Burgo[15] recently told me. "There is a craftsman," he said, "living in the region that is called Pilonicum,[16] a man most skilled in the blacksmith's art, famous far and wide for his notable manufacture of spears and arrows. He was not interested in making metal tools and other utensils that might satisfy domestic needs, but took special delight in sharpening those adapted to wounding and killing fighting men, so that there was already a considerable number of those who had been killed in battle by his inevitable swords. On one occasion this man was slightly wounded in the chest, and since he was far from home, he lay in bed in a stranger's house. When at length the wound healed under the care of a doctor, he recuperated there until he had somewhat regained his strength. And after his wife had sent a horse for his return home, he at once felt well enough to get up. But then a shocking marvel took place: his whole arm and shoulder were left lying there in the bed. And what was truly unheard of, he felt no inconvenience or pain, but standing there marveling at his loss as if it had happened to someone else, he suddenly realized that he was disabled, and kept looking at the arm wrenched from his body as it lay there before him." Surely, it was by the just sentence of God that he should suddenly lose the arm with which he had made these cruel weapons that inflicted sudden death. And so, he who had often caused unexpected damage to many by the genius of his savage art, now found that he was damaged in the member that had not inflicted a wound.

(11) But now to get back to the subject I had been discussing. Whoever is ashamed to take the discipline because of his bodily nakedness, undoubtedly flees with Adam from the sight of God as he walked about in paradise, and is guilty of mocking the suffering of the crucified Christ. Nor is he a fol-

15. Cannot be identified.
16. Cannot be identified.

lower of him who became an accursed thing that he might
bring us freedom from the curse [of the Law],[17] but rather imitates him who "looks down on all creatures from his loftiness,
and is king over all the sons of pride."[18] The latter, in fact, is
clothed in glory, of whom the prophet said: "You are adorned
with gems of every kind,"[19] but because of his exalted arrogance, he fell into everlasting confusion. But the former is he
of whom both persecutors and followers as one man agree that
he bore reproach. Those who plot against him say: "Let us condemn him to a shameful death,"[20] while those who do penance
exclaim: "We counted him smitten by God, struck down by disease and misery."[21] To these latter words the same prophet had
previously added: "He had no beauty, no majesty to draw our
eyes, no grace to make us delight in him. He was despised, he
shrank from the sight of men, tormented and humbled by suffering; we despised him, we held him of no account, a thing
from which men turn away their eyes."[22]

(12) Tell me, therefore, whoever you may be, you who proudly ridicule the suffering of Christ, you who, while disdaining to
be stripped and scourged with him, deride his nakedness and
all his sufferings as if they were trifles and nursery rhymes and
absurd dreams, what will you do when you see him who was publicly stripped and raised upon the cross, now conspicuous for
his grace and majesty, surrounded by hosts of angels, clothed in
boundless and incomparable splendor, presiding in ineffable
glory over all things visible and invisible? What, I ask, will you do
when you behold him whose disgrace you despise, seated on a
fiery throne in the highest tribunal, judging the whole human
race in a terrifying ordeal of justice? Then the sun will be darkened, the moon will be enveloped in darkness, the stars will fall
from heaven, the foundations of the mountains will tremble,
the skies will crackle with the harshest rays, the earth and its atmosphere will go up in flames, furiously rising to the heights,
and all the elements will likewise be destroyed.[23] And amid all of

17. Cf. Gal 3.13.   18. Job 41.25.
19. Ezek 28.13.   20. Wis 2.20.
21. Isa 53.4.   22. Isa 53.2–3.
23. Cf. Matt 24.29.

this, you in your splendid attire, finely and handsomely arrayed, what will you do? How can you be so bold, so daring in your presumption, that you can hope to participate in his glory, after refusing to bear his shame and ignominy?

(13) Who will associate you, so delicate and tender, with the company of the martyrs, on whose bodies not only the weals of the scourge but also the scars of countless wounds will be seen in all their glory? Christ did not blush at the infamy of the cross, and are you ashamed of the nakedness of your putrid flesh that will be devoured by worms? He was stripped, beaten, put in chains, spat upon, and his flesh pierced with fivefold wounds, that we might be cured from the invasion of vice, which enters into us by the five senses. And you, licentious, voluptuous, wanton, and soft-living man, do you not wish your treasured flesh to be uncovered before men lest—which God forbid—it be judged mortal and earthy, but rather be considered something noble? Three times in public the apostle Paul was beaten with rods, and he was not ashamed; five times in the court he was given thirty-nine strokes, and he rejoiced. Moreover, he said that he was happy to have suffered from cold and exposure.[24] Along with all his co-apostles, Peter was flogged and made to suffer in the council of the Pharisees, and all praised God and danced for joy that Jesus had found them worthy to suffer indignity for the sake of his name.[25] After he had removed his garments, wearing a linen ephod, David danced without restraint before the Ark of the Lord, and, seeking only the glory of God and not his own, putting aside the decorum of royalty, he celebrated in honor of the omnipotent God.[26] And Michal said to him: "What a glorious day for the king of Israel, when he exposed his person in the sight of his servants' slave-girls like any empty-headed fool!"[27] The daughter of a proud king was unable to endure the humiliation of her husband, and so did not understand the glory of his nakedness, endured in the service of God.

(14) Therefore, those who contend that one's body is not to be bared in the presence of the brothers, deserve to have such

24. Cf. 2 Cor 11.24–27.
25. Cf. Acts 5.40–41.
26. Cf. 2 Sam 6.14–15.
27. 2 Sam 6.20.

a teacher. And since pride causes their roots to shrivel and they never bear spiritual fruit, they deserve to hear the words that Scripture used of her: "And so, Saul's daughter, Michal, had no child to her dying day."[28] And such people should be severely repulsed by you, just as David crushed her with his reply: "In the presence of the Lord I will dance for joy, yes, and I will earn yet more disgrace and lower myself still more in my eyes."[29] Through Isaiah it seems that the Lord was speaking to Michal as well as to Isaiah's disciples who were living indulgently, when he said: "Now therefore listen to this, you lover of luxury, carefree in your ways. You say to yourself, 'I am, and who but I? No widow's weeds for me, no barrenness.' Yet suddenly, in a single day, these two things shall come upon you: barrenness and widowhood."[30] It is certain that the Holy Spirit, who resided in him, urged David to go naked; but the devil, who possessed her father, incited Michal to disparage him. And of this possession it is said, "that an evil spirit of the Lord suddenly seized Saul."[31] And indeed, without the slightest doubt we can believe that the Spirit of God prodded David to humbly expose his body in honor of the cross of Christ, while Saul, because of his arrogance, refused to divest himself of the spirit of pride that he might imitate Christ on the cross. And this pride so dissociated him from the very Source of humility, that not even Samuel was able to obtain forgiveness for him.

(15) The Lord commanded Isaiah, the most outstanding of all the prophets, publicly to go naked in the presence of all the people, and should a monk who, so to speak, is not worth a farthing, blush to take off his clothes before a few of his brothers? "Come," he said, "strip the sackcloth from your waist and take your sandals off," and then the text continues: "He did so, and went about naked and barefoot."[32] And we should note that the Lord was not speaking of a soft linen garment, or of one made of delicately woven cloth, but said: "Strip the sackcloth from your waist," that from the softness of the garment you might conclude how delicate and easy was the life of those who, even

28. 2 Sam 6.23.   29. 2 Sam 6.22.
30. Isa 47.8–9.   31. 1 Sam 11.6.
32. Isa 20.2.

under the Old Law, were imbued with the spirit of truth. Accordingly, both kings and prophets, and even the Savior and the apostles, never shrank from going naked when times of persecution demanded it, and do you, like some delicate little lord, fear to be seen naked, lest the eyes of the viewers be fascinated by the sight? Truly, your brothers are the young of ravens who are proud to bear the disgrace of their Lord.[33] As it is said, like a young cock, born of a white hen, you are happy to appear trim and splendidly equipped. But when in your pride you despise the blackness of ravens, you become white with the leprosy that the Ancient Law denounces.

(16) And so, my brother, what is this flesh that you are so careful to keep covered with clothes, and which you take such pains to foster like the son of a king? Is it not a mass of rottenness, is it not food for worms, dust, and ashes? But even in its present condition, it is not heeded by a wise man, but is rather looked upon as bloody matter, poison, foulness, and filth from repulsive corruption, which it will later become. What thanks can you expect from worms that will devour your flesh, which you so softly and sweetly nourish? So answer me, I say, why did Christ suffer? Was it to wash away his own guilt and to destroy the sins he had committed? But listen to what Peter says of him: "He committed no sin, he was convicted of no falsehood."[34] Therefore, what was the cause of his passion? And again Peter replies: "Christ suffered on your behalf, and thereby left you an example; it is for you to follow in his steps."[35] Accordingly, first Christ suffered, to be succeeded then in suffering by the apostles, whose example we are commanded to follow, just as one of them says: "Follow my example as I follow Christ's."[36] Why, then, do we read that Christ suffered? It was that we too might do likewise.

(17) I beseech you, my beloved brothers, stop your ears against the hissing serpents that speak of evil things, and keep them pure in the simplicity of the poor, crucified Christ Jesus.

---

33. Perhaps a reference to the legendary birds that tried to pluck the nails from the hands and feet of the crucified Christ.

34. 1 Pet 2.22.   35. 1 Pet 2.21.

36. 1 Cor 11.1.

Refuse to drink from the golden cup of Babylon and from the cup of God's wrath that are so alluringly handed to you,[37] and avoid the pestilential poison of the proud and of those who adulterate the word of God. Of such people the apostle says to Timothy: "Avoid empty and worldly chatter; those who indulge in it will stray further and further into godless courses, and the infection of their teaching will spread like a gangrene."[38] God forbid that either you or I should be exposed to this twin danger, which the apostle observed in various letters. To you he said: "As the serpent in his cunning seduced Eve, I am afraid that your thoughts may be corrupted and you may lose your single-hearted devotion to Christ."[39] But to me he said: "You make me fear that all the pains I spent on you may prove to be labor lost."[40] And of our adversaries he also said: "Such men are sham-apostles, crooked in all their practices, masquerading as apostles of Christ. But they will meet the end their deeds deserve."[41] Accordingly, a man of holy intent should not fear to participate in scourging and thus in the cross of Christ, nor should he be ashamed of his humiliation in being stripped of his clothes, since he said: "For whoever is ashamed of me and my words, the Son of Man will be ashamed of him, when he comes in his glory and the glory of the Father and the holy angels."[42] Certainly, one will never be embarrassed by the nakedness of his body if he bears in mind the rewards that await him, nor will he dread the sharpness of the blows that are over in a moment, if he considers beforehand the sweetness of eternal happiness that will be awarded him.

(18) Oh, what a happy and remarkable sight, when the divine Judge looks down from heaven and sees a man here below punishing himself for his sins. When the guilty one himself presides on the bench of his own conscience, he holds a threefold office: in his heart he becomes the judge, in his body the guilty one, and with his own hands he is happy to play the role of the torturer, as if the holy penitent were saying to God: "It is not necessary, Lord, for you as judge to pass sentence on me; there

37. Cf. Jer 51.7; Rev 14.10.
38. 2 Tim 2.16–17.
39. 2 Cor 11.3.
40. Gal 4.11.
41. 2 Cor 11.13–15.
42. Luke 9.26.

is no need for you to strike me and administer the penalty that I deserve. I am laying hands on myself, I am taking vengeance on myself, and make myself responsible for my crimes." And this, in fact, is just what the apostle Peter advises, when he says: "If you suffer, it must not be for murder, theft, or sorcery, nor for infringing the rights of others. But if anyone suffers as a Christian, he should feel it no disgrace."[43] But when this takes place, the demons take to flight, and dread to see what is conducive to Christ's glory and their own ignominy. The angels, on the other hand, are present at this public display, rejoice at a sinner's conversion,[44] and for joy announce the event to God, even though the invisible Judge is already viewing the same event with pleasure. This is the victim that is sacrificed alive, and is offered to God by the angels; and thus the human body, as a victim, is invisibly joined to that unique sacrifice offered on the altar of the cross. And thus, every sacrifice is concealed in this one treasure, namely, that which is offered by each member and by the head of all the elect.

43. 1 Pet 4.15–16.
44. Cf. Luke 15.10.

LETTER 162

Peter Damian to Peter, the archpriest of the canons of the Lateran, and chancellor of Pope Alexander II. The last of four tracts treating of clerical celibacy, this letter exhorts the archpriest Peter to use his good offices in combating the current evil of clerical marriage and cohabitation with women. Damian's primary argument against these practices flows from the respect due the Holy Eucharist, which, like the bread of the Presence in David's time, should be handled by men who are free from sexual contact.

(June 1069–1072)

O SIR PETER, archpriest of the Lateran canons, the monk Peter the sinner in the bond of fraternal charity.

(2) A lance is only as effective as the strength of a fighting man. For no matter how much care has gone into polishing and sharpening it, if the arm that hurls it is weak, no trophies of victory will be won. But where the soldier is vigorous, even a blunt sword will serve to cut down the foe and win the battle. As you know, even Goliath, who was armed with a mighty sword, not only lost, but was struck down and died.[1] With a worthless jawbone of an ass Samson also killed a thousand Philistines.[2] And so, when Jether, the eldest son of Gideon, was afraid to draw his sword, the Midianite kings, Zebah and Zalmunna, said to Gideon: "Rise up yourself and dispatch us, for you have a man's strength."[3] Accordingly, since I am fashioning a spear that will serve as a hammer in countering the lust of clerics, I could do no better than put it into your hands. In fact, I have observed you always burning with such ardent zeal in opposing

1. Cf. 1 Sam 17.50–51.   2. Cf. Judg 15.15.
3. Judg 8.21.

their profligate moral life, that you might be judged as being endowed with the fire of Phineas or Elijah, and that these clerics dread the attack of your reproaches more than they fear a papal decree. For like an excellent watchdog that guards the court of the king, with your loud bark you assail the nocturnal thieves and seize them in your teeth, lest they burn down the royal palace with the fires of their sexual desires.

(3) You are surely not unaware that the law of celibacy is so strictly and rigorously imposed on priests, deacons, and subdeacons, that by the common consent of all the Catholic Fathers they are utterly forbidden to contract marriage. And certainly, there is every good reason why, after the bishops, the snow-white splendor of chastity should flourish also in these three grades of clerics, since they are so closely associated with the sacred mysteries. For since the body of the Lord grew to maturity in the temple of the Virgin's womb, now too he seeks the purity of continent chastity from those who are his ministers.

(4) Surely, just as no male seed flowed into the virginal Mother of God when she conceived, but the power of the Holy Spirit overshadowed her, so too the same power of the Holy Spirit, which gives life, is present in the sacrament that is placed on the altar, and it is required that pure and unsullied hands reach out to touch it. But since elsewhere I have already treated this subject at great length, and in separate letters have assembled various texts from Scripture, first to Pope Nicholas of blessed memory, then to the bishop of Turin, and lastly also to the Countess Adelaide,[4] I refer you to them, venerable brother, invest you with them as with military weapons, and like another Joshua send you to destroy the city of Jericho. Therefore, it now remains for me to address a few words to these same clerics, so that the fire that burns in the furnace of my heart may escape through the open vents of my lips.

(5) In presenting my suit against you, you charmers, you womanizers, who find yourselves enslaved by the power of dom-

---

4. To Pope Nicholas, *Letter* 61 (FOTC, MC 3.3–13); to Bishop Cunibert of Turin, *Letter* 112 (FOTC, MC 5.258–85); and to Countess Adelaide, *Letter* 114 (FOTC, MC 5.294–305).

inating females, why do you overthrow the laws of canonical jurisdiction and violate the norm of ecclesiastical purity set up by the holy Fathers? You should be ashamed to bend your necks to the yoke of your lust, and trample on the decrees of the Holy Spirit made known to us through the words of the doctors. Obviously, the work of the apostles has been subverted by you, and the building that the doctors of the Church had erected has fallen to pieces at your attack. And thus it happens that the law of the Church, which the rank of clerics is known to have established, is once again destroyed by opponents of that same rank. Amnon and Absalom were brothers, born of the same father, but one of them killed the other.[5] Cain murdered Abel, the evil brother doing in the just one.[6] Frequently also, a bastard brother will kill the legitimate one, just as Jugurtha, according to the account of Crispus Sallust, slew Hiempsal and Adherbal.[7] Thus too, as it were, spurious brothers are killing their legitimate brothers, when those who profess to be clerics only in name, destroy the decrees of the holy Fathers. And it seems that they are annihilating the very decisions that they have no fear of annulling. It would seem, moreover, that we have an apt symbol of these clerics in Abimelech, son of Jerubbaal, who, as Scripture reports, was born of a concubine he lived with in Shechem.[8] For on a single stone block he killed all seventy of his brothers, the sons of Jerubbaal. And what is meant by these seventy men, if not their counterpoise, the preachers of the Church? Of them the evangelist Luke says: "After this the Lord appointed seventy men and sent them on ahead in pairs to every town and place he was going to visit himself."[9]

(6) This rank of preachers was already prefigured by those of whom the Lord said to Moses: "Assemble seventy elders from Israel, men known to you as elders and officers in the community; bring them to me at the door of the Tent of the Presence."[10] The same mystic number is undoubtedly recognized as

5. Cf. 2 Sam 13.28–29.

6. Cf. Gen 4.8.

7. Cf. Eutropius, *Breviarium* 4.26 (MG Auct.ant. 80–82); Sallust, *Bellum Iugurthino* 12.5 and 26.3, ed. A. Kurfess (Leipzig: Teubner, 1957), pp. 62, 74.

8. Cf. Judg 9.1.　　　　　　　　9. Luke 10.1.

10. Num 11.16.

referring to preachers in the account of the people of Israel encamped at Elim, where there were twelve springs and seventy
palm trees.[11] For what was meant by the twelve springs, if not
the holy apostles, who never cease irrigating the parched land
of the human heart with the waters of their sacred preaching?
And what should we understand by the seventy palm trees, if
not the ranks of lesser priests who were commissioned to announce the victories of Christ to the world? The palm, in fact, is
customarily used to crown victors, and in these seventy, the
number ten goes seven times, since in carrying out the commands of the decalogue the sevenfold grace of the Spirit[12] is in-
dispensable.

(7) Nor must we forget that before this people had reached
Elim, they had camped the day before at Marah, where, since
the water was so bitter that they could not drink it, the Lord
showed them a log which they threw into the water, and then it
became sweet.[13] Now since men refuse to drink this salty water
because of its bitterness, prefiguring the death-dealing letter[14]
of the Old Law that no one was able to fulfill, to these waters we
apply the wood of the cross by mixing them with the events of
the Lord's passion, and at once, through the mystery of spiritual interpretation, they become sweet enough to drink. And so,
the people left Marah and came to Elim, turning their back on
the dreadfully bitter letter of the Law, and in their joy moved
on to the fresh springs of the apostles and to the sweet fruit of
the palm trees. They rejected the servitude of the Law, and
sought out the sweet freedom of grace found in the Gospel.

(8) But to get back to what I began to say, since the seventy
men killed by Abimelech prefigure the preachers of the
Church, what should we understand by Abimelech, who was
their brother, even though illegitimate, if not lustful and carnal
clerics who are indeed brothers of Catholic and holy bishops
according to the ecclesiastical order that they received, and yet
are considered bastards by reason of their wayward life and the
depravity of their ignoble deeds? Such men kill their brothers

11. Cf. Exod 15.27.
12. The seven gifts of the Spirit are named in Isa 11.2 (LXX).
13. Cf. Exod 15.23–25.   14. Cf. 2 Cor 3.6.

when they destroy the decisions of the holy Fathers, when by their evil lives they run roughshod over their ordinances and decrees, and this killing takes place on a single stone block. This stone is the Church of the Savior, of which Zechariah says: "Yes, I will bring my servant the Shoot, for here is the stone that I set before Joshua, a single stone on which are seven eyes."[15] Both texts aptly speak of a single stone, so that the unity of the Church may be favorably noted. And of her the bridegroom says in the Song of Songs: "There is one alone, my dove, her mother's only child."[16]

(9) I am saving for a higher mystery, if one is here to be found, the identity of the seven eyes on this single stone. Who are they, if not those seventy men, that is, the holy doctors, joined in the unity of the Church's peace, and adorned with the sevenfold gifts[17] of the Holy Spirit? For with these eyes holy Church is able to see, with them she decides where she should step in order to act correctly, so that[18] by following God's commandments she may not violate the norms of an upright life.

(10) Therefore, the bastard and spurious Abimelech kills his seventy legitimate brothers on a single stone block, when a part of the clerical order deviates from the noble life of ecclesiastical chastity, and submits to the obscene laws of lust. And when this group decides that the sacred canons are to be rejected, with a certain cruel streak they implicitly kill the authors of these canons, holy and noble men, the sons of Gideon, that is, of the Savior and of the Church. For they are in possession of counterfeit canons and of certain novel documents filled with sophistical arguments, by which they urge their followers to imitate their doctrine and attack the stronghold of ecclesiastical chastity. This is, in fact, prefigured by the siege of the castle of Shechem, of which the historical account has this to say of the murderer of his brothers: "When Abimelech heard that all the occupants of the castle of Shechem had gathered together, he and his people went up Mount Zalmon; there, picking up an ax, he cut brushwood, and hoisted it on his shoulder. He said

---

15. Zech 3.8–9. 16. Song 6.8.
17. Cf. Isa 11.2 (LXX).
18. Reading *ut* for *ac*, following MS G1.

to his men: 'You see what I am doing; be quick and do the same.'"[19] And the text continues: "So each man cut brushwood; then they followed Abimelech, and surrounding the fort they set it on fire. And so it happened that with smoke and fire a thousand persons were killed, men and women together, all occupants of the castle of Shechem."[20]

(11) This is not the place to use one's ingenuity in explaining the symbolism of sacred history. It will suffice for me to examine the matter summarily, only so far as it suits our purpose. By the brushwood we understand short excerpts from the Scriptures, which wicked men violently tear out of context to support their contentions, and with smoke and fire kill great numbers of people, that is, the smoke of error and the fire of passion, so that the flames of lust might consume the mind of those who are deceived by their evil teachings and so that the darkness of their vicious doctrine might confound them. These indeed, are the remains that were seen in the ruins of Sodom and Gomorrah after these cities had been destroyed: "Next morning," Scripture says, "Abraham rose early and went to the place where he had stood in the presence of the Lord. He looked down toward Sodom and Gomorrah and all the wide extent of the plain, and there he saw thick smoke rising high from the earth like the smoke of a limekiln."[21] Again when he besieged the town of Thebez with his forces, Abimelech seemed to prefigure the attack on chastity. "There was a tall castle in the middle of the city," as Scripture affirms, "and all the citizens, men and women, and the princes of the city took refuge there. They shut themselves in and went on to the roof, standing upon the battlements of the castle."[22] The city is the universal Church, the castle of chastity is its high point, in which both men and women, the strong and the weak, take refuge, and also the princes of the city, namely, the order of clerics who wield authority in the Church. And when Abimelech came up to the castle, the battle became more fierce, and, approaching the gate, he tried to destroy it by fire.

19. Judg 9.47–48.
21. Gen 19.27–28.
20. Judg 9.49.
22. Judg 9.51.

(12) In the same way senseless and wanton clerics attempt to set fire to the castle of chastity as they exhort many to follow the example of their voluptuousness and burning madness. Firebrands in hand, they attack the castle of chastity as the impure enkindle the chaste with the flames of their pernicious arguments. But who will end this battle? On whom does this struggle bestow the trophies of victory? Scripture says: "And then a woman threw a piece of millstone down on Abimelech and fractured his skull. He called hurriedly to his armor bearer and said: 'Draw your sword and dispatch me, or men will say of me: A woman killed him.' So the young man carried out the order and killed him."[23]

(13) But that we may not linger too long on these words, the piece of millstone that fractured the skull of Abimelech, is nothing but the stone which Daniel saw, hewn from a mountain, not by human hands,[24] namely, the Lord himself, who says in the Gospel: "Any man who falls on this stone will be dashed to pieces; and if it falls on a man he will be crushed by it."[25] Now the woman who threw the stone is the sacred law that threatens infamous men who despise purity with the unexpected judgment of Christ. Of it Jeremiah says: "Do not my words scorch like fire, says the Lord? Are they not like a hammer that splinters rock?"[26] Abimelech's armor bearer is the devil, who hands the weapons of passion and sharp arrows of lust to all who attack the castle of chastity. Of these missiles the apostle says: "With all these, take up the great shield of faith, with which you will be able to quench all the flaming arrows of the evil one."[27] And the prophet adds: "There is Assyria with all her weapons."[28] And he who was struck by the piece of millstone, hurled by the woman, was cut down by the sword of the armor bearer, because the devil dispatches with the sword of everlasting death all the opponents of chastity, whom sacred Scripture threatens with the sentence of divine punishment, so that as he was their servant in the battle, he may afterwards be their tormentor in hell. And the weapons he once provided for them in

---

23. Judg 9.53–54.
25. Matt 21.44.
27. Eph 6.16.

24. Cf. Dan 2.34.
26. Jer 23.29.
28. Ezek 32.22–27.

fighting against purity, he will then use to cut their throats as they deserve.

(14) So now let these degenerate and lustful clerics, these flawed deserters from the noble ranks of their order, seize their weapons, like Abimelech, and kill the legitimate brothers on a single block of stone. Let them push the attack and storm the castle of Thebez, the fortress of chastity. But all their fighting has only this conclusion, that after they are struck by the stone, they will also be dispatched by their own armor bearer's sword. Those who used the sword to kill their brothers on the stone, are struck by a stone so that they may not escape the sword, so that first the weight of God's sentence might crush them, and the vengeful sword of the evil spirit might cut them down, while at the same time we know that it is not absurd to say that Christ can be prefigured by Jerubbaal, and the Antichrist by Abimelech.[29] For just as the latter is the son of the concubine, the former is the son of the synagogue that has been discarded. But by the seventy brothers who, as Scripture says, were killed by Abimelech, we should understand the seventy peoples of various tongues whom the Antichrist shall persecute at the end of the world.[30] But to get back to the topic I started to discuss, I have still more to say about this clerical madness.

(15) Evidently, like the sons of Jacob, they are indeed endowed with their father's rights, but because they are base and stained by bastardy, their origins are not legitimate, but rather ignoble, because they spring not from wives, but from concubines. For as Scripture says: "None of their bastard offshoots will strike deep root."[31] They are not the children of Leah or Rachel, but prove rather to be sons of the slave girls, Bilhah and Zilpah, in the servile deeds of their degraded way of life.[32] Now Bilhah has the meaning "of long standing."[33] And those

29. This seems to be a unique reference to Abimelech as a prototype of the Antichrist.

30. The seventy peoples of various tongues may be a paraphrase of the nations from the four quarters of the earth, spoken of in Rev 20.7.

31. Wis 4.3.

32. Cf. Gen 30.

33. Cf. Jerome, *Nom. hebr.* 3.23. Cf. Damian's treatment of these names also at *Letter* 153.35–36.

who live by the flesh prove that they are not born of the new
way of the spirit, but of the carnal seed of our old human nature. Again, in our language Zilpah means "lips that move."[34]
This is a proper description of their mother, for when they
preach the truth, their lips appear to be moving, but their
heart is not in what they say. And it was surely said of them:
"This people honors me with their lips, but their hearts are far
from me."[35] As if he were addressing them in person, the apostle also reproached them: "You, then, who teach your fellow-
man, do you fail to teach yourself? You proclaim, 'Do not steal';
but are you yourself a thief? You say, 'Do not commit adultery';
but are you an adulterer? You abominate false gods; but do you
rob their shrines? While you take pride in the law, do you dishonor God by breaking it? 'Because of you the name of God is
dishonored among the Gentiles.'"[36]

(16) Truly, by their evil lives they do violence to the word of
God, which they pronounce with their lips; and as they speak,
they appear to be descendants of the honored nobility of the
patriarchs, but by living in disgraceful filth, they demonstrate
that they originate in a brothel. Abraham, we know, had one
son by his wife but begot many sons by concubines, yet he kept
them away from his legitimate son so long as he lived. For they
could not become coheirs with their brother if they were born
of slave girls. And so, what does Scripture say? "Abraham gave
all that he had to Isaac, but to the sons of his concubines he
gave presents."[37] Indeed, so long as Abraham lived, all his children boasted that they were the sons of Abraham; but when at
the end he gave his whole patrimony to one of them, who truly
bore the name of son, he obviously omitted those who bore the
disgrace of concubinage. Therefore, bastard clerics now seem
to live in common with the legitimate sons of Abraham, but later they will be denied participation in his inheritance, because
now they take their pleasure with women, as if these were the
presents they received from their father.

34. Cf. Jerome, *Nom. hebr.* 11.28.
35. Isa 29.13, which is quoted in Mark 7.6.
36. Rom 2.21–24; cf. Isa 52.5.
37. Gen 25.5.

(17) But they reply: "Did not the apostle say, 'Because there is so much immorality, let each man have his own wife and each woman her own husband. The husband must give the wife what is due to her, and the wife equally must give the husband his due'?[38] Please note," they say, "that these words of the apostle are of general application, and while granting each one the right to marry, they do not appear to exclude us." To which I may retort: If by these words the restraint on conjugal incontinence is relaxed, then the same freedom should not be denied to bishops, monks, or even abbots. And since both sexes are bound by the same law, even holy virgins should be urged to enter the married state. But what ears, incessantly attuned to the doctrine of the Church, could calmly bear to hear such an idea and not promptly react in horror at such a monstrous sacrilege? But some who find this matter agreeable to them, promptly have recourse to the plea of poverty, using it as a pitiful excuse to shield their actions: "We cannot live," they say, "without the solicitous care of a woman, because we lack adequate income for our household."

(18) To these, on the other hand, I might say, that while in your case food is limited, so too is the family that must be fed, and your table, which is not spread for a banquet, is not expected to support many guests. Hence it follows that poverty in need of solitude should teach one to shun the company of women, and thus prevent the bearing of swarming youngsters, eagerly waiting to be fed.

(19) Truly, by what audacity are they not horrified at approaching the divine mysteries, since before touching the Bread of the Presence David reverently asserted that both he and his men had kept themselves from women during the past three days. For the priest Abimelech had said to him: "I have no ordinary bread available. There is only the sacred bread, but if your young men are pure, especially from contact with women, they may eat it."[39] Here we should note that in saying that those who would eat holy bread must be pure, especially from contact with women, he clearly taught that no stain of sin, in fact, no sin

38. 1 Cor 7.2–3.
39. 1 Sam 21.4.

at all is more opposed to the sacred mysteries than unlawful co-habitation with women. Moreover, since among men of the Old Testament such great fear surrounded the imperfect image of the Body of the Lord, how much reverence should be shown to the reality itself? And if relations in marriage prohibited access to the showbread, how much more must concubinage be removed from contact with this most sacred sacrament? What a crime! Hands that were consigned to consecrate the life-giving food of angels on the heavenly table, are not appalled at handling the filth and foul contagion of women. Men who, while engaged in these terrifying mysteries, associate with angelic choirs, now fall, as though rushing headlong from heaven, into the arms of polluted women, and like swine wallow in the mud and vermin-infested sloughs of lust, "where their worm shall not die nor their fire be quenched."[40] Heaven is opened, the highest and the lowest are joined as one, and the cleric is not ashamed to involve himself brazenly in unclean affairs. Angelic spirits stand by in awe, divine power comes down into consecrating hands, the gift of the Holy Spirit flows into the offering, the High Priest himself, whom the angels adore, does not remain aloof from the sacrifice of his body and blood, and he who burns with the fires of hellish lust has no fear of being present.

(20) If the man who was not wearing his wedding clothes was bound hand and foot and thrown out into the punishing darkness,[41] what hope can there be for one who was admitted to the heavenly banquet, and not only fails to appear in the beauty of spiritual attire, but even reeks of the squalor of befouling debauchery? If he whose garments fail to please his fellow guests is punished by wailing and the grinding of teeth, what judgment awaits him who in his very being is saturated with ghastly filth, pollutes the purity of the marriage banquet, shocks the sensibilities of the white-clad assembly, and dares to touch the King himself with his unclean hands? The earth opened up and swallowed Dathan and Abiram for having de-

---

40. Isa 66.24, which is quoted in Mark 9.48.
41. Cf. Matt 22.13.

fied Moses and Aaron.[42] For the same offense, fire from heaven suddenly came down and consumed Korah and the two hundred and fifty men who were with him,[43] and how shall he continue to live who with such cruelty and shameful behavior sins, not against a man, but against the very Creator of men? Obviously, clerics of this sort send a delegation to the Lord, not in so many words, but in the language of their deeds and the purpose of their intention: "We do not want this man as our king."[44] And of these it will surely be said: "But as for those enemies of mine who did not want me for their king, bring them here and slaughter them in my presence."[45] To be sure, they were happy to have Pharaoh as their king, but refused to have the God of Israel rule over them. Yet the former put them to slave labor on clay and brick-making,[46] as he forced them to engage in filthy and soiling work. With the products of their hands they also mixed straw, that is, useless and unproductive deeds, destined for the fire that cannot be quenched.

(21) That prophetic girdle, moreover, of which Jeremiah speaks, aptly applies to these clerics: "These were the words of the Lord to me: Go and buy yourself a linen girdle and put it round your waist."[47] And a few verses later, he said: "Go at once to the Euphrates and hide it in a crevice among the rocks."[48] When he had done this, and had hidden it at the Euphrates as he had been ordered, the Lord at length said to him: "Go at once to the Euphrates and fetch back the girdle. And so I went to the Euphrates," he said, "and picked up the girdle from the place where I had hidden it, and I saw that it was spoiled, and no good for anything. And the Lord spoke to me: Thus will I spoil the pride of Judah, the gross pride of Jerusalem. This wicked nation has refused to listen to my words, and has followed the wickedness of its own heart. So it shall be like this girdle, not good for anything."[49]

(22) Whom does Jeremiah here represent, if not the Lord? And what is meant by the girdle, if not the rank of the clergy?

---

42. Cf. Num 16.31–33.
43. Cf. Num 26.10.
44. Luke 19.14.
45. Luke 19.27.
46. Cf. Exod 1.14.
47. Jer 13.1.
48. Jer 13.4.
49. Jer 13.6–10.

The entire Church is the garment of Christ, of whose members it is said through the prophet: "You shall wear them as your jewels."[50] But as a girdle is close to a man's body, and fits more snugly than other clothes, so the order of clerics is brought more intimately into the service of God than other men; as in the text cited above, God said of the people of Israel: "For just as a girdle is bound close to a man's waist, so I bound all Israel and all Judah to myself, so that they should become my people to win a name for me, and praise and glory; but they did not listen."[51]

(23) To whom, I ask, could these words apply more aptly and more directly than to clerics, who are especially commissioned to proclaim the name of God, his praise and his glory? And just as Israel and Judah were God's peculiar people among all the nations of the earth, so now clerics are uniquely associated with Christ, and are preferred to all the members of the Church. They are the linen girdle bound to God's body in close familiarity. Only after much effort does linen become white; and clerics, by diligently pursuing the study of the arts for a while, and then over a period of time rising in the ranks, only with difficulty are promoted to the high goal of sacred orders. Otherwise, if one were to be obstinate in interpreting this passage as a historical fact occurring in Scripture, and not according to the spiritual sense, how could Jeremiah, with hosts of Assyrians and Chaldaeans besieging Jerusalem, leave the city wearing this girdle, and hide it along the Euphrates, which runs its course so far away? And later also, after much time had elapsed, how could he safely return and find it completely rotted, as Scripture asserts, since Jerusalem was surrounded by trenches, ramparts, fortifications, and with munitions on all sides? For, at the time when the same prophet tried to leave the city and go to his village at Anathoth, lying three miles from the city,[52] he was promptly arrested at the gate, brought before the officers, flogged severely, and like a fugitive or a traitor was

---

50. Isa 49.18.
51. Jer 13.11–12.
52. At Anathoth Jeremiah owned a plot of land; cf. Jer 32.6–7.

thrown into prison.[53] And so, since it does not make sense to interpret all this as a historical event, it follows without question that there is here a mystery of allegorical significance. Therefore, in the light of what was said above, the linen girdle is an excellent figure of the order of clerics.

(24) But that he was ordered to put this girdle at the Euphrates, that is, in a damp area, and in a crevice of the rocks, namely, in an obscure and dark place, what is meant by this, but that portion of the clerical order that is living under the shadow of passionate desire and in a flood of lust? Of their leader the Lord said in the book of Job: "In the shade he lies, in coverts of the reedy swamp, where the shade covers his shadow, and willow trees on the stream surround him."[54] And to show how much he enjoys living with his friends on the river, the Lord promptly added: "If the river grows violent, he is not disturbed; he is confident though the Jordan surges about his mouth."[55] And when it is said that [the girdle] was placed in a crevice of the rocks, this can easily be understood to mean, within the walls of the Church. For clerics are confined, as it were, in the crevices of the rocks, when they are ordered to perform their ministries, frequently and devotedly, within the boundaries of the Church. And so the girdle rotted when put in a humid place, because the prophet asserts of those who live in a spate of lustful desire: "The cattle have rotted in their own dung."[56] The cattle, indeed, begin to rot in their own dung, when carnal and foul men conduct their lives in the stench of lust. It was also found to be good for nothing, since the Lord also says: "No one who sets his hand to the plow and then keeps looking back is fit for the kingdom of God."[57] This is like saying quite frankly: Whoever, in keeping with the law of his class, once grasps the handle of the plow of chastity, and then, because of the fires of lust, afterwards turns his eyes toward Sodom, and from now on has lost hope of ever reaching the mountain top, shows that he has become totally unfit for the

53. Cf. Jer 37.
55. Job 40.18.
57. Luke 9.62.
54. Job 40.16–17.
56. Joel 1.17.

kingdom of God. And thus, like the girdle that was put in a damp place, clerics become wholly rotten as in their drunkenness they fill their fat bellies with wine, and drown themselves in a flood of filthy lust and befouling passion. And so, they are good for nothing, for the more portly they become, the worse is their decay, as their souls waste away in horrid squalor. And in the psalm it is also said of them: "They are corrupt and have become loathsome in all their ways."[58]

(25) But you, my venerable brother, armed with these and other weapons of Scripture, engage the hostile forces of Midian, and with the spear of God's Word transfix Zimri and Cozbi, living shamefully in their brothel, so that along with Phinehas you may deserve to receive the peace of the Lord's covenant, and the right to the eternal priesthood. "Tell him," says the Lord, "that I hereby grant him my covenant of security of tenure. He and his descendants after him shall enjoy the priesthood under a covenant for all time, because he showed his zeal for his God and made expiation for the children of Israel."[59] Therefore, one need not fear human hostility if he is rewarded with the peace of God's covenant. Moreover, because Moses killed an Egyptian, he at once abandoned Egypt as a fugitive; but afterwards, as if interest had accrued, he became the ruler of the whole people of Israel. For as Scripture states: "He saw an Egyptian strike one of his fellow Hebrews, and promptly struck him down and hid his body in the sand."[60] And you also, when you see an Egyptian, that is, the prince of darkness, beating one of your brothers, namely, in the ranks of the clerics, with the rod of lust, or rather, which is more to the point, killing him with a deadly spear, promptly draw the gleaming sword of the Word to strike a telling blow and cut down the man who injured a fellow member of your own class, that is, "use argument, reproof, and appeal, with all the patience that the work of teaching requires."[61] But since, as the same apostle asserts, there are some who "will not stand wholesome teaching, but will follow their own fancy and gather a crowd of teachers to tickle their ears, they will stop their ears to the truth and

---

58. Ps 13.1.
60. Exod 2.11–12.
59. Num 25.12–13.
61. 2 Tim 4.2.

turn to mythology."[62] Do not give up, but do what follows: "But you yourself must keep watchful at all times; face hardship, work to spread the Gospel, and do all the duties of your calling."[63]

(26) By so acting, attract all whom you can, but leave those who are stubborn and who obstinately rebel, in the filth of their obscenity. For this is burying the Egyptian in the sand. Sand, indeed, is dry and brittle soil, which is unable to support the foundation of a rising structure. Consequently, the Church should be built, not on sand, but on rock, that it will stand forever. "On this rock," says the Lord, "I will build my Church."[64] Therefore, those who construct their foundation on the rock of the Church, remain firm and steadfast in performing good works. Of these the Lord says in the Gospel: "Every one who hears these words of mine and acts upon them, is like a man who had the sense to build his house on rock. The rain came down, the floods rose, the wind blew, and beat upon that house; but it did not fall, because its foundations were on rock."[65] But those who are fragile and made of dust, and, like a reed bed, are swept by the driving winds of carnal desire, must undoubtedly be compared to a patch of sandy soil. Of them the psalmist says: "Wicked men are not like this; they are like dust driven away by the wind."[66] And the Lord says: "But what of the man who hears these words of mine and does not act upon them? He is like a man who was foolish enough to build his house on sand. The rain came down, the floods rose, the wind blew, and beat upon that house; down it fell with a great crash."[67] And so also in the book of Kings he says: "All the objects in the house of the Lord which Hiram made for King Solomon were of brass. In the plain of the Jordan the king cast them in clay ground."[68] Now, since these vessels symbolize carnal men, it is said that they were made of brass and not of gold; and so they were cast, not in the mountains, but in the plain, because men who are prefigured by them do not climb to the

---

62. 2 Tim 4.3–4.
64. Matt 16.18.
66. Ps 1.4.
68. 1 Kgs 7.45–46.

63. 2 Tim 4.5.
65. Matt 7.24–25.
67. Matt 7.26–27.

heights of virtue, but settle in the valley of a wanton and voluptuous life. They are not beaten, but cast, because they are not
pounded by the hammers of the cross and of penance, but are
bent by the pleasures of vice and loosened by the waters of the
most shameful desires. And just as the girdle was placed at the
Euphrates, so these vessels are said to have been cast near the
Jordan; and not in the firm and solid soil, which might provide
a base for the casting, but in earth composed of clay and sand
that produces sudden fragmentation.

(27) Accordingly, venerable brother, like Moses you should
cut down the Egyptian who struck your brother, using the
sword of severe correction, and you should hide him in arid
souls that are like sand, that in death he may occupy the clay-
bound grave of earthy men, there to produce worms of concupiscence. Let him refrain from beating true Israelites with the
scourge of his temptations. It was not by accident that the Lord,
the head of his chosen ones, was interred in a sepulcher made
of stone, while the Egyptian, who symbolizes the devil, was
buried in the sand. For the devil, whose name means "flowing
down,"[69] lays claim to those who, like sand, always fly in all di-
rections to their ruin. But those who belong to Christ remain
constant and firm in their holy purpose. The grave is the home
of the dead, and since the devil is dead because he is dissociated from God, who is life itself, he undoubtedly causes every
soul in which he dwells to become a grave. Hence the prophet
says: "There is Assyria with all her graves."[70] Therefore, let the
Egyptian die, struck down with the sword of your holy eloquence, and let a grave in the sand receive him, so that after
Pharaoh has been drowned, and with the banner of chastity going before them, the people of Israel may go up to the promised land, singing their hymns of triumph.

69. Cf. Jerome, *Nom. hebr.* 73.17.
70. Ezek 32.22.

LETTER 163

Peter Damian to the archpriest Peter, to whom, perhaps, he also addressed *Letter* 162. This fragmentary letter, preserved only in the *Collectanea ex opusculis Petri Damiani* of John of Lodi, includes the interpretation of two passages from Jeremiah. In both he deplores the sad departure of the soul from the body of a sinner, and the sorry fate that awaits it in eternity.

(After June 1069)

ND NOW I will summon all the families of the kingdoms of the north, says the Lord, and they shall come and each shall set up his throne before the gates of Jerusalem, against her walls on every side. I will state my case against them for all the wrong they have done in forsaking me."[1] Surely, if these words were not meant for others besides the citizens of the earthly Jerusalem, they would not be proclaimed in the holy Church today. Accordingly, who are these families of the kingdoms of the north, if not the great number of evil spirits that proudly reign in the frigid souls of men separated from God? Each one of them sets up his throne before the gates of Jerusalem, as they surround the city they are besieging, on guard lest the unhappy soul, which formerly they ruled in its frigid state, go free as it leaves the body, and so that they may now drag it with them into fiery torture. Oh, how lamentable, how doleful is this belated and fruitless repentance,[2] when the sinful soul begins to be released from the prison of its flesh, in which it was held fast, as it looks to the past and to the future. Behind it, the soul sees the short and narrow course of

---

1. Jer 1.15–16.
2. A prose counterpart of the following commentary may be found in Peter Damian, *Letter* 66.9–12 (FOTC, MC 3.50–54). For a poetic version, see Peter Damian, *Rhythmus* B.5 in M. Lokrantz, *L'opera poetica di S. Pier Damiani* (Stockholm, 1964), 88–89.

its mortal life now complete, and lying ahead the unending span of the ages. It perceives the time it has lived as a moment that quickly passed away, and beholds before it the infinite duration of time that is now beginning. That which went by in an instant is most short indeed, while the path it must now take will never have an end.

(2) "These are the words of the Lord: I pursue them," namely, the citizens of Jerusalem, "with sword, famine, and pestilence, and make them an object of execration and horror, of derision and reproach."[3] And why this is to happen, he explains in what follows: "Because they did not listen to my words," says the Lord, "which I sent to them by my servants the prophets, rising by night to send them."[4] By saying "rising by night," he indicated the solicitude and the speed of his message, so that listless inactivity would not be found in those who preached his word, but rather in those who should listen. And so, when almighty God, speaking to men in human fashion, said that he had awakened in the night, and by so doing, seemed to have interrupted his sleep, what valid objection can we make if, in keeping with what we deserve, he should wish to answer us as we face the ultimate danger of dire necessity: "Even though I am the Creator, it is on your behalf that I became a creature. On your behalf I suffered insults and shame, endured the cross, and bore all the torments that you deserved. Why did you not listen to me, why did you refuse to observe the sacred rites and precepts of my law?"

(3) Moreover, if once he reproached [the Jews] for not receiving the servants he sent to them, how much more terrible will be his indictment of us, since he came himself? If he upbraided them for interrupting his sleep, how much greater will be his charge against us, since he died and was buried for us? Because they despised his servants who were sent to them, God did not deliver the Jews who were confined by the siege of encircling armies. And how will he listen to Christians who turned their back on the precepts of the Gospel sent by his Son? For

3. Jer 29.17.
4. Jer 29.19.

he who does not listen to God, will not be heard by God. There is one thing to which the mind of any member of the faithful must give diligent and full attention, and must always carefully question, namely, whether his actions are pleasing to God, and whether God is satisfied with his life and works. For, to what avail is anything that a person achieves, if it is not acceptable to God? And so David says: "The Lord has sought a man after his own heart."[5] Accordingly, if the Creator is not now pleased with a man, that man will afterwards be unable to delight in his Creator.

(4) To this point we read in the *Life of the Fathers* that when a certain false hermit, a famous man of great reputation, came to the end of his life, a spirit of hell came to him, carrying in his hand a fiery trident. And then the spirit heard these words: If this soul did not allow me to dwell in it for even one hour, you too should show no pity in tearing it away." With that, the evil spirit thrust his fiery trident into the heart of the dying man, and tore out his soul as he had been commanded to do. . . .

5. 1 Sam 13.14; Acts 13.22.

LETTER 164

Peter Damian to Pope Alexander II. Back in Fonte Avellana after attending the Roman synod in July 1069, Damian expresses his weariness and disgust with these gatherings, and vows never again to attend. In this spirit of frustration, he criticizes two current usages in the Church: (1) the almost universal practice of anathematizing by papal decree, without discriminating between greater and lesser offenses; (2) the prohibition that neither cleric nor layman might expose to higher authority the failings of his bishop. The major part of this letter deals with the second problem of episcopal immunity, and its sources.

(August 1069)

O HIS LORD, Pope Alexander, the monk Peter the sinner offers his service.

(2) You have written to tell me that I should write to you; you have directed that I should frequently send you my trifling pages, even though they reflect my lack of culture. Truly, I would rather weep than write; in fact, I should weep the more because I am unable to weep. Consequently, I left the synod over which your holiness presided, then so worn out and drained, with my spirit so burdened with agenda and as unyielding as a rock, that it could neither be softened by the rains of compunction, or lifted somewhat out of its doldrums by the grace of intimate contemplation. To my way of thinking, what was given to me as a penance, was promised to the saints as a gift of grace. For it was said: "God will wipe away every tear from the eyes of the saints."[1] And in the psalm it says: "He has rescued my soul from death, my eyes from tears."[2] Accordingly, what was granted to holy men as a reward, is inflicted to tor-

1. Rev 7.17; 21.4.
2. Ps 114.8.

ment me as I deserve. Wherefore, I have made up my mind that as long as I live I shall absent myself entirely from Roman synods, unless unavoidable necessity compels me to go.

(3) Moreover, it seems to me that there are two practices frequently employed by the Apostolic See that need thorough correction, if this should meet with your approval: first, that an anathema is attached to almost all decretal letters,[3] and secondly, that no member of any diocese, whether cleric or layman, is permitted to expose the failings of his bishop.[4]

(4) Your tender kindness is not unaware of the enormous danger to man's salvation presented by the first of these, of the bottomless abyss opening up for those who are in sin, and of the disaster for souls that it occasions. For it is said in these documents that whoever does not observe this or that, or certainly, whoever makes void what had previously been sanctioned, or has violated it in any way, let him be anathema. Here we should note how hazardous this is, and how great the danger of suddenly rushing to one's damnation, so that even before one falls into the pit of eternal death, or is aware that he has been even slightly pushed, his foot, as it were, is already caught in the hidden snare, just as he thought he was walking along at a free and easy gait.

(5) Therefore, if anyone should fail to observe this apostolic ordinance, or should transgress in even some slight or minor matter, like some heretic or as one found guilty of the gravest crimes he is at once made liable to the sentence of excommunication. And although, according to the norms of justice, a greater delict is punished in one way, and a lesser in another, here the same indistinguishable penalty, namely, excommunication, is assigned to all, whether they have sinned gravely or venially. Nor does one suffer either the loss of his freedom, or confiscation of property, nor is he assessed a financial penalty, after the manner of the courts or the decisions of secular law, but is instead deprived of God, the author of all good things.

(6) Thus, from another man a human being receives the

---

3. Cf. Ryan, *Sources*, no. 107, p. 64.
4. Cf. Ryan, *Sources*, no. 284, p. 129.

kind of punishment that almighty God himself does not expect for a transgression of his law. For he states that "he who cares more for mother or father than for me," and he does not immediately add, "let him be anathematized or cursed," but says only, "is not worthy of me."[5] And in the law it is stated that only "an eye for an eye, a tooth for a tooth, a bruise for a bruise, and a burn for a burn"[6] shall be required, and one who is guilty is not promptly expelled from the synagogue, nor condemned with a curse. Nor do the stoics consider all sins to be equal and therefore subject to indiscriminate punishment, but the amount of penalty must always be meted out in keeping with the type of fault.[7]

(7) I might add that neither Pope Gregory nor the other Fathers who from time to time presided over the Apostolic See, are known to have practiced this custom in issuing their decrees, and hardly ever is excommunication added to their statutes, except when they end with a short statement of the Catholic faith. Wherefore, if in your holy prudence you find it advisable, let this customary formula be removed in the future from decretal letters. In its place either an amount of pecuniary fine or some other penalty should be assigned for not observing them, lest what for some is seen as a means of safeguarding their provisions, should for others result in disaster for their souls.

(8) This statement, moreover, in which it is said: "No member of any diocese is allowed to bring the failings of his own bishop, and anything else that is in need of correction, to the attention of a greater church,"[8] is totally awry, and completely opposed to ecclesiastical discipline. For who is in a better position to hear of the faults of bishops than he who holds the office of superior? And thus, he surpasses all brother-bishops, so that while others are not permitted to do so, he alone may correct the errors of bishops because of the privilege of his own see. What kind of arrogance is this, what haughty disdain, and

---

5. Matt 10.37.
6. Exod 21.24–25.
7. Cf. Cicero, *Paradoxa stoicorum* 3.20–26, where just the opposite is stated.
8. Cf. Ryan, *Sources*, no. 284, p. 129.

finally, what an excess of pride to allow a bishop, right or wrong, to live as he will, and what is the extreme insolence, to deny his subjects the right to be heard? This is especially true, since they may not appeal to the courts of margraves or dukes, nor apply for a decision from secular judges, but must rather approach the Church and present episcopal affairs in need of judgment to their own bishop, so that a case which might be laughed out of court by going to secular authority, may be seriously and properly corrected when brought before an episcopal tribunal. There, to be sure, the charge will be equitably handled, so that one who is accused might give evidence of his innocence, or humbly confess that he is a sinner.

(9) Nor should one use the excuse of pleading that he ought not be charged by those who are his subjects, lest he appear to cover up his transgressions and escape justice, as he attempts to divert the injury rising from the allegation to someone else. For who is unaware that Peter, the prince of the apostles, received power from on high, was given the authority of binding and loosing whatever he wished in heaven and on earth,[9] walked on the water,[10] healed the sick by having only his shadow fall upon them,[11] killed liars with the sword of his word alone,[12] and by his prayers brought the dead back to life?[13] Yet when this man of such lofty merits went at the inspiration of the Holy Spirit to visit Cornelius, who was a Gentile,[14] some of the faithful who had been converted from Judaism raised the issue of why he had gone into the house of strangers to the faith, presumed to eat with them, and, what was more, received them in baptism. He, I say, who was endowed with the incomparable power of so many heavenly gifts and was outstanding in his performance of so many miracles, did not use his authority to rebuff the questions of his subjects, but humbly replied by citing his reasons, and, like a truthful reporter, properly explained the case: how he had seen a receptacle lowered from the sky, like a sheet of cloth, containing creatures that could walk or crawl or fly, and how he had heard a voice that said:

9. Cf. Matt 16.19.   10. Cf. Matt 14.29.
11. Cf. Acts 5.15.   12. Cf. Acts 5.5.
13. Cf. Acts 9.36–42.   14. Cf. Acts 10.17–23.

"Up, Peter, kill and eat."[15] He also told them how three men had come to him, asking him to go to Cornelius, and how finally the Holy Spirit had ordered him to go with them. And just as the same Holy Spirit had come down upon those who had already been baptized in Judea, he descended upon the Gentiles, even before they had received baptism.

(10) Therefore, when his disciples found fault with him, and Peter chose to conceal the authority over the Church that had been given him, he might have replied that the sheep committed to his care should not dare to accuse their shepherd.[16] But if he had interposed his rightful prerogative against the complaint of the faithful, he would clearly not have been the doctor of clemency. Hence, he did not curb them by using the preeminence of his privileged position, but rather appeased them by his humble reply; and just as though his own word did not suffice to establish his credibility, he also produced witnesses: "My six companions here," he said, "came with me."[17]

(11) And so, when a bishop is challenged about his actions, he should learn to give an account in all humility, not haughtily playing on the eminence of his high office, nor thinking that he has been wronged when he is corrected by one of his subjects, but should consider him rather as a counselor or as a doctor who will attend to his wound. When the prophet Nathan reproached David so harshly and severely, did he incur the anger of the king? Did the latter confront the prophet with the dignity of his royal authority, and repel him as if he were insulting him? Instead, as soon as he recognized that he was sick, he gladly accepted the remedy, laid bare the wound, and did not shudder when the knife was applied. Take note of the humble patient who said: "I have sinned against the Lord," and listen to how quickly the medicine took effect: "The Lord has laid on another the consequences of your sin: you shall not die."[18]

15. Acts 10.13.
16. Cf. Ryan, *Sources*, no. 285, p. 129, who cites Ps.-Fabian II, c. 22, in Ps.-Isidore; see Jaffé, 93; Hinschius, 165; *Collection in 74 Titles*, Tit. IX, c. 78, in *Diversorum patrum sententiae sive Collectio in LXXIV titulos digesta*, ed. John T. Gilchrist, Monumenta iuris canonici 1 (Vatican City, 1973).
17. Acts 11.12.
18. 2 Sam 12.13.

(12) King Ahab, on the other hand, by disdaining to listen to the prophet who upbraided him, was unable to avoid the avenging sword that threatened him. The Lord said: "Because you let that man go when I had put him under a ban, your life shall be forfeit for his life, your people for his people."[19] And thus David, by listening with an open mind to the accusation of guilt leveled at him, escaped the sentence of death that he deserved, but Ahab, by revealing his anger when he was corrected, and by wickedly showing mercy to an unworthy king, was not pardoned.

(13) Did not the women who hospitably welcomed the Savior, quarrel among themselves, as one complained about the other for forcing her to get on with the work alone?[20] But Mary might have answered after the fashion of our bishops: "You have accused me, and condemned my idleness and negligence." Certainly, not every complaint is to be immediately called an accusation. For a compassionate complaint is one thing, while a jealous and hateful accusation is quite another. The former happens that some fault might be corrected, but the latter is meant to condemn someone who has sinned.

(14) It is clear that Paul rebuked Peter and opposed him to his face, and in the presence of all told him that he was wrong.[21] Yet Peter did not take offense at this accusation, but accepted it patiently and in good nature, since he obviously understood that it did not proceed from spite but from charity.

(15) But now one will say: "I am the bishop, I am the shepherd of the diocese. I should not have to put up with these bothersome accusations from the sheep in my charge, and it is my prerogative, for the sake of the faith, to have them tolerate my wayward habits."[22] Yet tell me, whoever you might be, have you never read what was written in the Gospel: "If your brother sins against you, go and take the matter up with him, strictly between yourselves, and if he listens to you, you have won your brother over. If he will not listen, take two or three others with

---

19. 1 Kgs 20.42.   20. Cf. Luke 10.38–42.
21. Cf. Gal 2.11–14.
22. Cf. Ps.-Anaclete III, c. 39 in Ps.-Isidore; see Jaffé, 4; Hinschius, 85; Burchard I, 136 (PL 140.586D); *Collection in 74 Titles* IX, 74, ed. Gilchrist.

you, so that all facts may be duly established on the evidence of two or three witnesses. If he refuses to listen to you, report the matter to the Church"?[23]

(16) Therefore, if a case involving any of the brethren is to be brought to the attention of the Church, why not one that involves bishops? Moreover, if a bishop who is a sinner in the Church, refuses to be interrogated in the Church, who would then brook coercion by the laws of the Church? Again, as you claim, if it is not permitted the sons of the diocese even to hint at an accusation against you, are witnesses to be brought in from elsewhere, since by living outside the diocese they do not know you and what you are doing? Blessed Job says: "Have I ever rejected the plea of my slave?"[24] And you state, "God forbid that I should stoop to be tried by my cleric." And almighty God exclaims in the words of Isaiah: "Give the orphan his rights, plead the widow's cause, and then come and accuse me."[25] If he, who is the Judge of all things, does not consider it beneath his dignity to be accused by his servants, do you who are a servant flinch at appearing at a trial with your fellow servant? And you who are earth and ashes, worms and dust, do you find it something despicable to humble yourself according to the example of your Maker? You should especially remember what Scripture says: "If they have chosen you to be their ruler, do not put on airs; behave to them as one of themselves."[26] Who, in fact, is unaware that the Israelites acted shabbily toward Samuel, and unjustly threw him out of office? And while he might deservedly have denounced them for acting improperly, he gave none of his accusers any further reason for charging him, and asked them whether he had ever been harsh in his dealings with them: "Here I am," he said, "lay your complaints against me in the presence of the Lord and of his anointed king. Whose ox have I taken, whose ass have I taken? Whom have I wronged, whom have I oppressed? From whom have I taken a bribe, to turn a blind eye? Tell me, and I will make restitution."[27]

23. Matt 18.15–17.   24. Job 31.13.
25. Isa 1.17–18.   26. Sir 32.1.
27. 1 Sam 12.3.

(17) Now, since such incomparable, eminent, and lofty men did not bridle at accounting to their subjects for their own actions, what a figure of arrogance, what scornful pride it is, that in our day a bishop should feel so mighty that he could hide behind the dignity of his office and not appear in court, as justice required, to reply to the sons of his diocese who insisted that they had been aggrieved.

(18) Therefore, this pernicious custom must be eliminated from the discipline of the Church; this clever attempt at subterfuge must be abrogated, so that anyone who would dare to employ such perverse excuses based on pride, should not be afforded immunity for the crime he has committed. Consequently, a free approach must be provided for just complaints, and appeals to a primatial see must be allowed for those known to be oppressed by their bishop,[28] lest he who in his pride refuses to consider his brothers as his equals, should boast of the uniqueness of his high prerogative. He, moreover, who wields the rod of correction over others, should be aware that the vigorous discipline of the Church is superior to him. And he who does not speak humanely, but like rolling thunder terrifies others with his booming voice, should at length recognize that he is a man, and in humility learn to speak in human words. And thus, as this arrogant prelate is deprived of his boastful eminence, and subjects are relieved by the authority of a greater church, conflict everywhere will be put to rest, and out of fear of a synodal trial, all members of the Church will live together in peace.

28. Cf. Ps.-Melchiadis I, c. 4 in Ps.-Isidore; see Jaffé, 171; Hinschius, 243.

LETTER 165

Peter Damian to the hermit Albizo and to the monk Peter. In a pessimistic mood, following his return to Fonte Avellana from Rome, where he assisted at two synods, Damian deplores the vile condition of the world rushing to an imminent end. And yet, men who by their monastic profession have renounced the world, renege on their promises and involve themselves in worldly affairs. He inveighs against monks who depreciate the laws, amass money in defiance of their commitment to poverty, desert their monasteries for vain travel, dress in fine clothes, and associate familiarly even with the excommunicate. Carried away by his denunciation of these false brethren, he paints a picture of worldly corruption that can only be the prelude to final disintegration. Lacking the customary salutation from "the monk Peter the sinner," this letter addresses the hermit Albizo and Peter the rhetorician.

(August 1069)

 S YOU KNOW, my dear brothers, the venerable hermit Albizo[1] and brother Peter, formerly a rhetorician, but now a philosopher of Christ, it was often my custom to engage you in friendly discussion of the contempt we should feel for this world. You are aware of how I deplored our own imperfection, and also complained about certain brothers in this sacred order who were moving along dangerous paths. The world, in fact, is daily deteriorating into such a worthless condition, that not only has each rank of secular and ecclesiastical society collapsed and fallen from its [former] state, but even monastic life, if I may put it so, has declined and lies prostrate, deprived of strength to climb to its accustomed goals of

1. Perhaps the same Albizo who accompanied Damian on his visit to the urban hermit, Teuzo, living in Florence; cf. Peter Damian, *Letters* 37 and 44.3 (FOTC, MC 2.71–72 and 222). Peter the rhetorician is otherwise unknown.

perfection. Decency has gone, honesty disappeared, religious devotion has fallen on bad times, and like an army on the march, the throng of all the holy virtues has withdrawn at a distance. "All are bent on their own purposes,"[2] and, despising every aspiration for heaven, greedily yearn for the earth. And since, as the world is coming to an end, they never cease longing for the world, it seems that after experiencing the high seas and being carried to the shore, they row in vain toward land and still stubbornly try to operate the boat. And because peace and quiet are without a doubt the objective of all our effort for those who at length await a resting place, as a punishment they are worn out by their useless endeavor.

(2) But be that as it may, the children of this world are swamped by a flood of stormy secular affairs, and they now scatter the seeds to which they are especially addicted, so that afterwards they may reap the fruits on which they had not planned. Yet, as the apostle says: "What business of mine is it to judge those who are in the world?"[3] We who are known to have renounced the world, who brag that we have escaped shipwreck in an earthly storm, why do we again fall back into it, as if we were violently swallowed up by some whirlpool? Why do we return to those things that we have despised for the love of God, there to be rekindled by the flame of evil desire? Why are we not ashamed, at the urging of improper ambition, to resort to that which neither earthly rights nor the authority of God's law had forbidden us to have? We have determined, moreover, that what once was rightly ours should now be ours no longer, and what was in our control, should pass to the ownership of others. What sort of decision was this, that we should involve ourselves in such a dangerous encounter, that we now find it necessary to fight against the decrees of all human and divine laws whose security we enjoyed? Without the slightest provocation and of our own accord, we rashly stir up war, and now have no fear of fighting against the decisions of sacred Scripture.

(3) Who, I ask, compelled Ananias and Sapphira[4] to surrender their own property? But because both of them kept back a

2. Phil 2.21.   3. 1 Cor 5.12.
4. Cf. Acts 5.1–3.

part of the money as if they wished to support themselves for many years, they did not escape the penalty of sudden death. And because they were not satisfied to live according to the rules of those who had renounced their property, they were forced to undergo the punishment of liars and to suffer a sad and untimely death. And these people, indeed, like unlettered folk who had recently embraced the faith, had not yet perhaps fully learned the precepts of the Gospel. And since the sacred books of the new doctrine had not yet been published for all to read, still those who as novices in the faith had seemingly sinned without being fully aware, by a severe yet kindly judgment they were punished only, as we might believe, by suffering bodily death. But we who know all the books of God's word, who diligently read the lives and admonitions of countless holy fathers that were produced after the golden age of the apostles, what excuse can we offer when called before the judgment seat of Christ, what cause can we find for avoiding the issue? With a far nobler advantage in sight, not only have we left behind every earthly gain and profit, but have vowed, not to men but rather to God himself, to consider them an everlasting abomination. Therefore, if we still have coins in our purse, if as an affront to him who sees our inner motives, we hold back any amount of money, what can we say in explanation? What kind of defense can we employ to clear ourselves? In addition, I might state that Ananias and Sapphira, while their faith was still insecure, were unable to find any material support in the community, since at the very beginning of the Christian religion, Church structures had not yet been built.

(4) But we who everywhere about us see such generous endowments of the churches, so that daily while the world is diminished because its possessions are despoiled, the Church is most abundantly enlarged, if we count on earthly gain for future sustenance, just as we grew rich by providing for ourselves in the past, we show that we are devoid of the treasures of the faith. Of which the apostle says: "We have this treasure in pots of earthenware."[5] And as we break the pledge we made to

5. 2 Cor 4.7.

Christ, we can only fear the penalties that await this breach of promise, rather than hope for the reward that follows from our conversion. For when two people enter an agreement, there is consent on both sides, so that when one party fulfills the conditions of the promise, he at once receives the benefits that had been determined, while, on the other hand, he who fails to carry through, incurs the loss that accompanies his broken word.

(5) Now, in the contract we made with our God, it was we undoubtedly who said that in following Christ we promised to renounce the world and everything for which it stands. And following that, it was God who replied: "I tell you this: in the world that is to be, when the Son of Man is seated on his throne in heavenly splendor, you, my regenerated followers, will have twelve thrones of your own, where you will sit as judges of the twelve tribes of Israel."[6] And this will follow if we observe the stipulations of the proposed agreement. Otherwise, if we look back, we shall promptly hear the terrible pronouncement of a threatening God: "No one who sets his hand to the plow, and then keeps looking back, is fit for the kingdom of God."[7] And so, we have heard that not just any sort of reward was promised to those who totally renounced the world, but thrones on which they would preside as judges, the same men, in fact, who formerly had feared to be judged for their own sins. Indeed, it was proper that this exchange at the right hand of the Most High should take place, so that they who by their love of perfection had become poor for Christ's sake, now made rich, might take their place at his side as senators of the heavenly court, as it is written: "Her husband is well known in the city gate when he takes his seat among the senators of the land."[8]

(6) But when one who by amassing earthly things returns to those he has left behind, just as he is estranged from the world he decided to abandon, so too is he no longer fit for the kingdom of God that had undoubtedly been given him, but that he did not choose to accept. He is like the stupid traveler who cannot return to the place on which he irrevocably turned his back, and has not reached the destination toward which he

6. Matt 19.28.   7. Luke 9.62.
8. Prov 31.23.

planned to go. For when we renounced the world, we determined that God was to be our possession, and that in consequence we were to become his property, so that he would be our portion, and we the inheritance that was his alone. We used the words: "You are my portion, O Lord";[9] and he said to us: "You are the work of my hands, you are my inheritance, O Israel."[10] But of earthly inheritance it was written: "If you begin by piling up an inheritance in haste, it will bring you no blessing in the end."[11] Therefore, if almighty God himself condescended to be our portion, what kind of wealth, I ask, can one acquire, that one should accumulate in addition to this outstanding treasure? For this treasure is of such great value that, if it were all one had, all riches would truly be possessed along with it. Indeed, all the treasures of wisdom and knowledge are hidden in the heart of Jesus.[12] But if in addition to this, one so endowed should wish to acquire other exotic wealth, association with these base and worthless riches at once becomes totally improper, and irritated by its shameful companionship, this treasure that we thought was ours, is lost, and in this way escapes the grasp of its frustrated owner: "For no one can serve God and money."[13]

(7) Wherefore, O monk, do you wish to have Christ in your purse? First throw away your money, since the two do not belong in the same pouch; for if you put both together, like a foolish owner you will find one without the other. Clearly, the richer you become by owning the trifling profits of this world, the poorer will you be in possessions that have true value. Accordingly, if you have money, quickly dispose of it, so that Christ may find the treasury of your heart laid bare. Your mighty guest wishes to come down into the narrow confines of your lodging-place, and he wishes to live alone without others in the room. For if the vast expanses of heaven and earth are unable to contain him, how can you expect to have him live with strangers in a tiny corner of your house? So, let earthly money make way for the arrival of heavenly treasure. "Can light

9. Ps 118.57.
11. Prov 20.21.
13. Matt 6.24.

10. Isa 19.25.
12. Cf. Col 2.3.

consort with darkness?"[14] What has God to do with worldly wealth? Therefore, get rid of your money that is liable to damage from rust and moths and theft. Let the storeroom of your heart be bare, that it can be filled with heavenly goods. The Lord says: "Do not store up for yourselves treasure on earth, where it grows rusty and moth-eaten, and thieves break in to steal it."[15]

(8) Money, indeed, is more dangerous for the soul when one is acquiring it, than when we retain it after it has freely come to us. In the latter case, by worldly standards it is just possession, while in the former, dangerous ambition often takes over. It would have been, therefore, more profitable for us calmly to keep what we owned, than to reclaim what we had given up, and that, not without a certain amount of ill will and solicitous concern. Hence, O knight of Christ, you should be ashamed to enrich yourself with worldly goods that are bound to perish, lest in the future you be forced to go naked and poor, and become a perpetual beggar. You have sworn to bear arms in a force that counts on lightly clad, fleet-footed fighters, but those who are weighed down, and are therefore sluggish, are prevented from guarding the camp, and are deprived of their pension. Such an army denies one so encumbered the right to serve, and for him who is forced into early and dishonorable retirement, it substitutes one who is free to march. Moneybags may not hang from the belt where only scabbards for two-edged swords are meant to be. The battlefront where massed troops are engaged in hand-to-hand combat, is no safe place to keep your idle money. In such a place, one does not securely count his coins, where, surrounded by the numerous enemy, he must constantly expect a discharge of arrows. For in such circumstances, when one is assessing the value of what he has in hand, often an unexpected arrow comes in from a hidden enemy, pierces the stomach of the man preoccupied with his money, and thus it happens that he who is unable to support himself without the aid of his property, now grieves at the sud-

14. 2 Cor 6.14.
15. Matt 6.19.

den change of fortune that causes him the irreparable loss of his life and all that he had. Accordingly, he who refused to live in freedom as a poor man with Christ, after becoming rich without him, is compelled to die miserably as a slave of money. Listen to what the word of God promises to the rich: "Weep and wail, you men of great possessions, for you have received your consolation."[16] Do not overlook what James says: "Weep and wail, you men of great possessions. Your riches have rotted; your fine clothes are moth-eaten; your silver and gold have rusted away, and their very rust will be evidence against you and consume your flesh like fire."[17]

(9) I beg of you, you money-worshiping monk, have you not heard what the fires of avarice will bring you? Have you not heard of the end to which your money hoard is leading you? It is surely just, that he whose soul burns with lust because of love for his flesh, should afterward find his very flesh burned up as if for a midday meal. Now the furnace of your soul is aglow with the invisible ardor of concupiscence, and it is fitting that afterwards our material body should also be consumed in un-quenchable fire. So listen, you worshiper of money—that I call you a money-worshiper, I derive from what you are doing, and not from any desire to tag you with a term of abuse—for since you love money, you seem to worship it. And since the Lord says, in the words of the prophet: "Use your time and learn that I am God,"[18] the leisure time that you owe to God, you spend on money, devoting your time to guarding it. "For where your treasure is, there will your heart be also."[19] Wherefore, just as one who is devoted to Christ, is rightly called a worshiper of Christ, so he who spends his time in caring for money, deserves to be called a worshiper of money. But perhaps I might still be thought arbitrary in pursuing my own ideas, if I do not cite the evidence of sacred Scripture to confirm the etymology of this ti-tle. For Truth itself says: "You cannot serve God and money,"[20] as if he were plainly stating: No one can worship God and mon-ey at the same time. And this is just the point that the apostle

---

16. Luke 6.24.   17. Jas 5.2–3.
18. Ps 45.11.   19. Matt 6.21.
20. Matt 6.24.

makes, when he says: "But be very sure of this: no one given to fornication or indecency, or the greed which makes an idol of gain, has any share in the kingdom of Christ and of God."[21] Therefore, after simply enumerating all these crimes, but calling only greed the service of idols, he clearly stated that the avaricious man is not a worshiper of God but of money, and by that token is practicing the cult of demons.

(10) But in spending too much time in explaining the word "money-worshiper," I am not giving enough attention to getting rid of this hoard of money, much less to destroying it. Therefore, now that I have satisfied you on why I called you a money-worshiper, you should heed what I am about to say. Listen to the words of Truth itself as he addresses you and others like you: "Those who are rich," he says, "will find it hard to enter the kingdom heaven."[22] And this condemnation applies to those who, according to worldly standards, are wealthy, as well as to those who, after abandoning all things, return to their vomit.[23] Unless they come to their senses they will find it impossible, or extremely difficult, to gain the kingdom of heaven.

(11) But perhaps some hare-brained individual from among this group who idolize money will reply to my argument: "Why do you so sharply attack me for my riches, since you can surely see that I am content with very little, and own only a few pennies? And while I act in this manner because of my own weakness, I am only trying to provide for future needs, and have no hope of ever getting rich. Certainly, as all my brothers in the community can testify, I do not take a thing from the property of the monastery, 'not the least thread of cloth or shoe lace,'[24] and if I rid myself of these trifles of my own, how am I supposed to live?" Do you not see that this proprietor of ours, or better, this money-worshiper as I called him above, is using the plea of poverty so as not to be faulted for being rich, and covers up this deadly vice with specious arguments, so that, like a tomb filled with rotted corpses, he might appear white because he is covered with lime?

---

21. Eph 5.5.
23. Cf. Prov 26.11 and 2 Pet 2.22.
22. Matt 19.23.
24. Gen 14.23.

(12) Come now, brother, if you are allowed to expect conveniences at the expense of the monastery, do you not put on clothes as soon as they are provided for you, but are not given money that you can keep for your own use? Why do you not employ the same approach also with gifts that are given you by laymen, namely, that after you have received money, you quickly buy what is necessary, and thus the poison of filthy lucre does not infect you? By so doing, your needs are quickly relieved, and the disease of money does not cover you with its foul sores. But why do you congratulate yourself that the amount of money you are using is small, as if you were secure in the way you were acting, since there can be no doubt that you are forbidden to have a penny, or even a farthing? He, indeed, who is prevented from having anything at all, may not seek refuge in using excuses to cover these smaller matters, for if the whole is given up, undoubtedly no part of it remains, especially since it is peculiar to the human mind that if one is poor, he is concerned with little things, just as when he is rich, his interest lies in that which is greater. For whether you are surrounded by a sumptuous flood of riches, or feel the pinch of poverty in personal things, this statement cannot be changed: "Where your treasure is, there will your heart be also."[25]

(13) Croesus and Amyclas[26] were two contrasting men of wealth, but they did not differ from one another in their attitude toward what they owned. For while the former counted his pieces of gold, the latter would estimate the value of his millet; they possessed distinct amounts of wealth, but did not differ in the love they had for their property. Moreover, if a small mouse or any other crawling creature should chance to fall into a large vat, would not men with axes promptly gather on the spot, pour out everything that the vat contained, while every one present was retching and gagging as they became sick to their stomach? If a tiny drop of poison is poured into a rounded copper bowl of garden greens, even though they appear to be most appetizing, will they not be judged totally unfit for eating?

25. Matt 6.21.
26. For Amyclas, see *RE* 1, 1999–2000. He is reputed to be the founder of the town of Amyclae in Laconia, lying in rich, fertile fields.

(14) And so, if just a minor amount of an evil substance will often damage large stores of good things, how can you flatter yourself and soothe your conscience, by saying that it is only a trifle for you to have private property contrary to what you promised at your profession? For according to the apostle: "A little yeast leavens all the dough."[27] And elsewhere it says: "Carelessness in small things leads little by little to ruin."[28] Nor did our first parents frequently indulge in the forbidden fruit, since we read that they were unfortunately seduced into eating it only once.[29] Yet they were therefore not made to suffer only momentary punishment because they did not persist in their wrongdoing.

(15) Accordingly, my brother, whoever you might be, if you take pleasure in acquiring wealth with which you may be able to ward off poverty in the future, as a prudent man look for true riches, and also dread the deprivations of real poverty. By comparison with this latter poverty, the former is easily disdained, and all the property in the world when compared to these true riches is held in contempt like seaweed along the shore that is trodden underfoot. Therefore, if you are earnestly trying to escape the need that accompanies this loathsome poverty, take pains to sow good grain in the field of your heart, for the apostle states: "He who sows in the Spirit, the Spirit will bring him a harvest of eternal life."[30] And again: "So let us never tire of doing good, for if we do not slacken our efforts, we shall in due time reap our harvest."[31] Bury this highest and unique seed in the furrows of your heart, for if it falls into the ground it dies, and bears a rich harvest.[32] Let this be your treasure, this the bounty of crops of various kinds. In it set your mind to achieving your objective, in it place all your hope in this life and in the next, "for the same Lord is Lord of all, and is rich enough for the need of all who invoke him."[33]

(16) Accordingly, if you endeavor to watch over this seed with all due care, you will find the rooms of the storehouse of

---

27. 1 Cor 5.6.

28. Sir 19.1.

29. Cf. Gen 3.1–4.

30. Gal 6.8.

31. Gal 6.9.

32. Cf. John 12.24–25.

33. Rom 10.12.

your heart filled with gold and silver and a treasure of every kind of wealth, and your barns will be overflowing with new crops beyond compare. Always be vigilant in protecting this treasure, and guard it day and night with the utmost solicitude. In this one thing above all others, you will be rich, nor will you want for anything that you need. In this, indeed, you will possess the gold of divine wisdom, the silver of edifying eloquence. In it you will have the varied raiment of a seemly and upright life: the twice-dyed dalmatic of twofold love and the sleeveless tunic of chastity, the gray garment of patience, the flaming, rose-colored robe of divine fervor, the purple stole of royal dignity. Since wool is dyed in the blood of the murex[34] to give it a purple color, whoever sits so attired on the throne of right judgment, that he might quickly apply violence in mortifying all the enticements of his flesh and the barbarous attack of the vices, such a one, in truth, is called a king, and is clothed in the splendor of spiritual purple. In this treasure you will have the fragrant, long-lasting ointment of ever-verdant hope, signifying that you are called to an inheritance that nothing can spoil or wither, kept for you in heaven.[35] Along with it you will wear the ring of faith, the armbands of excellent deeds in the active life, and also the bracelets of mystical contemplation. "For his left arm is under your head, his right arm is around you."[36]

(17) And what more may I offer you? At times you will enjoy in this treasure the gems of all the virtues, the pearls of all spiritual gifts. Nor will you be denied herds of all clean and unclean animals that they may come under the control of your jurisdiction. The unclean beasts of the vices, to be sure, will be tamed at your command, while the clean, which relate to your spiritual nature, will provide you with food for a most delicious repast. The flock, carefully tended for its woolly fleece, will furnish the meat of sweet innocence for your table, while the flesh of domestic animals will always be at hand to make you grow in the riches of God's love. All kinds of fowl will grace the table of your mind with a sumptuous spiritual banquet, and the ox whose proud neck is made to bear the yoke of your command,

---

34. A species of shellfish.   35. Cf. 1 Pet 1.4.
36. Song 2.6.

will bellow contentedly. Under your authority the unbridled freedom of the frolicsome horse will be curbed, causing him to chew in vain on the iron bit in his mouth. All wild beasts of vice, every monstrous reptile will fear the power that you exert. And in this life, in fact, all of these will freely contribute to your riches if, as I said before, you carefully guard this precious and exceptional treasure.

(18) In addition, how many greater gifts will come to you in the truly blessed life that lies before us, is, I must admit, beyond my capacity to discuss, nor is it within my power to lay them out before you. It will suffice only to refer in summary to the indescribable outcome of this exchange, for this is what awaits those who have perfectly left the world: "Things beyond our seeing, things beyond our hearing, things beyond our imagining, all prepared by God for those who love him."[37]

(19) Therefore, hide this treasure, namely Christ, our God and Lord, who became both redeemer and ransom for us; he who both promises and is the reward held out to us; he who is the life of men and endless existence of the angels. With great care hide this treasure, I say, in the receptacle of your heart. With it in your possession cast away all concern for anything else in this world. Take delight in speaking with him in unremitting prayer, and in this way constantly nourish yourself at the feast of holy thoughts. Let him be your food and also your raiment. But if it should happen that you are also in need of some tangible convenience, do not hold back, but place your trust in the firm promise he made to you when he said: "Set your mind on God's kingdom before everything else, and all the rest will come to you as well."[38] For if he could satisfy the thirsty throng of Israelites by commanding water to gush from that dry, metallic rock; if for long periods of time he could serve heavenly manna to the hungry; if he could order vast flocks of quail to light in the camp of these people who complained of their lot, would he be unable to provide for the necessities of one little man who is constantly requesting his assistance? And for him who for almost forty years kept the clothes

37. 1 Cor 2.9.
38. Matt 6.33.

of that great multitude intact, would it be difficult to replace your tattered old garments with new ones? Truly, we of little faith must urge ourselves to hold fast to Christ, for fainthearted diffidence makes Christ a pauper, while full confidence causes him to be rich and generous in dispensing his gifts. Take care to be concerned only with those things that he commands, and let there be no doubt at all about those that he promises. Let the tax collector feel safe when the debtor is prompt to pay. There is no reason to be apprehensive when he who never lies has given his word. The creditor can breathe easily when Truth itself is bound by his promise.

(20) I have attempted to be brief in speaking of monks who possess property; and now I come to a discussion of those who delight in constant travel on horseback. I suppose that it could hardly escape your memory, my dear brothers, that many times when we were together, we deplored this evil practice of the monks, and with fraternal charity felt sorry for these restless brothers who were being destroyed by the vice of wanderlust. For there are many who, while they were living as laymen, found it repulsive to run here and there under the press of working in the world, so that out of love of freedom, they deliberately chose to embrace the peaceful life of the monastery. But now they are so on fire with the ardor of pernicious restlessness, that if there should be a time when an occasion demanding a long journey is not forthcoming, they act as if they were confined in some dark and horrible prison; of this the cleverness of the ancient enemy is not unaware.[39] Those whom this wicked horseman still rides, he consequently urges to go abroad by prodding them with his importuning spurs, so that they may perish as they return to the frivolity of the world, and to divert others from following the path of true salvation. There are also many others living in the world, who totally despair of being saved in any other way from the billowing waves of this earthly sea, unless they take refuge in the port of monastic pursuits under the leadership of Christ.

(21) But when laymen observe those who were only recently

39. Cf. Damian, *Letter* 153.39.

so fervent in despising everything that belonged to the world, now eagerly returning to the whirlwind of secular affairs, involving themselves in the mud and filth of the same wallow from which they had escaped, they stand in amazement, sigh deeply in their inmost being, and are overwhelmed by feelings of despair. Each of them laments to himself in these or similar words: "Woe to me, in what can I trust to ensure my own salvation? Why did I place myself in jeopardy by deciding to enter that order? In no time at all I have lost both my body and my soul. Voluntarily and with open eyes, I nearly threw myself into the fire. For who had ever been more eager to enter the monastery than he? Who had seemingly ever hastened to join the service of Christ with more heartfelt purpose? But now, forgetting all that he had promised, he constantly busies himself with earthly matters, deals with the world, breathes its very atmosphere, and after becoming unlike me in continually practicing a life of mortification, he now lives in the world exactly like me. Truly, as is quite evident, his body was able to alter its outward appearance, but his spirit remained permanently mired in its previous condition. What good does it do me to accuse those who incited him to change his life? In engaging in spiritual combat, to be sure, I have been deprived of a comrade, but in other earthly affairs, I have not lost a companion. For he is certainly at my side in practicing law in the courts, is never absent when we plead before judicial tribunals, eagerly enters the halls of princes with me, and together with me whispers profound bits of worldly wisdom into their ears.

(22) "But why do I dare call him a companion, since he is not an associate in the usual sense, but in all that we do, he precedes me as if I were his servant. In fact, from his change of lifestyle he has gained such esteem from the crowd, that at his arrival, all will rise; whatever he asserts, they believe as if it were some prophetic oracle, and reverently give him their devoted attention. Accordingly, in a naturally human sense they do not consider his change of heart to be anything but productive, because one who has put aside secular attire, but has not changed his attitude, is only a sly change artist, who has thus acquired a fuller measure of worldly honor."

(23) And so, while detractors utter these and similar complaints, who can estimate the number of souls for whom these roaming monks provide the occasion for damnation in the world? For they surely think it easier to be damned in secular garb, than by following the example of lost souls, to have both of them, as they say, lose the world together. And indeed, we should not be surprised that those who observed all of this are scandalized, since such action is certainly opposed to God and contrary to sacred authority. For the apostle says: "A soldier on active service for God will not let himself be involved in civilian affairs; he must be wholly at his commanding officer's disposal."[40] And the Lord himself admonishes his disciples in these words: "Do not let your minds be dulled by dissipation and drunkenness and worldly cares."[41]

(24) Now, from this poisonous root of restlessness so many shoots of vice come forth, that whoever is known to foster it, like a dried-up tree he loses every fruit of monastic perfection. And just as unripe figs cannot survive if exposed to the wind, so too the fruit of good works is wanting in him who is buffeted by the varied temptations of the world. For this vice is so unruly, that once it gains control of a monk's disposition, in great part any medley of virtues that is present will soon depart, and monsters of vice will invade his breast, as if it were a workroom that belonged to them. But now to cite just a few examples from among many, a monk who travels about cannot observe the fast, because his status as a guest does not allow it; he will not be able to chant attentively, because he will be disturbed by the constant chatter of those walking about him. He will not keep watch in nightly prayer vigils, because he is never alone; he will not engage in genuflections, because the hardships of the journey are at variance with his customary devotions; he will never be able to observe silence, since there will be frequent occasions when, even against his will, he must relax his tongue.

(25) What shall I say about his lack of attention to reading and prayer, since for him impending necessity often requires that he abandon his own interests and, instead, concentrate on

40. 2 Tim 2.4.
41. Luke 21.34.

those of the world. Charity is diminished in him, because in the soul that experiences the winds of so many secular affairs, the fervor of interior love grows lukewarm. Chastity will also be routed from his soul, because his spirit will frequently be pierced by arrows of lust resulting from the sight of carnal images he beholds about him. The vigor of patience will also be broken, because for anyone who attempts anything at all, when events suddenly turn up that stand in the way of what he wishes to do, he who hurries to disentangle his business, is unable to bear his setback quietly, and then gives vent to such intemperate words, that when he is able to relax, they severely punish him with avenging tears. The rule of sobriety is not observed, because when the banquet table is laden with elegant food, he must be careful to play the role of the courteous guest, since he thinks it rude not to comply with the request of his host, and thus takes pleasure in indulging his appetite under the guise of charity. But at that moment doubt often arises in the mind of the servant of God, lest in observing the rules of abstemiousness, he is at the same time acting the hypocrite, which is a detestable vice. And so, some will totally disregard the bounds of temperance, so that not even the appearance of hypocrisy will be present. But in this way he who thinks he is acting discreetly, is not practicing discretion at all. For he knows how to make correct decisions, if he is able to distinguish virtue from vice; but he who uproots the wheat together with the tares, is doubtlessly ignorant of the norms of discernment. Therefore, anyone who does not exceed the limits of sobriety, motivated only by the thought of heavenly reward, will trample hypocrisy under the feet of humility, and will eagerly await the prize for observing moderation.

(26) But to continue our discussion of the wandering monk, he does not have tears of compunction to shed for his sins, because an arid soul that moves through the heat of an earthly way of life, grows dry, since he does not deserve to be saturated with the dew of the Holy Spirit. Filled with the uncleanness of worldly thoughts, he cannot externally shed tears, because his head is not watered with the moisture of interior grace. At times, perhaps, when others are around to hear him, he preaches; but

suddenly vainglory seizes him, and like one leaping from ambush, it kills the one who was trying to help others. But if he takes precautions against this happening, and remains silent, he is ashamed at not being able to finish what he had set out in grace to do. If he puts on grave airs, which is the proper attitude to assume, he begins to fear that as an impostor he will be accused of hypocrisy. But if he relaxes somewhat from engaging in rigorous mortification, in this too he is far from secure, fearing that by his example he will lead others to destruction. If he should wish to bring peace and harmony to those who are at loggerheads, and tells them the truth, he does not achieve their reconciliation; and if he is satisfied to lie, he does not avoid falling into sin. When he wishes to censure others for their faults, he considers it no minor offense that he has caused his neighbors to hate him. But to see a thing and hold one's tongue, what else can one call this but giving consent to those who are doing evil, and that, indeed, in the case of those who still glow with some little spark of heavenly fervor? On the other hand, in regard to those who are cold, those who, after turning their backs on the camp where God is served, return to their former wicked life at the whirling mill of this world, let anyone who wishes say how culpably they are acting, or how rashly they are living. For me it appears more advantageous to weep for them with loving compassion, than to write about their detestable deeds, lest by my censorious words I appear to defame those for whom we should only shed tears of pity.

(27) But this I say without fear of contradiction, that since in our day the world is so thickly set with insidious snares that anyone in the monastery who plans to live an upright life, must cautiously take pains to avoid moving about in it, and if he frequently takes trips, he will not escape the traps that are placed for him; and like a tree that has been stripped of the bark that protects it, he will not bear the fruit of virtue, nor be able to avoid the decay of vices that swarm over it like scavenging worms. When he gets back to his own monastery, however, he comes face to face with this pressing throng of everything he had seen and heard that seems to have accompanied him, and so the noise of the tumultuous affairs that he had physically put

up with on his travels, now assail him much more fiercely in spirit, and with much more vigor. This is especially so when he earnestly begins to pray, for then fantastic thoughts and the images of things he had seen come back to him, so that wherever he is, he imagines himself present in the theater, or seated among those who are pleading in the courts. And the man truly struggles, and tries to chase these thoughts away as if they were flies circling about his face. But as soon as they leave, they promptly return; once they are driven off, they are right there, as if they were trying to capture him who would escape from them, and striving to recall him to servitude under them.

(28) Then the unhappy soul learns how much it means to it that it has foolishly exposed itself to the whole wide world. It wastes away like something dried up, somber, and insensitive, hard as a rock, nor is it able to shed tears, nor see the light because it is everywhere enveloped in darkness. It tries to attend to the mystic imagery of the psalms, but is repulsed like intolerable brightness that hurts one's inflamed eyes. It yearns with all its might to engage in higher things, but, overburdened by its own weight, it is forced to lie disgraced in the doldrums. And these prophetic words are aptly applied to it: "He has cast me into a place of darkness like a man long dead. He has walled me in so that I cannot escape, and weighed me down with fetters; even when I cry out and call for help, he rejects my prayer."[42] It grieves, worries, and laments, and because it is not permitted even to weep over its own miserable state, it is thrown into confusion by the sharp pain and bitterness that pervade it. At least it is able to voice these words of woe that the prophet uttered: "For these things, therefore, I weep over my plight, my eyes run with tears; for any to comfort me and renew my strength are far to seek."[43] But how unhappy is the soul when it sees itself in this lamentable state, and still is unable to lament; when it beholds how far removed it is from salvation, as if it had been plunged into some deep pit of misery. If there were only some way to weep, some way to arrive at forgiveness

42. Lam 3.6–8.
43. Lam 1.16.

for its sins. And thus, since he cannot mourn over his guilt, it seems to him that he has not yet taken a single step along the road that could lead him to salvation.

(29) Similar to his situation is that in which the prophet says, when speaking in the person of sinners: "My heart is consumed with longing for your ordinances at all times."[44] Now, one who does not yet long at all times for the law of God, which undoubtedly comprises his ordinances, but is already consumed with longing, in some way approaches it from afar, but has not yet scaled the heights of perfection. Hence the soul of this miserable man is so filled with darkness and confusion, that wherever it turns, it sees itself living in the world, while it clearly knows that the world exists outside of it. He is therefore in the world, which has no part in him, since in his mind he conjures up fantastic images of the world that he has physically deserted. Now this disaster in the human soul is both sin and the punishment for sin. Indeed, it is right and just, that what one has voluntarily accepted, must be endured against his will. And being more specific, we may say that he who does not wish to live within the confines of his order, when he is able to do so, can never do without the world, even after he has left it.

(30) And so, the soul of man, constrained by the burden of such extreme poverty and need, grieves and laments and deplores its miserable condition, because by the vice of restlessness it has lost the purity of its innermost retreat, and is again mired in the filth of the world like a pig in its wallow.[45] Then it bitterly charges itself with fickleness and inconstancy, violently accuses itself of vagrancy and deceit, and in truth agrees that God's decree is just and equitable, as it says with the prophet: "The Lord is good to those who hope in him, to the soul that seeks him; it is good to wait in silence for the Lord's deliverance. It is good, too, for a man to carry the yoke from his youth; he shall sit alone and hold his peace, because he has taken it upon himself."[46] For if it had loved solitude, it would rejoice

44. Ps 118.20.
45. Cf. 2 Pet 2.22.
46. Lam 3.25–28.

that it had been elevated above itself; but it now deplores that when it goes into the world, it sees itself lying prostrate under its own burden.

(31) There is also something else which, even though all other obstacles were removed, should be enough to restrain monks from gadding about in the world. For who in our day is able to find a group of laymen among whom there is not someone who is under the ban of excommunication because of his sin? For years now, all sorts of crime have sprung up throughout the world, every shameful act now flourishes, and daily this condition becomes more widespread the closer we come to the end of the world. Wherefore, it is impossible for a monk who goes out among the people, to avoid meeting persons who are excommunicated or, which is nearly the same, those who should be excommunicated. For he will come in touch with murderers, perjurers, and the incestuous; with arsonists and adulterers, and even if he finds them repulsive, he often greets them with a kiss, and if necessity demands, eats with them from the same dish, even though the apostle exclaims: "You must have nothing to do with any so-called Christian who leads a loose life, is unclean, or a robber or a drunkard. You should not eat with any such person."[47]

(32) And indeed, it is most abominable and totally out of place to associate with those who are separated from God, especially for monks who are united with God with such a special, and, I might say, such a domestic familiarity, that after renouncing the world, they are unalterably dedicated to speaking with God alone. Just as one must be careful to avoid the head of the reprobate himself, so too must we shun his members, except when we are trying to convert them.[48] Certainly, the same rejection and abomination is now deserved by those for whom, in the words of Truth itself, the same fire is prepared, since to those who will stand on the left hand, he says: "The curse is upon you; go from my sight to the eternal fire that is ready for

47. 1 Cor 5.11.
48. Cf. Burchard XI, 3 (PL 140.858C), and XI, 5 (PL 140.859C–D), from Regino II, 413 (PL 132.362C), and II, 415 (PL 132.363B); see also Ryan, *Sources*, no. 266, pp. 122–23.

the devil and his angels."[49] Therefore, we must not associate in crime with those whom we see on their way to another homeland, lest the inordinate love that brings us together, also involve us in the same torments of ultimate retribution.

(33) Now to make it abundantly evident how much keeping company with the wicked harms the good, let me cite the obvious reason that some of them have been recently excommunicated by episcopal decree, while others ought to be denied association only by the canonical sanction of the holy Fathers. But regarding those who were recently excommunicated, there can be no doubt that anyone who has commerce with them, will incur a similar sentence of condemnation.[50] Regarding those, however, who for crimes committed should obviously be condemned by canonical authority, but have not yet been excluded from union with the Church by an actual decision of the living bishops, some are in doubt whether one may safely consort with them; but if we reflect on the matter more carefully, we find hardly any difference between them. For whether one is legally condemned by contemporaries or by the ancient Fathers, it is the same; nor does temporal difference absolve one who is bound by reason of committing the same offense, and the disparity of age does not prejudice the juridical decision where the same fine rule of law determines the sentence.

(34) But I can more easily demonstrate the case that I am favoring, if I cite the actual words of the Fathers who are handing down excommunications, both ancient and modern. In fact, the sacred canons say: "He who does this or that, shall be excommunicated." Accordingly, for those who use the same words, we should obviously interpret their sentence in the same way, and since every decision of current holy bishops depends upon the decrees of the ancient Fathers, the former would never presume to condemn anyone except those whom they knew had already been condemned by the latter. Hence, recent bishops do not innovate in sentencing just anyone, but by following

49. Matt 25.41.
50. Cf. Burchard XI, 3 (PL 140.858C), and XI, 5 (PL 140.859C–D); cf. also XI, 32, 34–35, 38–39, 43–44 (PL 140.866C, 866D, 867A–B, 867D–868A); see also Ryan, *Sources*, no. 267, p. 123.

their example confirm the sentence of the ancients already decreed. Therefore, we must reach the conclusion that, just as we are to avoid association with those who are excluded from membership in the Church by the decision of recent synods, so we must also avoid contact with those whom the ancient Fathers decided to banish.[51]

(35) And so, this is not some minor consideration in determining that a monk should refrain from moving about in the secular world, and remain permanently in the cell to which he had retired, because it is most unfortunate when one is indeed able to curb his own excesses, only to be contaminated by another's faults, not to sin with others, and to suffer the punishment of another's crime. For we are bound by the guilt of the wicked when, throwing caution to the winds, we are united with them in friendship. And thus Jehoshaphat, who was so greatly admired for the good deeds of his earlier life, was almost threatened with death for showing friendship for King Ahab, and by the prophet the Lord said to him: "Do you take delight in helping the wicked and befriending the enemies of the Lord? You deserve the Lord's wrath. Yet there is some good in you, for you have swept away the sacred poles from the land of Judah."[52] Indeed, by the very fact that our life is characterized by friendly relations with the wicked, we are already at variance with him who is the supreme Good. Who is not terrified by the words of the apostle in which he admonishes us and calls us back from close relationships with evil men: "We command you," he says, "in the name of the Lord Jesus, to avoid any brother who wanders from the straight path and does not follow the tradition you received from us."[53] Therefore, if we must cautiously withdraw from all those who, in our opinion, are not living according to the tradition of the apostles, how many laymen are there with whom we may safely have friendly relations? Moreover, he who shows his contempt for apostolic traditions,

---

51. Ryan, *Sources*, nos. 267–68, pp. 123–24. Damian enlarges the number of excommunicates by including also those guilty of crimes for which excommunication was decreed by the ancient canons.

52. 2 Chr 19.2–3.

53. 2 Thess 3.6.

and either by his manner of living or his teaching endeavors to introduce some new doctrine, does not deserve to associate with orthodox and religious men, as the apostle John testifies when he says: "If anyone comes to you who does not bring this doctrine, do not welcome him into your house or give him a greeting; for anyone who gives him a greeting is an accomplice in his wicked deeds."[54] Evidently, after hearing these words of apostolic truth, we should obviously agree with them, because those who physically associate as friends with persons living in sin, participate in their guilt and together with them are liable to a harsh sentence at the last judgment, even though in this life they have not committed sin in their company.

(36) There is also another vice, which I have attacked elsewhere, that frequently besets a wandering monk, because, in fact, one can never simply shake off the leprosy of poisonous possessions without finding it necessary to retain some of them for travel expenses. From this a love of costly attire has its origin, so that, as he moves about in public, he may not appear as a beggar. For when one is preoccupied with the fine quality of his outer clothes, the entire inner disposition of a person is eroded. I do not know why it happens, but this deceitful madness so blinds the eyes of an obstinate man, that he is neither able to see what people perceive as integrity, nor is he concerned with what causes him to appear honorable in the sight of God. And truly, it is madness and deceit. It is madness for us in our pride to despise the decrees of him who judges in secret, and by our fastidious dress to set our mind on winning the favor of public opinion. It is also deceitful, for inasmuch as it displeases the eyes of the heavenly Judge, it also lessens us in the estimation of men; and in the very desire to appear more important in the eyes of men, it somehow exposes one to the teeth of public detraction. And since splendid attire causes all eyes to be centered on us, it also sharpens the tongues of hostile critics who are only waiting to tear the fancy dresser to pieces.

(37) For when someone sees a monk dressed in fine and costly garments, does he not at once consider him to be devoid

54. 2 John 10–11.

of the spirit of God, striving for earthly goals rather than those of heaven? From a person's attire one can infer what his inner disposition is like, and from his external appearance can judge the quality of his purpose. And this agrees with the authoritative statement of the Gospel, which says: "You will recognize them by the fruits they bear."[55] To be sure, these monks do not come to us dressed as sheep, since sheep's clothing bespeaks humility and innocence, not arrogance or plunder. Their attire is aptly called plunder, since it is bought in quantities that allow two or three changes. Such a monk is certainly guilty of the sin of plunder, since one who is addicted to pride in choosing the clothes he will wear, purchases only for himself what ordinarily would be enough to clothe also one of his brothers. He is undoubtedly practicing plunder, if out of vanity he squanders his money on one garment, when it would be enough to buy two, and thus allows his neighbor, whom he should love as himself, to go unclothed.

(38) But there is a difference between these monks, decked out in festive clothes, and the hypocrites of whom the Gospel speaks, since the latter, as Truth itself asserts, "came to us dressed up as sheep, while underneath they are savage wolves";[56] the former, however, are inwardly bloated with the wind of vain glory, which they pass with utter abandon, but outwardly wear clothes they have plundered, as I have already demonstrated, and in so doing, arrogantly appear dressed up as wolves. Therefore, since the Lord said to the Jews concerning John: "What did you go out to see? A man dressed in soft garments? Surely you must look in palaces for that,"[57] obviously the monk who makes a display of his costly clothes, does not bear arms for the heavenly King, but is engaged in the service of this world; and even though externally he seems to offer God the tribute of his obedience, it becomes evident that by seeking to win human applause, he is devoted to his own aggrandizement. Moreover, if under the pretext of obedience elegant attire is allowed, to whom could this permission be more freely granted than to

55. Matt 7.16.   56. Matt 7.15.
57. Matt 11.8.

blessed John, who after being endowed with special dedication to God's will, came with a new message to turn the hearts of fathers to their children, and to prepare a well-disposed people for Christ the Lord?[58] Could the Lord not have provided sandals for himself, as the wicked pagans divided only his garments among themselves? For if his sandals had not been lacking, the account of sacred history would not have kept silent about them.

(39) When the king of Nineveh wore his robes of state, he deserved to have his city destroyed; but when he put on sackcloth, he turned back God's anger by his humility and contrition.[59] Hezekiah also, when he was attired in all his royal splendor, was alarmed when he heard the threats of the terrible king of the Assyrians. But as soon as he wrapped himself in sackcloth, and was not ashamed to send a message to the prophet by officers also clothed in sackcloth, he received word from him that God's victory was close at hand, and that good times would ensue. And as Scripture reports, this promise was quickly fulfilled. For that night the angel of the Lord struck down a hundred and eighty-five thousand Assyrians, and somewhat later the two sons of Sennacherib, though guilty of patricide, murdered [their father] as he deserved.[60]

(40) Do you see, therefore, what a great difference there is in the sight of God between dissolute and rough clothing? Are you not aware that while elegant garments cause the Judge to become angry, inexpensive and poor garb appeases him; and while the former had made a person deserving of punishment, the latter commends him as one worthy of forgiveness? Isaiah, the greatest of all the prophets, clearly shows how God regards splendid garments, since at his command he took off his clothes, and for three years went about naked and unshod.[61] Therefore, let human pride blush, and let the miserable soul that is corrupted by the disease of egotism be put to shame, while the instrument of God's word, the temple of the Holy Spirit, that publisher of God's plan, did not hesitate to appear

58. Cf. Luke 1.17.
60. Cf. 2 Kgs 19.1–7, 35–37.

59. Cf. Jon 3.6–10.
61. Cf. Isa 20.3.

naked before the people. And the unhappy man, who has never deserved the slightest mark of familiarity with God, puts on airs by scrupulously grooming himself in luxury, and, as he disguises himself in wickedly pretentious garments, is not ashamed to appear licentious in his own estimation, and to have the eyes of the heavenly Observer turn away from him. And thus, in fact, as this arrogant vesture is considered despicable in the sight of God, he who wears it is consequently judged worthy of disgust.

(41) But now pay close attention to Isaiah as he took off his clothes. When he went about in his usual attire, did he indulge in fine, soft garments? So, let us examine the historical account, just as the prophet tells it, and listen to what the voice of God commanded him to do: "At that time the Lord said to Isaiah, son of Amoz: Come, strip the sackcloth from your waist and take your sandals off."[62] Now he who was ordered to remove no other kind of clothes, but only the sackcloth that was around his waist, clearly demonstrates how much value he set on disfiguring garments. Oh, how many ornate supper-rooms of kings and princes there were in the world at that time! How many bedchambers, decked in purple, and dominated by frescoed cupolas! How much jewelry of the wealthy, covered in sparkling gems! How many ceilings paneled in cedar and cypress wood! And still, turning his back and despising all of these, almighty God saw fit to construct a human temple for himself, using this man who was clothed in ugly sackcloth, and through him as his instrument, revealed to mortal men his secret mysteries.

(42) So let this monk, clothed in his fine, new robes, learn how poorly he has bargained, since, in his desire to appear important in the eyes of men, he has undoubtedly become vile in the estimation of the heavenly Judge; and the more lavishly he is honored by men, the more he is despised by God; and as he causes all eyes to admire him, he clothes himself in darkness, hidden from the view of God's grace.

(43) But as the occasion presented itself for me to speak of

---

62. Isa 20.2.

the foibles of dress, and as I have said a few things about those who delight in wearing fine clothes, let me now briefly address those who are infected with the same disease, but suffer from a different madness. For there are some who use the uncouth appearance of their garb to win the approbation of the crowd, and they enjoy this situation the more, in that while they appear humble by reason of the calculated cheapness of their clothes, their fame may be sung by everyone. They are pleased when they are the topic of conversation, when they are pointed out as someone special, while they plot to appear so unconcerned about their unsightliness, so conspicuous in their very obscurity, so esteemed for their humility. In fact, it is the deception of a sly and tricky devil that degrades them so that they may boost their self-esteem, and that disfigures them so that they might shine like stars in the eyes of onlookers.

(44) Compared, moreover, with the practice of the above-mentioned monks, the amount of money they spend is different, but the product they agree to buy is just the same. It is egotism that is up for sale at a bargain price, but the purchasers present are not the same. Some take from their bags their cheap clothes and offer them in exchange, while others try to pay the price with their expensive attire. But while all of them try to get their share, those who offer their poor garments are usually preferred to all other buyers. For those who wear fine clothes, as was said above, often suffer general attack from detractors for the very thing they thought would win them favor; but those who are satisfied with poor and inexpensive garb— and I am still speaking of monks—for whatever reason this happens, whether from good or evil motives, are usually judged by people to be holy men, so that the more lowly one appears because of his outer dress, the more worthy of reverence he is often thought to be.

(45) Moreover, anyone who expects a heavenly reward for wearing disheveled clothes, must not cease to trample all applause and human esteem under foot as if it were mud and filth, and must reveal himself to onlookers exactly as he judges himself to be within the secret recesses of his own conscience. Therefore, when Saul's daughter, Michal, scolded David and

said: "What a glorious day for the king of Israel, when he exposed his person in the sight of his servants' slave girls like any empty-headed fool,"[63] that he might show that interiorly he possessed the same humility which he displayed in public, David did not grow angry and answer in haughty words, but humbly replied: "Before the Lord I will dance for joy, yes, and I will earn yet more disgrace and lower myself still more in my own eyes."[64] In these words we see the model of true humility, since it is demonstrated to be no less internal than external. For the more unsightly some people appear in their external deportment, the greater is the internal esteem they have for themselves. Truly, they wish to be seen in public as someone quite different from what secretly they know themselves to be; and the more they humbly disparage themselves before others, the prouder they are of themselves when they are alone. But to display his humility before others, David said: "I will dance, and I will earn yet more disgrace." And to show his interior humility, he added: "And I will lower myself still more in my own eyes," as if he were obviously saying: I will humble myself in public, that I might give others a salutary example; I will be interiorly humble, that I might persevere in humility, the foundation of salvation. Accordingly, he who lives so artlessly that in the unsightliness of his garb he shows himself to be the same as he would wish to be in the opinion of his viewers, truly bears the stigma of Christ,[65] and, dead to the world, takes up his cross to follow him. He becomes more important in the sight of God, the more despicable he is thought to be in human estimation, and as a most productive bargain, he who is abased by his external garb, shines with the brilliance of internal grace.

(46) There are also some who, while properly motivated, are long accustomed to wearing unseemly attire. But if it should ever happen that they are able to put on somewhat better clothes, they disdainfully reject them out of pride in their unrestrained humility; while some are ashamed of their rags, these others blush at putting on costly garments. In fact, they put up with elegant attire, yet they enjoy the rough texture of despica-

63. 2 Sam 6.20.   64. 2 Sam 6.22.
65. Cf. Heb 13.13.

ble clothes; all bodily adornment becomes disgraceful for them, and ugliness becomes respectable. Indeed, Esther was the model for such monks, when she said: "You know in what straits I am, O Lord: I loathe that symbol of pride, the headdress that I wear when I show myself abroad; I loathe it as one loathes a filthy rag; in private I refuse to wear it."[66] These monks, to be sure, burn with the ardor of holy desire, but they still struggle against the temptations of their passions. But there are others who have reached such heights of mortification, that they seem to have become insensible to both, and as they usually choose to be clothed in poor attire, so also, when occasion demands, they are not disturbed by costly and elegant clothes, viewing both situations indifferently, not affected by the luxury or distressed by the coarseness.

(47) The model for these monks was Judith, who usually wore sackcloth, but when required by the occasion, complemented her bodily beauty with jewels and other finery, as Scripture attests when it says: "Judith removed the sackcloth she was wearing and took off her widow's weeds; then she washed and anointed herself with rich perfume. She did her hair, put on a headband, and dressed in her most festive clothes. She put on sandals and anklets, bracelets and rings, her earrings and all her ornaments, and made herself very attractive."[67] Yet, despite all this personal adornment, this holy woman took pains to guard her humility, and never lost the spirit of poverty with which she was endowed.

(48) But while I have attempted to divest this wandering monk of his precious garments, the man I have been satirizing has escaped my grasp as I argued with him. He is now so far away that I can hardly see him, and I find myself with only his clothes in my hands. But throwing these garments aside, I will continue to follow him, and when I get hold of him, I will try, if possible, to make him stand still. Therefore, let the monk who is addicted to the vice of wanderlust be aware that, unless he retreats from the world, and untiringly prepares himself for the

66. Esth 14.16.
67. Jdt 10.2–3.

service of God in some solitary place, he will not be able to reach the heights of perfection, or worthily guard the stronghold of the religious life. So long as Dinah, the daughter of Jacob, lived in the tents of her father, she was able to preserve her virginity. But once she went out to visit the women of the country, her virginity quickly came under assault, and she was shamefully dishonored by a stranger's lust.[68] So long as the wife of the Levite lived in the heart of the hill country of Ephraim, and kept busy with her domestic duties, she remained faithful to her marriage obligations. But out of affection for her widowed mother's family, she visited her hometown and her relatives, and on the way back, fell prey to a band of lecherous attackers, who raped her and left her to die. And so, while physically suffering disaster by putting her virtue in danger, she was exposed to wanton attack that also took her life.[69] While Absalom's sister, Tamar, lived a simple life with her brother, she had no difficulty protecting her maidenhood. But when she visited Amnon, David's son, and there took care of her brother, she was forced to mourn the loss of her stolen virginity, and at length, feeling that it was safer to stay with him than to leave, after it was too late, chose to live in quiet seclusion in preference to dangerous wandering.[70]

(49) You too, if you wish your soul to remain steadfast in its virginity, if you consider it an abomination to fall into the hands of foul and violent seducers, choose seclusion, retreat into a solitary place where you can live alone, forcefully barricade your ears and your eyes from the foolishness of worldly affairs, and despise all conversation with sensuous men, as more productive of destruction than of edification. For according to Solomon: "Handle pitch and it will make you dirty."[71] Therefore, take refuge within the chamber of your own conscience, close all the doors of your house, bolt all your senses with the strictest discipline, so that no one may enter. The spring that is dammed up to prevent outflow in any direction, rises in flowing swells to a higher level, but if, on the other hand, it is

---

68. Cf. Gen 34.1–2.
70. Cf. 2 Sam 13.1–14.

69. Cf. Judg 19.1–28.
71. Sir 13.1.

drained off through many channels, as soon as the heat above it becomes more intense, it will run dry. We may be sure that, if the doors to the roof of the palace had been closed, keeping David from walking there, his desire for Bathsheba as she bathed would not have been aroused;[72] but because he did not guard his eyes, he fell headlong into the ruinous pit that yawned before him. Because he merely failed to curb his sight, he greased the path that led to his total downfall, as Jeremiah so aptly said: "My eye has wasted my soul."[73] Therefore, if such a lofty pillar of heaven fell so ignominiously only because of his unguarded eyes, what should be thought of us weak and little men, who by running about in the world totally abandon the interior life, and engross our sight and hearing and all our senses in imbibing the vanities of the world?

(50) What a difference there is between monks who love a life of solitude and those who live without restraint outside the monastery, can be readily seen in the two sons of Isaac. For it is written that "Esau became skillful in hunting, a man of the open plains, but Jacob led a settled life and stayed among the tents."[74] Accordingly, the latter, prudent in his simplicity, and circumspect regarding his own welfare, received from his father the blessing reserved for the firstborn, while the former, skillful only in his folly because he lived by the sword, agreed with his brother like an attendant in the service of his master. Yet, if Jacob had not lived among the tents, he would not have been blessed as the firstborn, while if Esau had not roamed about in the fields, he would not have lost his birthright. The former remained quietly at home, and by God's favor usurped another's right; but the latter, preoccupied with his hunting, lost what was rightfully his. Now, if those who wander about in the world should persist in offering excuses, bragging that they were observing the precepts of obedience, they should not forget that, in going hunting, Esau obeyed his father's command, and still was unable to serve a meal for his father, nor did he win the blessing that his birthright deserved. Consequently, if

---

72. Cf. 2 Sam 11.2.   73. Lam 3.51.
74. Gen 25.27.

one is habitually enticed by something evil, and succumbs to the temptation of his own free will, he commits sin, even though he is apparently obeying the commands of others. For when it is said that "Isaac favored Esau because he kept him supplied with venison,"[75] it becomes evident that, in order to provide food for his father from the chase, Esau was not so much obeying parental instructions, as he was paying tribute that had long been customary. And so, one who satisfies his own desires by gadding about in the world, and still claims that he is obeying the instructions of his superiors, should know that God does not believe such specious arguments, but rather judges the hidden purposes of men according to their conscience.

(51) It should be noted, however, that so long as some monks are engaged in their roaming, they do not commit serious sin; but after their return, acting as if they were drunk on the wine of secular affairs, suffer a mighty fall. They come back, indeed, but their eyes are filled with the smoke of worldly deeds, and therefore upon reaching their own house, they cannot see where they should walk in performing good works. This is exactly what the story of Esau clearly hinted at. For when he came in from the country, complaining about being exhausted, he struck a most damaging bargain with his brother, and while allowing his mighty appetite to get the better of him, he sold his birthright for a paltry bowl of lentil soup.[76] Thus also, one who was preoccupied with external affairs, was unfaithful to himself, and lost what was his when he physically returned to the interior life without doing so in spirit.

(52) It is also the case with those who suffer from the vice of wanderlust, that because of the dust in the eyes of the spirit, while not taking precautions against stumbling into the pit of sin, afterwards they pay no heed to why they have fallen. And so, by failing to give careful consideration to their sins, because of their muddled judgment they minimize their faults by not straining off a gnat, even though they have swallowed a camel.[77]

---

75. Gen 25.28.
77. Cf. Matt 23.24.

76. Cf. Gen 25.29–33.

We know that Esau was not free from this kind of blindness, as sacred history reports when in the next sentence it says: "Esau swore an oath and sold his birthright," and then added: "Then Jacob gave him bread and the lentil soup, and he ate and drank and went away without more ado. Thus Esau showed how little he valued his birthright."[78]

(53) Wherefore, from these two brothers it becomes perfectly clear how great a difference there is between monks who reside in their monasteries and those who are vagrants. For if Esau had not been so unsettled in his habits and so profligate of himself in his travels, he would never have lost the spiritual blessing of his father along with his birthright; and if Jacob had not confined himself to his domestic surroundings, he would have remained the poor younger son in the line of succession. The former, despite his skill and ingenuity, was deprived of his legal rights, while the latter, by acting calmly and simply, won a privileged position over his brothers[79] who were subject to him. When the one was at length worn out by his constant chase through forests and valleys, he lost his preeminence as the first-born; but the other, by enjoying his leisure in a pleasant environment, was raised by God to leadership over tribes and nations.

(54) Therefore, with Esau, let the monk, whoever he may be, discontinue his frequent excursions from his monastic retreat. With him he should cease involving himself in secular affairs under the guise of obedience, lest, like him, he eventually find himself a sorry exile from the land of God's blessing, associated with the very author of all pernicious wandering. Like Jacob, let him rather show that he prefers to stay at home; like him, let him live simply among the tents, so that he may refresh God, who, as the true Father of the elect, desires a meal of good works, by preparing, not game from the forest, but meat from his own flocks when he serves the food that pleases him, not procuring it from holiness that is only superficial, but from

---

78. Gen 25.34.

79. Damian has "brothers" (*fratribus*), although Jacob seems to have had only one brother (see Gen 25–27).

virtues that proceed from a good conscience. God, moreover, ordained that the hides of the victims were not to be offered to him in sacrifice, but instead commanded his people to present the entrails along with the very best parts. Therefore, in explaining the rites for burnt offerings, Moses gave orders, saying: "Strip the hide from the victim and cut its body into pieces,"[80] in which precept one can also find a symbolic sense if he examines it carefully. For we "strip the hide from the victim" when we remove the outer appearance of virtue from the eyes of our mind; we "cut its body into pieces" when by subtle discrimination we ponder its inmost parts, member by member, that what externally appears sound and healthy, is not inwardly porous and suffering from the vice of hidden vanity. For in thanksgiving for the gifts he had received, David promised to offer fat beasts as sacrifices to the Lord, when he said: "I will offer you fatted holocausts, and burn rams as a savory sacrifice."[81]

(55) Whoever, then, delights in undertaking secular projects, removes the choicest parts of the fatted animal he is sacrificing, along with its entrails, and tries to burn in God's honor only the hide of the victim that he is forbidden to offer. But he who would present a savory sacrifice to God, should seek solitude, devote himself to the life of the spirit, and keep his soul sound and unsullied in its original virginity, by avoiding all commerce with the brothels of the world and refusing to submit like a prostitute to foul seducers. And so, that he might be pleasing in the sight of the spiritual bridegroom, he should not, like Jezebel, paint his eyes,[82] that is, cover himself with the deceits of worldly trappings, but like Judith, anoint his body with rich perfume,[83] and apply to all the senses of his immortal soul the ointment of chastity, lest through incontinence he fall dead and rot in the stench of impurity.

(56) Therefore, let the chaste soul confine itself to the inner recesses of holy Church, and thus always find its repose in the marriage chamber of the eternal King. It should not seek the affection of close relatives or of other associates, but find its de-

---

80. Lev 1.6.
82. Cf. 2 Kgs 9.30.

81. Ps 65.15.
83. Cf. Jdt 10.3.

light in the embrace of the true spouse alone. For it was not in vain that Scripture says: "Listen, my daughter, hear my words and consider them: forget your own people and your father's house, for the king desires your beauty."[84] Let the holy soul sleep in the chamber of this spouse, away from the turmoil of all worldly disturbance; let it be enkindled with the fires of chaste love at the side of the author of its chastity, as it repeats the Song of Songs: "The king has taken me into his chamber; we shall rejoice and be glad for you."[85] And again: "My beloved is for me a bunch of myrrh as he lies on my breast."[86] But if on some occasion it should seem necessary to leave this pleasant atmosphere, the soul that is absorbed with God should not rush out and lightheartedly wander about, eagerly seek contact with relatives, nor become excited by the deceptions of the world, but should pause and seriously take counsel with itself, saying: "I have stripped off my garb; must I put it on again? I have washed my feet; must I soil them again?"[87]

(57) Accordingly, if its special bridegroom should observe this longing present in a holy soul, since he is undoubtedly the prince of peace, he grants it unencumbered repose and spiritual calm, and gently puts to rest all disturbances that might assault it. For this is what he says in the Song of Songs: "I charge you, daughters of Jerusalem, do not rouse her, do not disturb my love until she is ready."[88] But on the other hand, the prophet has this to say to the soul devoid of God, that yearns for secular involvement, using the figure of Babylon: "Down with you, sit in the dust, virgin daughter of Babylon, sit on the ground: there is no throne for the daughter of the Chaldaeans."[89] In this citation, I think, the human soul is called a virgin, not in the sense of being unsullied, but only because it is unproductive. And since Babylon may be understood to mean "confusion,"[90] the unproductive soul is called the daughter of Babylon which, since it does not bring forth good works, and is not subject to the norms of virtuous living, seems to be the off-

84. Ps 44.11–12. 85. Song 1.3.
86. Song 1.12. 87. Song 5.3.
88. Song 2.7. 89. Isa 47.1.
90. Cf. Jerome, *Nom. hebr.* 3.18.

spring of confusion as its mother. But if it is not called an unproductive virgin, but is said to be unsullied, after it has lost its
salvation, it is known for what it was, and the confusion is increased. And so, God properly upbraided it and said: "Down
with you." The human soul, indeed, stands proud when it is eagerly aware of what God holds in store for it. But it falls from
this state, when to its shame it is defeated and subjects itself to
the passing fancies of the world. And in the next breath it is
well said: "Sit in the dust." Falling from its high estate, it sits in
the dust, because by deserting the things of heaven, it is spat-
tered by earthly concerns and soiled by lying in filth.

(58) And then, by coming back to the same idea, the text
continues: "Sit on the ground," as if, by making its reproach
more obvious, it were saying: Since you do not choose to direct
your life by heavenly norms, humiliate yourself by wallowing in
earthly affairs that are below your dignity. And so, the text in-
evitably continues: "There is no throne for the daughter of the
Chaldaeans." Now the Chaldaeans are said to mean "the headstrong."[91] They are extremely headstrong, because by going
their own way, they are not able to safeguard even their own
moral actions. Earthly desires are headstrong because they render the soul hard and insensitive, not only to the commands of
the Creator, but frequently also to physical punishment. There
is no throne for the daughter of the headstrong, because the
soul that is born from evil desires to love of the world, is hardened by these same desires. Because it subjects itself to earthly
passions, it loses its ability to judge, and there is no throne on
which it might preside, since it lacks a sense of discretion,
seemingly restrained from sitting in judgment because it wanders about seeking satisfaction in external delights. For it is obvious that the soul that has lost its ability for inner deliberation,
in countless ways dissipates itself by its longing to fulfill its desires outside itself, and because it pretends to be acting intelli-
gently, is blinded to the point where it is unaware of what it is
doing. By the just sentence of God, it is frequently left to its
own deserts, and is allowed to endure the wearisome service of

91. Cf. Jerome, *Nom. hebr.* 4.22.

the world it so eagerly sought. And so, the text cited above aptly continues: "Never again shall men call you soft-skinned and delicate: take up the millstone and grind meal."[92] But it is evident that her parents are gentle with their delicate daughter, and do not load her with hard and servile tasks.

(59) Accordingly, almighty God seems to call this tender daughter when he invites a beloved soul to abandon the wearisome servitude of this world, lest, while enduring the burden of external affairs, it grow callous to the internal yearning of the spirit. But the soft-skinned and delicate daughter of the Chaldaeans is not invited, because the soul devoted to evil desires is abandoned to the service of the world, which it so eagerly sought, that it might live as a slave girl in the outside world, since interiorly it failed to love God as his daughter. Hence she is commanded to take up the millstone and grind meal. The millstone goes round and round, and thus the meal emerges. All mundane affairs are, indeed, a millstone, because, as they accumulate many concerns, they lead human minds about in circles. And what they issue forth is like meal, because in a heart that is led astray they always beget trifling thoughts. At times, however, one who remains alone is thought to be of some importance; but when engaged in some form of active life, his true value is revealed. And hence the text I cited at once continues: "Uncover your shame, strip your shoulder, bare your legs, and wade through the rivers."[93] By performing some external task, shame is uncovered when in its vain display of action the soul is recognized to be low and worthless, while before when it was at rest, it was thought to be of great value. The soul strips its shoulder when it displays its deeds that formerly were unknown. It bares its legs when it shows to what lengths its desires will go as it longs for worldly wealth. It also wades through rivers, because the soul constantly seeks the activities of this world that daily flow onward to their end, and by abandoning some and following others, seems always to cross from one river to another.

92. Isa 47.1–2.
93. Isa 47.2.

(60) But I have said all this, that I might indicate where the soul, driven from the throne of its holy purpose, and addicted to the vice of wandering, now lies, because if it ceases to strive for goals that are above it, it will forever fall in its own esteem. It is raised to the heights, however, if, after abandoning the love of temporal things, it holds fast to the hope of an immutable eternity. Nor do I wish to imply by these words that a monk should obstinately purpose to remain at all times in retirement, nor that on occasion he should not agree to leave the monastery when extreme necessity demands. Yet I rather advise that he do so temporarily and only rarely, with the knowledge that by wandering through the world he cannot practice the spiritual life, nor reach the heights of perfection even if he makes every effort to do so.

(61) But I am greatly displeased to note that among all the types of men who deviate from their sole purpose, holy hermits are also found, attacked by the disease of pestilential wanderlust and, if I may be permitted to say so, stirred up by some devil called Vertumnus.[94] Among the ancients the Vertumni were said to be demons at whose instigation men became giddy and unstable. Those, indeed, may rightly be said to suffer from their attack, who, while staying in their cells only during the Lenten season, run here and there throughout almost the whole year, and thus spend their life in aimless wandering. These hermits, in fact, while living temporarily in seclusion, and then more frequently going out among the people, brag that they are leading both kinds of life, namely, the contemplative and the active. But it is clear that in neither do they produce a full harvest for salvation, and while congratulating themselves that with Jacob they have joined in some kind of spiritual union with two spouses, they follow their own whims and are going in the opposite direction. Contrary to the usual interpretation, these hermits would have us believe that Rachel was dull-eyed and Leah childless, the one with obstructed vision and the other suffering from unfortunate sterility. Because

94. An Etruscan deity, understood by the Romans to be the god of the changing year and of change in general. It is also used as a symbol of instability.

men of this kind run about in public, and are consequently held in low esteem by the people, they will never be able to bear spiritual sons for God; and as they return from the world like drunken men, they find it impossible to penetrate the secrets [of contemplation]. For anyone who wishes to use his mind to approach this inaccessible light, must spend extensive periods of time cleansing the eyes of the soul from every blemish of worldly activity. Barring that, as the soul raises its sight to view the highest truths, the dust of earthly concerns will block its vision, and it will behold only the darkness it had left behind, rather than comprehend the light toward which it was striving.

(62) To this I might add that, for those who constantly switch from one lifestyle to another, the life of seclusion seems more harsh, the more accustomed they become to excursions into the world, so that the eremitic vocation becomes an intolerable burden for them, and their very cell a horror. For habit makes the cell sweet for the monk, while wandering makes it seem dreadful. For those who gad about, the cell is a prison, but for those who live there permanently, it is a most pleasant little room. Silence causes the persevering monk to be wide awake, while for one who goes abroad, it puts him to sleep. Temperance strengthens the body accustomed to fasting, while a surfeit of delicious food causes it to grow weak. The moderate practice of praying through the night sharpens the edge of a man's mind, but twice going to sleep makes it dull. Frequent conversation begets hunger in the heart of a monk, but quiet solitude safeguards the soul in the disciplined practice of its accustomed continence. Speaking of secular topics subjects the soul to passions and desires, while unremitting meditation on sacred Scripture renders it dead to the world. A monk's poverty gives his mind security, and security is the mother of purity. On the other hand, an abundance of earthly things gives rise to the stings of uneasiness, and uneasiness is the root of anxiety. Unwashed feet, neglected hands, and unkempt hair are like an anchor constantly keeping a monk to his cell; but careful solicitude for one's tender body, on the contrary, is the lure and the occasion for going out among the people.

(63) Therefore, whoever wishes the eremitical life to be a pleasant experience for him, must constantly strive to persevere in it with a steadfast spirit, and must never vary his life-style if he would bear the easy yoke of the Lord without disturbance. The continuous practice of the eremitic life is a source of refreshment, but when interrupted it becomes a torture. By an unbroken life of solitude the soul is enlightened, sins are laid bare, and whatever a person had concealed from himself is exposed. When water is drawn from a pond, and whatever did not belong there is removed, the fish that are high and dry can be seen by men; and when the flood of worldly concerns spills forth from us, whatever was wont to swim in the depths of the emerging torrents, comes to light. So too with the hunter. After blocking various paths, he surrounds the animals' wooded haunts with dense brush, purposely leaving only one avenue of escape for the fleeing game, and there from ambush positions himself with his ready spear. And thus, with a minimum of effort and anxiety, he leisurely waits at the only exit for the approach of the nimble game that he was unable to pursue in the unbounded depths of the forest. And when we obstruct the path of worldly activity for vices that try to escape and be free to engage in evil deeds, we set our traps, as it were, in only one place, because our constant struggle is with thoughts alone. And thus, the wild beast of our vices is easily captured, since the only thoroughfare of human thoughts is effectively guarded. The fowler, too, will cover every fountain and spring with heavy foliage, thus forcing the birds to gather at one source of pure water. And since this is the only watering hole left open, and by surrounding it with traps,[95] he is successful in netting a goodly number of fowl. Therefore, that we may easily set snares for the soul's various passions, after obstructing the streams of secular concerns, we should strive to fight manfully only against the onslaught of our thoughts, so that after our vices have been prevented from going into action, with only our thoughts flying about, they may easily fall into the trap that our holy prudence has devised.

95. Lit., "surrounding it with images of mousers," i.e., of hunting cats.

(64) It should be noted, however, that the servant of God is frequently deceived by people dedicated to worldly interests when they urgently invite him to settle quarrels among those who are at odds, or to engage in some task that would benefit the Church, exaggerating the present threat and the common danger to many [souls] unless he visit them. And if he comes, they repeatedly assure him that he may act as he chooses, and all will come to a happy conclusion. For when the ancient enemy sees that the knight of Christ, who is involved in sacred combat, cannot be deterred from his purpose in any other way, he falsely conjures up some specious plan of achieving greater success, so that, as he concentrates on the larger objective, he will temporarily postpone the good to which he is presently dedicated. But anyone who has frequently experienced the customary deceits of this world, will be wise enough to reject these vain suggestions and will carefully guard against making these fruitless efforts. For in some circles, the authority of a monk who is not on the scene is great indeed; but if he should be present, it is judged to be of little value. And often great respect is shown for the writings of some outstanding man, but little regard is accorded him if he is there in person. In fact, among laymen a religious is something like a painting. Indeed, if one stands some distance from it, a painting is viewed eagerly and with keen interest; but if one is close up, it is thought to be of little value. And a religious who is not at hand is regarded with respect; but if he is present, he can easily be overlooked. And this, the apostle states, is just what happened to him: "His letters, so it is said, are weighty and powerful; but when he appears he has no presence, and as a speaker he is contemptible."[96] Those, then, whom he had frightened by the force and seriousness of his letters, he left unimpressed when he was with them in person. So why should we wonder if this happens to upright men, since the Gospel account asserts that something quite similar took place with the head of the elect, our Redeemer himself: "When Herod," it says, "saw Jesus he was greatly pleased; having heard much about him, he had

96. 2 Cor 10.10.

long been wanting to see him."[97] But let us observe how this great and enduring desire that Herod had falsely entertained for the Lord he had never seen, would end once he had an opportunity to meet him. This, in fact, is clearly stated, when a little farther on the text continues: "Then Herod and his troops treated him with contempt and ridicule, and sent him back to Pilate dressed in a white robe."[98] Notice how that crafty fox scorned him whom he had wanted to meet, and how he ridiculed the man he had wished to see. And with a love for dishonest living he sought life by sending him back to Pilate, and so he remained dead because of his wickedness.

(65) Therefore, one who serves in the army of God and is thus on his way to reside in his eternal homeland, must seek to despise the evil, flattering promises of the world, and dread to entangle himself in any way in the snares of secular concerns. He has his own function allotted to him; let him know that it is enough for him if he is able to carry out his duties assigned under obedience. He should call to mind what was written in this regard: "Be careful not to engage in too many transactions."[99] Let secular matters be handled by laymen. It should suffice for servants of God to show that they are dead to a world that is on the verge of destruction. Just as it is absurd to prefer evil things to those that are good, so too is it foolish to consider the best to be inferior to something that is good. Because Mary had chosen the part that was best, she thought that it sufficed for her, and did not involve herself in what was good for Martha, that is, performing her many tasks.[100] And because Moses, who had left human contacts behind, twice fasted for forty days, he was also twice deemed worthy to receive the law written by the finger of the Lord.[101] But Aaron, who was commissioned to care for the people, is remembered as a maker of idols.[102]

(66) And so, it frequently happens that he who is not content to look after himself, and leaves the monastery to promote the salvation of others, is forced to put himself in danger, and like a man reaching out to help someone who is gasping for air

97. Luke 23.8.
98. Luke 23.11.
99. Sir 11.10.
100. Cf. Luke 10.40–42.
101. Cf. Exod 24.18; 34.28.
102. Cf. Exod 32.1–6.

in a shipwreck in a stormy sea, he puts himself in jeopardy of drowning in the furious waves. In the dark night of this life it is safer for us, as we stand on the shore, to produce a light for those who have suffered shipwreck, than out of compassion for them to swim out at the peril of our lives, so that when we have shown them the right direction, they may reach the safety of the harbor, and not cause us to drown in the wild sea as we try to reach them. At the crest of Mount Rephidim Moses prayed, while Israel under the leadership of Joshua fought in the valley. But if Moses had come down to the plain to help his people, Amalek undoubtedly would have cut the fleeing Israelites to pieces. If he had lowered his hands to seize his weapons, after the slaughter the enemy would have won an easy victory. All of this is clearly learned, if we carefully note the actual account of sacred history, where it says: "Whenever Moses raised his hands, Israel had the advantage, and when he lowered his hands even a little, Amalek had the advantage."[103] And so the hands of one at prayer strengthened the hands of the fighters, and because the former were peacefully extended to heaven, the latter that engaged in battle were victorious over the fallen foe. The latter, indeed, were involved in combat, but the former undoubtedly won the victory, because praying hands were used in begging God to grant success for those that did the fighting. On the other hand, when Balaam son of Beor went into battle along with the Midianites, he was put to the sword with those whom he had tried to help.[104] And rightly so, for he who is not content with his own responsibility, puts himself in danger of sharing the fate of others. This unfortunate man deserved to fall in battle, a victim of enemy swords, for if he had remained out of combat, he might have used his prophetic voice to announce the outcome of the battle.

(67) This was not the case with Elisha, who did not accompany Jehoram, the king of Israel, into battle against Moab, but thought it sufficient to forecast the result of the war and his future victory over the fallen enemy.[105] But why do I say that he

---

103. Exod 17.11.   104. Cf. Num 31.8; Josh 13.22.
105. Cf. 2 Kgs 3.13–19.

never followed the royal forces into battle, since when Naaman traveled from the distant lands of Syria, and with his horses and chariots humbly stood at the entrance of Elisha's house, the latter did not deem it proper to go out to meet him, did not open the door that he might enter, but sent out a messenger to tell him what he should do? And besides, Naaman had at hand a great supply of worldly possessions that apparently had been given to him. For, as sacred history attests: "He was the commander of the army, a great man highly esteemed by his master, because by his means the Lord had given victory to Syria. He was also," as the text explains, "a powerful man of great wealth."[106] And on this trip he did not travel empty-handed, but with substantial resources. In fact, as the text tells us, "he brought with him ten talents of silver, six thousand shekels of gold, besides ten changes of clothing."[107] Scripture does not say what kind of garments these were, but who can doubt that they were precious, heavily laden with silver and gold? How many monks there are today, men vowed to the religious life, who, if such a powerful and famous man had deigned to knock at their door, would not have hurried to greet him with great respect, humbly begged him to come in, and employed flattering words which would not only have been advantageous but also highly pleasing to the visitor? And if they had been repeatedly asked, they would never have refused to accept his gifts, especially if there were a somewhat greater number of brothers in the house who had to be fed. But Elisha, the disciple of the Holy Spirit, rich in hope, and highly endowed with the treasure of faith, even though he was supporting a hundred sons of the prophets under his tutelage, turned down the money, rejected the gifts, and in praiseworthy fashion refused to receive recompense for a considerable favor, lest what he had freely accepted should appear to be sold at the expense of the giver. But when Naaman came, it was not his pride but his prudence that told him not to rise respectfully, lest he show reverence for a stranger who still put his trust in earthly glory, already at that

106. 2 Kgs 5.1.
107. 2 Kgs 5.5.

time anticipating the figure of apostolic dignity which Paul would later display, when he said: "As long as I am the apostle of the Gentiles, I will give all honor to my ministry."[108]

(68) Should not [Elisha] be considered a humble servant, letting Naaman stand proudly outside his gate, yet who allowed a woman to entice him from Mount Carmel, where he was staying, and not only did he accompany the Shunammite woman, but in fact he also followed after her? For when she said: "As the Lord lives, and as you live, I will not leave you," Scripture then continued, saying: "So he got up and followed her."[109] And did he not show his contempt for the rich presents offered him, and still did not refuse to accept a donation of ordinary barley loaves from the man who came from Baal-shalisha?[110]

(69) But in shielding the prophet from accusations of acting arrogantly, I lay myself open to some demanding questions. Can someone not raise this issue against what I have been saying: "If such a great prophet accepted bread that had been offered him, and agreed to leave his hermitage when begged to do so by a woman, how can a monk not be allowed to go out into the world, or be hindered from taking gifts?" To this let me reply in just a few words: "I do not absolutely forbid a monk to accept gifts, for when this happens discreetly and in moderation, and when fraternal charity demands, I advise it, as, for example, in accepting necessary items that one needs, similar to the prophet receiving bread, but refusing what he might consider superfluous, just as the prophet turned down money."

(70) That Elisha, however, left his mountain retreat to revive the son of the Shunammite woman, is something that monks in our day might admire but not imitate. It is, of course, permitted for a monk to go out into the world as he wishes, so long as he is able to bring a dead man back to life. For such a prophetic trip is not wholly unknown, both as a display of power in the miracle of restoring human life, and as a symbol of a mystery that has spiritual significance. What its meaning might be, is not an idle concern if we only briefly examine it. For the ser-

---

108. Rom 11.13.   109. 2 Kgs 4.30.
110. Cf. 2 Kgs 4.42.

vant whom Elisha sent, carrying his staff, was not able to revive the son of the Shunammite woman. But when Elisha himself came and stretched out upon the dead child, putting his body on that of the boy, walked up and down the room, and then breathed into his mouth seven times, he at once revived him by means of this symbolic act of compassion. Surely God, the Creator of the human race, as if grieving over the dead boy, took pity on us, seeing us lying dead, killed by the arrow of iniquity. And through Moses he published the terrible decrees of the Law, as if sending the servant with the rod. Through the Law God took up the rod, when he said: "Whoever does any of these things, shall be put to death."[111]

(71) And so, the Law was unable to revive us from sin and death, but by the gentle breath of grace God lovingly brought us back to life. And the servant with the staff could not restore the dead child because, as Paul asserts: "The Law brought nothing to perfection."[112] But the prophet himself came, humbly stretched himself out upon the dead body, and placed his limbs on a level with those of the deceased, "for although he was in the form of God, yet he did not think to snatch at equality with God, but made himself nothing, assuming the nature of a slave. Bearing the human form, he was born in the likeness of men."[113] He walked up and down, because he was calling the Jews, who were close at hand, and the Gentiles, who were far away. He breathed seven times upon the dead boy, because the sevenfold grace of the Spirit[114] enkindles those who lie dead in their sin to receive the divine gift. And at once the boy was alive and sat up, because he whom the rod of terror was unable to revive, came back to life through the spirit of love.[115]

(72) Who, therefore, would dare to follow the example of the prophet in leaving his abode, since it is obvious that he cannot equal this power or this mystery? Hence, the warrior of Christ should be constantly on guard, ready for action in the heavenly army, armed with the shield of faith. He must always

111. Exod 21.12–17.   112. Heb 7.19.
113. Phil 2.6–7.   114. Cf. Isa 11.2 (LXX).
115. Cf. 2 Kgs 4.34.

be prepared to fight to protect the stronghold of his leader, lest perhaps enemy swords find him wandering outside the camp, and kill him. So long as Abner was in camp with the troops, he was a terror to the opposing forces. But after he laid down his arms, he was killed by a less skilled swordsman and made to pay for the recent death of Asahel.[116] If Uriah, moreover, had been satisfied to live in his own house, he would undoubtedly have avoided the king's anger and deceit. But because he chose to sleep away from his own home and among strangers rather than in his own chamber, he brought the letter that resulted in his death to the commanding officer of the forces attacking the city.[117]

(73) Formerly, indeed, the world felt a need for those who would announce the good news; but those days are over and times have changed, in which a monk might profitably advise laymen and would find it useful to implant spiritual ideas in the minds of worldly men. Now such unhappy people consider any discussion of the spiritual life to be based on fables, and even though they might listen to salutary admonition, they refuse to observe it. Moreover, if we look back with the eyes of faith to times that used to be, we find that in the present age the past has deteriorated like fruitful branches producing sterile offshoots.

(74) Who does not marvel that Nineveh, a great and spacious city, should so easily turn away from its evil practices at the preaching of one man, and that countless men, along with their women and children and even their cattle, would be led to do penance?[118] In our day who would presume to prescribe three days of fasting even for men—and I do not mean those of tender age or of the weaker sex—that would forbid them to drink water or eat any food at all? Note that among these Gentiles even the cattle abstained for three days at the call of the prophet, while the very people who live under the regimen of the Gospel refuse to fast longer than one day. The former wholeheartedly assemble to do penance at the preaching of one man, while the latter constantly listen to crowds of preach-

116. Cf. 2 Sam 2.14–32; 3.27.   117. Cf. 2 Sam 11.9–17.
118. Cf. Jon 3.3–9.

ers and are absolutely unwilling to obey. Who is not astounded that all the men of Judah and Benjamin who had married foreign women, not only dismissed their illicit wives at the advice of Ezra the priest, but also gave up the children who had been born of them?[119] Who is not aware of the great love that men have for their wives, and how deep is their paternal attachment to their children? Who does not know what grief and bitterness can assail the hearts of men who must dissolve this double bond, or how vehement is the fire of paternal love and conjugal affection that burns in the soul of married people? But these men, endowed with true love for God, rejected this false image of affection, and that they might be truly loving in spirit became praiseworthy for their inflexible attitude toward flesh and blood. They armed themselves against the order of nature, that they might faithfully serve the Author of nature. And so, they forgot the children they had begotten, that they might be included among the heirs of their true father, and for the purpose of restoring the bonds of heavenly peace, abrogated the union of conjugal living. They were unable to practice fidelity to their marriages when a greater faith in their own Creator was enkindled. Certainly, we may aptly apply to them the words spoken by Moses: "Who said to his father and to his mother: I do not know you; and to his brothers: I do not acknowledge you: and their own children they did not recognize. They have observed your word and kept your covenant."[120]

(75) Who, I ask, is now able to break up incestuous marriages with even the most insistent preaching? Who can succeed in convincing, I will not say the people, but even one person, to repudiate an illicit marriage? The sacred canons protest against such a crime, human laws penalize it, preachers of the Church oppose it, and all of these together cause incorrigible men to scoff at them as if they were empty tales told by old women, rather than to feel remorse and amend their ways.[121]

---

119. Cf. 1 Esd 10.3, 7–14.

120. Deut 33.9.

121. Cf. Peter Damian, *Letter* 19 (FOTC, MC 1.171–93), *passim;* Ryan, *Sources*, nos. 4–14, p. 269, where Damian shows his familiarity with ecclesiastical and civil law forbidding marriages within certain degrees of kinship.

And besides, as you know, this very year a council was twice convened by the Roman Pontiff, where at length all who were living in incestuous marriages, contrary to the decrees of the canons, were excommunicated.[122]

(76) But who can find even one person among so many thousands who is forced to give up such an abominable and unfortunate union? In fact, as they dig a deeper pit of damnation that will swallow them, who among such people afterwards refrains from entering the church? Or, moreover, who is there that is aware of these events, and refuses to have anything to do with them? Therefore, this deadly disease spreads through all, because the interwoven network of apostolic excommunication ensnares all of them. Indeed, anyone who fortunately marries into a distinguished family, and is flattered by the endearing charm of his wife's sinfully enticing figure, especially if she brings with her a substantial dowry, or if her ability to bear children rouses within him the hope of future offspring, purposely decides to abandon God rather than dissociate himself from such an auspicious marriage. But if these people have experienced the misfortune of an unhappy marriage that excludes pleasures, the husband fabricates a false family tree, and forges documents that contain the names of unknown ancestors, and calls on certain old men to certify this allegation, even though he knows that because they are dead they cannot testify. Hence he is his own accuser, as a guilty man involves himself in the crime, thus exaggerating the heinous deed, and searches for the evidence whereby he can extricate himself from such a dangerous shipwreck.

(77) Let a monk, therefore, now leave his monastery, desert the salutary retreat where he is at peace, and spend his life pursuing fruitless goals under the guise of saving souls. For was there ever a simonist, who on the basis of my advice and warning willingly resigned his office? What violent usurper of another's rights ever restored the inheritance he had stolen to those who had been evicted from their paternal lands? Who was ever

---

122. Cf. Ryan, *Sources*, no. 270, pp. 124–25, where he argues for 1063 as the date of these councils. But see G. Lucchesi, *Vita*, nos. 214–16, proposing 1069 as the year in which these councils were held.

surrounded by an army in the field, and if he could fight on equal terms, returned home under the protection of a truce without first shedding blood? What public officer ever allowed a poor debtor to go free without paying interest on his loan? What debtor ever acted in good faith to guarantee the rights of the heirs of his creditor? Everything in the world is confused, and all the decrees of religion and faith are brought to naught. Justice is sold by judges; in the hands of lawyers truth is clouded by the darkness of specious arguments. Laws are subject to corruption, and money is the excuse of lawbreakers. Gold now presides over senators and passes judgment from the bench, and like some emperor publishes its official edicts. Just as a king in his private offices deliberates on the state of the realm and on the whole of its affairs, so too gold hides behind the scenes and issues its decrees in public. It is carried hidden in a small cloth, and when the debate is over, it makes judicial decisions. And it often happens that underhanded financial motives boldly declare a reward for those whom the evidence convicts, while, on the contrary, those whose conscience assures their innocence, are found guilty by the judge because of their poverty. Money, to be sure, has influence on the laws, and a deceptive interpreter perverts obscure passages in its interest. In the case of the rich, money softens the heart of judges with the oil of iniquity, but toward the poor it compels the judge to apply the full rigor of the law. And so, today avarice, the root of all evil, becomes ever more pervasive; and like branches of a poisonous plant spreads the monstrous depravity of deadly vices throughout the whole world.

(78) These days of ours, to be sure, the apostle had in mind when he spoke to Timothy about the future: "There will be terrible times in the last days. Men will be lovers of self and of money, proud, arrogant, abusive, disrespectful of parents, ungrateful, profane, inhuman, implacable, slanderous, licentious, brutal, strangers to all goodness, traitors, adventurers, swollen with self-importance. They will be men who put pleasure in the place of God, men who preserve the outward form of religion, but are a standing denial of its reality."[123] And having said these

123. 2 Tim 3.1–5.

things, he promptly added, "Keep clear of men like these."[124] Did Timothy have to wait for the end of the world, since as the apostle enumerated for him the depravity of men that would be found in these last days, he at once added that he should avoid them? Or did he rather generally impose his command on this one disciple who would represent those who, as he foresaw, were to be entrusted with his office at the end of the world? Therefore, since what he said was not, "Preach to these," or, "Announce to them the words of life," but rather, "Keep clear of such men," he attempted to show the rash insolence of our own times, and kept all arrogant men away from fruitless preaching.

(79) What do we monks have to say to all this, since we exceed the bounds of our competence and claim for ourselves the rights of another's office? If Paul forbade his disciple, who was especially commissioned to this duty, to preach to the incorrigible, how can we be so bold as to rudely involve ourselves in the office of preaching, which was never delegated to us, and, by placing our salvation in jeopardy, toil in vain as if these others were making progress?

(80) Therefore, abandon all interest in unprofitable activity. You should judge it unnecessary to involve yourself in fruitless labor. Having gathered all its strength, your spirit should concentrate on itself and alertly prepare for battle against its untiring adversaries. It should interiorly abound with charity toward all, but should consider it useless to become involved in external affairs in the interest of another's salvation. When people come, one should give them salutary advice, but at no one's urging should you lightly put aside the treasure of your own life of solitude. Let imperial documents be brought by his majesty's messenger, let papal bulls be sent to us by the authority of the apostolic see, let a synod be assembled, and the total business of the council be placed in the hands of upright men. Let the monk promptly prostrate himself on the ground, reverently show his respect for these sacred writings, but irrevocably hold himself aloof from serving at this gathering, saying to himself: What business have I with the kings of this world? Why should I

124. 2 Tim 3.5.

involve myself in synods and councils? Let it suffice for me constantly to weep for my sins, let it be enough for me to demonstrate that I am dead to this world.

(81) Monks, I beg you, do not rush in to the courts of kings under the guise of ecclesiastical concern; do not disturb princes in audience with them, as if you were carefully using the occasion to advise them on their spiritual welfare. Believe one who has experience in these matters, believe one who has grown weary in zealous pursuit of these goals. I have often spoken with his majesty the emperor, telling him what I thought should be said, and at papal invitation I have participated in councils. But one who pursues these matters in our own day, seems to be planting seeds on a sandy beach.

(82) As often as I was present at synods, I observed some among the bishops who had deadly sins on their conscience, not only secure in their own regard, but even boldly prepared to defend the sins of others. These men, as was said, had first bought with Simon,[125] and then afterwards, like Gehazi, had sold the gifts of the Holy Spirit.[126] They were so adept at "making excuses for their sins,"[127] that among other evil deeds they were known to be not only defenders of simoniacal heresy, but even promoters thereof. What monk would presume to mutter a word that was hostile to them? Who would dare claim the freedom to accuse them of crime or to defend justice? At once they would become furious, promptly they would attack and insult us, and after the quarrel had run its course, command us to be silent, telling one another: We came to this council to decide on this matter.

(83) But what novel presumption! We are subject to the decisions of dead men, and they have been made judges of bishops under whose jurisdiction they were legally installed. At one time I replied to them: Venerable fathers and lords, just as it is your special prerogative to judge, so also is it allowed lesser members of the Church to speak their mind in the council, nor does any canonical authority forbid younger men to propose

125. Cf. Acts 8.18–20.   126. Cf. 2 Kgs 5.22–23.
127. Cf. Ps 140.4.

what they think is for the well-being of the Church, so long as the affairs here discussed are terminated by an expression of papal decision. But when this or something similar was humbly proposed to them, it never received a tolerant hearing, but whatever I had to say in the council was totally construed to my disadvantage and was haughtily called a judgment.

(84) I have briefly brought up these matters, so that one without this experience might learn from me how much it behooves him carefully to avoid such affairs. From one who has preceded him, one may learn whether he can trust the unknown waters of some subsequent enterprise. Merchants will promptly stop selling their wares at the announced price if they observe even one person leaving their stall empty-handed, without taking something with them. Should repeated crop failure mock the efforts of the farmer, he will discourage any others from cultivating his sterile field. When he who scours the seas returns home frustrated, worn out from his labor with nothing to show but his empty nets, he easily calls off those already stripped for action from searching this area of unproductive waters. And so, it should suffice that I have tried to do these things, not for me alone but for all my brothers, that when one's effort proves to have been useless, it should serve as a warning, not just to one individual but to many, to stay clear of fruitless labor.

(85) Therefore, any monk who is striving to reach the heights of perfection, should restrict himself to living within the confines of his monastery, should love spiritual leisure, and should be horrified at wandering about in the world as he would at plunging into a pool of blood. The world daily becomes more and more polluted by the contamination of numberless crimes, so that every holy soul is besmirched only by calling it to mind. And while new ways of acting are always added to the old, what else is this but surely preparing for the advent of Antichrist, so that now toward the end of time as he comes into the world, he may freely enter with no impediment in his path? And since his entry is undoubtedly prepared by our sins, for this very reason we must curb our way of life which would assure him that he can freely come into our midst.

(86) Therefore, let every brother now chastise himself in the narrow confines of his cloister, that a home of infinite dimensions may be made ready for him in heaven. For Jeremiah says: "How great, O Israel, is God's dwelling-place, how vast the extent of his domain! Great it is, and boundless, lofty, and immeasurable."[128] One should now restrict himself with the chains of the fear of God, that afterwards he might obtain the freedom of true liberty. Finding one's repose in Christ, he should hold nothing in common with the world, so that, as the apostle John prescribes, he should serve him, not only in spirit but also in the flesh: "Do not set your hearts," he says, "on the world or anything in it. Anyone who loves the world does not have the Father's love in him."[129] The servant of Christ should be renowned for showing no affection for the world, and as a proof thereof, he should even loathe serving the needs of the body. This very denial of the body should confirm the devout soul's aversion for it, so that the more one is removed from harmful acquaintance with the world, the more closely will he be joined in familiar intercourse with God. Let him now weep and mourn as he goes with downcast eyes, so that later he may raise his sight to behold him who is to come on the clouds of heaven with great power and majesty,[130] as it is written: "Stand upright and hold your heads high, because your salvation is at hand."[131]

(87) O, what few words are needed to pronounce and inwardly consider this everlasting sentence, when reprobate souls will weep and tremble as they say: "You mountains, fall on us, and you hills, hide us from the face of the One who sits on the throne,"[132] and when "the sun will be darkened, the moon will not give her light, and the stars will fall from the skies."[133] Then, indeed, every eye shall see him, and among them those who pierced him; and all the peoples of the world shall lament in remorse.[134] What human mind can conceive, and what tongue can express the great joy to be experienced then by the elect,

---

128. This citation is from Bar 3.24–25, and not from Jeremiah.
129. 1 John 2.15.   130. Cf. Matt 24.30.
131. Luke 21.28.   132. Luke 23.30; Rev 6.16.
133. Matt 24.29.   134. Cf. Rev 1.7.

and what unutterable happiness of the blessed when the world
falls to pieces and they no longer must endure such great dangers, and with the coming of the immortal bridegroom they
run joyfully to meet him with lamps aglow.[135] When those devoted to the world are falling into the fires of hell to endure
their punishment, the blessed will rise to receive the reward of
never-ending glory. When undying death suddenly snatches life
from the damned, glorious incorruptibility swallows up the
mortality[136] of the blessed by the power of the resurrection. The
holy soul should ceaselessly hold before its eyes this unique
spectacle that is the wonder of all ages. By profound meditation
it should vividly call to mind this terrifying picture of the judgment that is to come. Even now the chosen one should visualize
himself as he is brought before the judge's tribunal, there in
fear and trembling to consider himself driven under harsh examination to give an account of his life. Let him become a
stranger to the world, that by a more bounteous supply of grace
he may enter into more intimate union with God. And so, in
this way by dying he may live, removing himself from earthly
vexations, and, like one already placed in his grave, sweetly rest
in yearning only for his Creator. And thus, may his life be hidden in God,[137] that when Christ comes, he too may be found
worthy to appear with him in glory. Amen.

(88) Now, therefore, my dear brothers, as one of you follows
the cenobitic way of life, and the other imitates the example of
the eremitic vocation, I recall for you the purpose of this letter,
so that as the beginning was originally meant for you, so too the
conclusion of this little work, now completed, may also come to
an end with you in mind. And so, you have seen how quickly
this short life passes away, and you have noted that this world
gives ever more evident signs that its end is near. For the earth,
having exhausted its generative juices, unwillingly, as it were,
tolerates the plow as it denies a harvest to those who cultivate it,
like the womb of an old woman that has withered away and
grows old while there is still blood in her body, and though
every effort was made at begetting, it still does not suffice for

---

135. Cf. Matt 25.6–7. 136. Cf. 2 Cor 5.4.
137. Cf. Col 3.3–4.

bearing children. In addition, water also becomes sterile, so that now the fisherman refuses to invest in nets, as the profit of a meager catch is not proportionate to the hard work in this liquid element. Nor do I forget you, O air, once so fruitful, but now, as you fail to cooperate with the various tricks and snares designed to catch birds, you send the fowlers, worn out from their fruitless effort, back to tilling the soil. But a short while ago, those whom you caused to look to the heavens in snaring your gifts, now that they might remember to whom they should be grateful for the means of sustaining their life, you subject to living like farmers. And those for whom in your generosity you ordained that all rough fare give way to the delicacies you provided, now by withdrawing your hand you force to hoard leftover vegetables from the tables of the rich, as if they were the choicest food.

(89) Consequently, as was said above, the world, as if weary over a long period of time, now fitly shows in all its members that it has become feeble with age because the end of its course is at hand. To this we may add that men now grow old in their youth, and while still in the spring of their lives become gray before their time. This is to say, that those whose age dictates that they should still flourish with the flower of immature comeliness, the aged world, by some violent use of its authority, commands that along with it those men should appear decrepit. Thus it happens that as fruit on a hollow tree, just as it is produced, falls before it reaches maturity, so also men, by the harsh outcome of events, if I may put it so, die before they have reached the fullness of their years.

(90) Therefore, since the world rushes headlong to its fall, and already gives every sign that the end of its course is imminent, and men too are daily snatched away prematurely by death, what remains to be done but, in this brief moment when we are living, to despise this life that is collapsing about us as if it had already come to an end, and strive with all the fervor of our soul to hasten toward that life which remains forever? Indeed, the reward held out to those who run is not negligible, and the course of our journey daily grows shorter. So, let no obstacle in this present life impede our path, let no sluggishness

brought on by carnal pleasure cause us to delay. Whoever now directs the penetrating eye of his faith to the rewards that have been promised, having broken the bonds of laziness, should transcend on the wings of a powerful hope all the barriers of earthly depravity that stand in the way. For he, indeed, who has called us from afar, reaches out his hand to us as we draw near, and like his dearest sons who are faltering on unsure knees, he strengthens us, inviting us caressingly and sweetly into the embrace of his love.

(91) Let us therefore confidently approach the throne of glory,[138] let us take up the banners of his great love, and what had been a mark of our rashness to seek that which was not promised, should redound to our shame if we refuse something that is offered to us. Let us now disdain to walk frequently in the mire of this filthy world, whose love, at God's inspiration, we have learned to tread gladly under the foot of an unfettered soul. Therefore, all bodily contact should be forbidden to him whom the soul does not love. We should judge him unworthy of our frequent visits, who ardently longs to exult at our downfall. Let our bodily absence also witness the animosity of our mind, nor should he be deemed worthy of repeated discourse with us, whose presence he habitually dishonors. Let him alone fall into the pit of his own designing, as he takes such pains to prepare deceptive traps for our every step. Thus while we peacefully take our rest, let him deplore his frustrated attempt at deceiving us, and cleverly wait for us to leave the house by night.

(92) But let the field of God's word suffice for our wandering. Let us continually proceed through this field, and there take our delight in spending our time. One can there run freely along the equally level plains of sacred history, and by the depth of mystical understanding, one can also, as it were, climb slowly to the heights of the rugged mountains that are found there. There we may enjoy sweet discourse with faithful friends, there we may sit down to the eternal banquet of varied splendor and heavenly delights. Yearning for this banquet, let the

138. Cf. Heb 4.16.

faithful soul derive its strength, nourished by the food of constant reading, and enhance its stature from the rich supply of the purest prayer. Let hunger for the world be left to those who disdain the banquet feast of God. We, however, have learned to yearn for this sumptuous food, which is wont to provide satiety and merriment for the hungry, and still is incapable of causing nausea for those who have had their fill. This food, indeed, sweetly fills the stomach of our soul, and still leaves nothing to evacuate. It allows absolutely nothing of itself to be voided, but spreads itself internally through all the veins and entrails, providing them with strength.

(93) Let the soul, therefore, insatiably occupy itself with being intent on these foods of the heavenly banquet, let the eye be constantly focused on them, let the tongue pronounce the words letter by letter, and the heart understand what is read and reflect on the secrets of their hidden mystery. By the practice of earnest recall, the sacred animals[139] continuously ruminate on this food, which through repeated meditation often flows back from the stomach of knowledge to the throat of memory. May the fasting soul, I say, always hunger for these foods, but once satisfied by them, may it never withdraw, and the more it is filled, the more may it yearn to taste them again. Consequently, let us occupy all our senses in seeking after this life-giving banquet, so that in becoming insensible to all worldly affairs, as truly dead to the world we may live for God alone. Accordingly, may the author and provider of this joyous food see fit to enroll us among his guests who were worthy to hear these words from the mouth of Truth itself: "And now I vest in you the kingship which my Father vested in me; you shall eat and drink at my table in my kingdom."[140]

My dear brothers, may almighty God, who is love,[141] graciously inspire your holy soul, that in your kindness you may always pray for me, a sinner. Blessed be the name of the Lord.

---

139. Cf. Rev 4.6–7.   140. Luke 22.29.
141. Cf. 1 John 4.8.

LETTER 166

Peter Damian to the monk Stephen. He recommends to his correspondent the daily recitation of the office of the Blessed Virgin and the constant reading of sacred Scripture. As was his wont, Damian reinforces his advice with *exempla*, furnished in this letter by his nephew Damianus.

(1069–1072)

O SIR STEPHEN the monk, the monk Peter the sinner sends greetings in the Lord.

(2) As you vigilantly school yourself in studying the psalms and in giving praise to God, I exhort you, venerable brother, and recommend that you also not omit the daily office of the blessed Mary ever virgin. It is surely proper that she, who is worthy to receive honor and praise from the angels, should also be frequently acclaimed by human beings, and that after God the whole world should extol her through whom it received the Author of its salvation. With supreme hope, indeed, we take refuge in her who, among all the senators of the heavenly court, received the place of honor in interceding with God.

(3) In this connection, my sister's boy, Damianus, a young man devoted to the religious life, was present as I was writing this letter, and recounted for me this well known tale that he had heard while studying in Gaul.[1] A certain cleric of the diocese of Nevers grew ill, and as the sickness now became more severe, he was at the point of death. As was his custom, he devoted himself to observing the holy practice of daily praying the

---

1. Cf. Peter Damian, *Letter* 125 (FOTC, MC 6.26), in which he refers to his nephew's education, possibly in the monastery of Adraldus of Bremen. See also his *Letter* 158, where he reprimands young Damianus for extending his stay outside the hermitage of Fonte Avellana.

various hours in honor of the blessed Mother of God. When it became clear to everyone that there was no longer any hope that he would live, and as his breath seemed to grow shorter as if it were anxious to leave the breast, suddenly the glorious Mother of the Lord appeared to him, and, pressing milk from her sacred breast, poured it, drop by drop, onto his lips. And what power there was in this divine remedy! At once his strength returned, his sickness left him, and quickly putting on his clerical vestments, he went to the church and joyfully took his place among his chanting brothers, and provided a marvelous spectacle for those who saw him. It was also said that even then some vestige of the milk could be seen on his lips. But what words the Blessed Virgin spoke to him, even though in passing they were told me, because I am not certain, I will not report them, since I am afraid to deviate, even slightly, from the truth. Nevertheless, one can conjecture from this that the glorious Virgin instilled the healing milk onto the very lips with which he had praised and honored her, so that by this member of the body by which the venerable cleric had exalted and glorified her, in a fitting exchange he should receive the medicine that restored his health.

(4) Furthermore, I also consider it necessary to suggest to your holy prudence that you constantly take the sacred Scriptures in hand and page through their folios. Be totally absorbed in them, spend your time with them, and always find your peace in them. Nor should you take pleasure in engaging in conversation with secular men, which frequently repels and disturbs the vision of the mind that seeks after God. Let your mind be occupied with these divine volumes, and, intent on them, always persevere with watchful concentration. When the ancient deceiver sees you thus engaged, he flees from you as from an armed enemy, and fears to attack when he finds you armed with these weapons and, so to speak, with an impenetrable cuirass.

(5) This same nephew of mine, whom I mentioned above, told me the following story which he had learned from reliable witnesses. There was a certain Norman who had with him a large number of gold coins, and with them planned to return

to the land of his birth. Because of crime he began to fear for his life, lest, in fact, if he traveled while carrying all this treasure, he should suffer an attack by Isaurian brigands.[2] And on a Saturday afternoon, as he carefully considered the alternatives, deliberating whether he should go or not go, and evening was approaching, suddenly the ancient enemy appeared, dressed as a traveler. Upon inquiry he learned what [the visitor] wanted, and made a bargain with his future traveling companion, promising to give him ten Byzantine gold coins, and thus committed himself to accepting him as his guide on the journey and the source of doubtful security.

(6) "Since night is approaching," his companion said, "after you have got your baggage together, take your rest and wait for me to return to you, as I will surely do, so that when I come back in the silence of the night and find you here, we may both set out on our way." The man believed what was said to him, and, surrendering to sleep as he had been advised, waited for his companion. That same night the crafty spirit came to him as he had promised, and said to him: "See, I have brought you back to your native land without any effort on your part, and without your even being aware of it. What I promised you, I quickly fulfilled." And when the man found himself on the banks of a certain river with which he had long been familiar, and suddenly and unexpectedly saw and recognized certain landmarks that were nearby, such as his former home, he shook with fright, and knew without a doubt that it was an evil spirit who had so quickly transported him there from a distant land.

(7) And then the fallaciously truthful spirit, or, I might say, the truthfully fallacious spirit, said to him: "See to it without fail that you return to me here next Thursday and pay me the debt you owe me." At that, the man promptly went to see a certain priest, told him in detail what had happened to him, and anxiously asked him what he should do about the debt he owed. Then the priest sprinkled him with holy water, fortified him

2. Because even the edited text of this letter leaves much to be desired, I have taken the conjectural reading *direptionis* in PL 144.420 D, instead of *directionis* found in the MSS. Damian's reference here seems to indicate the Isauri, a marauding tribe conquered by P. Servilius Vatia in 76–75 B.C.E.

with texts from Holy Writ and relics of the saints, told him to return to the appointed place, and commanded him not just to give the agreed sum of money to his wicked creditor, but to throw it into his face.

(8) And when they both came together at the place they had agreed upon, the man threw the gold coins into the air, and said: "Here, take your money." The devil stood some distance from him, and, afraid to come any closer, began to accuse him and severely complain at his behavior, saying to him: "Why are you coming at me fully armed, equipped with spears and swords as if you are preparing for battle? Why do you not trust me? Now I do not dare come closer to you, and, deprived of my reward, I am leaving." And suddenly he produced a whirlwind that darkened the air about me,[3] and with a great and furious thrust he vanished from the gaze of the trembling onlooker. At once he gathered up the gold coins from the ground where he had thrown them, and, returning to the priest, tried to inquire what he should do with them. But the priest strongly reprimanded him for having collected the coins, yet he advised him to use them to build a bridge that was greatly needed in that area and would truly benefit those who traveled across the river. Taking him at his word, the man humbly obeyed, and built the bridge as he had been commanded.

(9) But whatever he and the stone-cutters and masons put up with great effort, the devil violently tore down during the silence of the night. Three and four times, as was reported, the man tried to erect the bridge, but whatever he had laboriously constructed on a given day, was found destroyed the next morning through the nocturnal wiles of the devil.

(10) But passing over other similar *exempla*, if he who carried these sacred texts of Scripture and the relics of the saints appeared fully armed and formidable in the eyes of our ancient enemy, making it impossible to approach or get close to him, how careful must we be to gird ourselves with the weapons of God's word, and thus be able to triumph in our uncompromising struggle with the evil spirit, as the apostle exhorts us when

3. The Latin text reads, "about me," when more correctly it should read, "about him."

he says: "Take up the shield of faith, with which you will be able to quench all the flaming arrows of the evil one. Put on the helmet of salvation, and take up the sword of the Spirit, which is the Word of God."[4] Therefore, always wear this sword, my dear friend, by which the crafty one who tries to ambush you may be mortally wounded, that Christ may live in you victorious as in the most secure fortress among all his strongholds.

4. Eph 6.16–17.

LETTER 167

Peter Damian to Pope Alexander II. This short but highly auto-
biographical letter laments an injury done him by the pope, and
that despite his many services for him and for the Holy See. He
trusts that his complaint by private letter will be effective, or else
he will be compelled to notify others of the situation. He begs
assistance for the church of Gubbio under his charge, and absolution for the archbishop of Ravenna, under excommunication,
to ease the burden borne by the innocent people under his jurisdiction. The bearer of his letter carries other instructions not
committed to writing.

(About 1069)

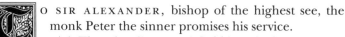 O SIR ALEXANDER, bishop of the highest see, the
monk Peter the sinner promises his service.

(2) That the diocese of Gubbio, which some time
ago was committed to my care by your predecessors, is now, sad
to say, in total confusion, and is like an abandoned field trodden underfoot, this I consider to have been brought about by
my sins and, which God forbid, I do not ascribe to any fault or
shortcoming on your part. Indeed, my many sins demand that
you should cut me to the quick, even with your own hands, you,
in fact, for whom I stood up bravely and fought against the
whole world, and, as a hardened and invincible adversary, exposed myself to the swords and arrows of almost the entire human race. Is this the reason, venerable father, why you rewarded me, that so often I found myself pleading your cause in the
councils of holy bishops; that in taking charge of your affairs as
your legate, I frequently spoke like a veritable advocate in the
assemblies of secular clergy and laymen? Is this, in fact, why
honors came my way, because I violently inveighed against your
enemies, overwhelmed them with my biting words, both in my

speeches and in my writings, praised you in the many tracts I wrote, and, to the best of my ability, promoted your memory with exalted praise, even among those who would come after us?

(3) Therefore, whatever I may have done, whatever I may have endured should be investigated with close scrutiny on your part, lest, urged on by a just complaint, I be compelled to make public what I have until now suppressed in silence, but which I can scarcely hide any longer. Rome does not yet know about this from anything I have said or written, nor has this matter, which could throw aspersions on Your Holiness's good name, yet come to the attention of others through me. Therefore, as is only proper, let him who has offended do penance, so that he who was harmed not be forced to heighten his just complaint. Let soothing oil soften the sharpness of biting vinegar, and let the mild and caressing flow of kindness be gently infused into the swollen stripes caused by severe lashes. Otherwise it will be necessary for him who has already borne so many blows, that he too. . . .[1] But, no, by restraining my bold tongue, I will put a curb on my freedom, place my finger to my lips, and, having suffered through this miserable episode, will in turn earnestly request mercy.

(4) Moreover, I beg indulgence of Your Holiness for the unhappy bishop of Ravenna, and humbly beseech you to absolve him, as you decided to do on a previous occasion. It is certainly improper that such a vast number of people perish because of the offense of one little man, and that the guilt of one miserable person should subvert the great endeavor of Christ, for which he shed his precious blood, and destroy the souls of so many innocent people.

(5) I do not, however, wish to overburden the eyes of Your Holiness with my many words, so all that needs be said, I have placed in the experienced hands of the bearer of this message. Therefore, let your holy and merciful disposition carefully listen to him as if I were there speaking to you, and so approve

---

1. Here Damian uses the rhetorical device of *aposiopesis*, i.e., breaking off in the middle of a sentence.

the two requests that I have cursorily and quickly here presented, so that I may not regret sending horses and messengers
over so many miles, and so that my spirit, which in your regard,
I will not say, became tepid, but rather began to grow cold, may
be rekindled in its desire for your former friendship.

LETTER 168

Peter Damian to Alfanus, the archbishop of Salerno.[1] Since his correspondent enjoys hearing of the spiritual progress others are making, he tells of the canons of Velletri, who formerly appeared incorrigible, but are now models of the common life. He then speaks of the marvels that occurred in the lives of men with whom he was acquainted, all serving the edification of Alfanus.

(After 1069)

ECAUSE I AM aware of your holy disposition, venerable father, especially that you rejoice when men are saved, so that when you happen to hear about souls that are making spiritual progress, it is as if you were partaking of the fine foods of an excellent repast.

(2) I call to your attention our canons, that is, those of the holy church of Velletri, who seemed to be incorrigible despite my frequent attempts and great effort, but who now by God's grace have come to their senses and follow the practices of the canonical life, not under pressure, but with a sense of joy. During the Lenten season, moreover, each of them daily recites an entire psalter; three days a week all of them in common abstain from wine and stew, and seem to be so fervent in observing the penitential life, that during the entire Lent that precedes Easter and that which we customarily celebrate before the nativity of our Lord Jesus Christ, each one of them on three days a week undresses himself before the brethren gathered in chapter, and after confessing his sins, allows himself to be scourged with a stout leather lash. And from this evidence of their holy

---

1. This letter has no salutation. But since in MS Cassino 359, p. 169, it follows directly after *Letter* 59, and in a later hand bears the conjectural *Ad eumdem* (to the same), it appears to have been sent to the same Alfanus. For *Letter* 59 see FOTC, MC 2.394–403.

zeal, you can clearly understand what you must conclude regarding the rest of their lifestyle and observances. Oh, how salutary is the use of the discipline, the mortification of the flesh, in which, when the body is laid bare in the sight of men, it appears to be garbed in sparkling attire before the eyes of God. Moreover, it has been scarcely a month since the following happened, to which I now refer.

(3) There was a brother, clearly of like mind with me, named Baruncius, a man outstanding for the sweetness of his charity, not a hermit, but living in a certain village subject to our hermitage. One day, as he was engaged in some necessary task, he became seriously ill. Upon learning that his death was imminent, he begged the brothers who were diligently taking care of him, to enjoin a penance for him to undertake. When they concluded that three, or at the most, four psalms were sufficient for such a holy and innocent man, he begged them to impose on him ten years of penance, which they should at once delegate to the brothers who lived in the hermitage, and who should carry it out as soon as possible. And so, on the following night as all of the brothers in their cells had taken off their habits after cockcrow and were taking the discipline, hastening to perform the penance before the man died, Baruncius said to brother Lambert, who was attentive at his bedside: "Why do you not get ready and put on your church vestments like the other brothers? For all the brothers of the hermitage are at this very moment standing around me where I can see them, and they are wearing splendid stoles and albs, and like monks chanting in choir are conspicuous for the brilliance of their shining vestments." Therefore, he urged him to dress according to their example. Here we should note that while the brothers who had taken off their clothes to apply the discipline were seen by him at a great distance, it seemed to him, not with bodily eyes, it would appear, but with those of the spirit, that they were garbed in beautiful garments. Likewise, he who told me of this event, the venerable brother Liuprandus, also brought to my attention another event, which will not fail to promote edification for those who hear of it.

(4) "At the beginning of this Lenten season," he said, "that

which by ecclesiastical custom precedes the Nativity of the Lord, such an attack of weakness suddenly overcame me, that I could scarcely keep my balance nor could I carry out my daily duties. And when a flood of dark and confused thoughts overwhelmed me, causing me to despair utterly of trying to fast, and I decided from then on to relax somewhat in my daily consumption of food, suddenly I fell into a light sleep, and began to nod over the book I was trying to read. Then I saw that my entire cell was filled with smoke, and, what was more, there were many people present, speaking to one another in loud voices. Just then our holy brother Juvencius, who is leading an admirable life in the same hermitage, rushed into my cell, and with threats of severe punishment, broke up the crowd, promptly pushing them out and violently forcing them to leave. 'Is it not the inviolable rule of this hermitage,' he asked, 'that no one would dare to converse in his cell, but should impose silence on all those who enter?' And then seizing a towel, he cleared the cell, driving away all the smoke and foul odors with which the room had been filled. When this happened, I was at once aroused from my sleep and awoke, and, not without experiencing heartfelt joy, was aware that my mind had been freed from all its darkness and smoky thoughts. With that, in fact, all wearisome temptation and weakness left me, and I discovered that I was possessed of such vigor and strength, that throughout that entire fast, which lasted until Christmas, I was hardly ever hungry at all, and, unless I am mistaken, there was never a day on which I partook of any food except bread and water."

(5) If only this had happened to Albuinus, the bishop of the diocese of Paris. After he had been fasting for seven months, if I remember correctly, and after two further days of fast were completed and it was now a Saturday, an especially fine wild [boar] that had been taken in the hunt was prepared for dinner. All at once a lethal appetite got the better of him; he decided to transfer the fast to some other week, and promptly ordered the cooks to roast the pork in elegant fashion. And so on that day this miserable man satisfied his gluttony to the hilt; on the next Saturday he died. And this he richly deserved, for in

the desert, as it were, he turned the sanctuary of the church into graves of greed.[2] But why should we marvel if on this occasion, where sin was so obvious, punishment was so justly applied, when frequently we see some wonderful thing happening, and do not understand the mystery of divine disposition, because the cause is not evident?

(6) And then there was Leo, formerly the bishop of Pozzuoli, but now a noble hermit, who recently told me and the brothers that when a certain man possessed by the devil was in the monastery that had been built in Parthenope[3] in honor of the blessed confessor Agnellus, he suddenly attacked a man standing nearby, struck him in his mad fury, and killed him. But who is able to penetrate the depths of God's justice! For soon after the madman had killed this innocent person, he was at once freed of the devil, restored to his former sanity, and never again suffered any attack of this disease. But when asked why he had committed this crime, he answered: "I did not see a man, but a black dog that was trying to bite me, and this, it seemed to me, is what I killed." Consequently, the cause of this event in the providence of God is not obvious, why, in fact, the former deserved to be suddenly cut down, or why the latter was found worthy of liberation from the devil. According to human estimation it seemed that the former was innocent when he was killed, but that the latter, to all outward appearance, should have been punished. But why should we marvel if the merits of others are not seen by us, since often the things that we ourselves do are unknown to us because of forgetfulness?

(7) The event I now relate happened a few years ago in Rome, as I learned from a devout priest named John, who informed me of it. It was the feast of the Assumption of Mary, the blessed Mother of God, when the Roman people customarily participate in prayers and litanies during the night, and with lighted torches visit churches in various parts of the city. On that occasion in the basilica that was built on the Capitoline Hill in honor of the Blessed Virgin, a certain woman saw her

2. Cf. Num 11.34.
3. A classical place name applied to Naples.

godmother, who had died about a year before. And when, because of the crowd that was milling about, she was unable to get close enough to speak to her, she tried to wait for her at the corner of a certain street, so narrow that, as she left the church, the old woman would surely be unable to get past her. And so the woman promptly asked her as she passed: "Are you not," she said, "my godmother Marozia who recently passed away?" That was her name when she was alive. She replied: "That is who I am." "And how," [the godchild] asked, "is everything with you?" She said: "Until today I was subjected to severe punishment because years ago when I was young, I defiled myself wantonly with other girls my age. But sad to say, I somehow forgot about this when I went to confession to a priest but did not confess it. But today the Queen of the World interceded for us, and freed me with many others from the place where we were being punished, and such a great number of people were rescued today from their torments through her intercession, that they exceed the entire population of Rome. Therefore, we are visiting the churches dedicated to our glorious Lady, and are joyfully giving thanks to her for her many merciful blessings." When with that her godmother was undecided whether the woman readily believed what she had said, she continued: "That you may know for sure that what I say is true, be warned that after a year has passed, on this very feast day, you will certainly die. But if you should live longer, which cannot happen, you will obviously prove that I was lying." And after saying this, she disappeared before her eyes. With that the woman put on sackcloth, and, paying heed to what she had heard about her death, began to live more circumspectly. What more need I say? After almost a year had passed, on the vigil of the Assumption she took sick, and passed away on that very feast day, just as it had been told her. Here we should note, and not without great fear, that for the sins she had committed, but had forgotten, this woman had to suffer punishment until the virgin Mother of God intervened.

(8) In the same vein, Rainaldus, the bishop of Como, told me this story, which, he said, he had learned from the venera-

ble Humbert, the former bishop of Santa Rufina.[4] "In the silence of night," he said, "while a certain priest was sleeping, his
godfather, who had died, appeared to him in a dream, and
called out to him: 'Come and see this marvel, which you will
not consider a waste of time.' He led him to the basilica of
blessed Cecilia, where in the atrium were seen Agnes, Agatha,
and Cecilia herself, and a choir of many blessed virgins, all ele-
gantly garbed in luminous gowns. They were all busy preparing
a magnificent throne that stood higher than the surrounding
seats, when suddenly the Blessed Virgin Mary with Peter and
Paul and David, together with a large, radiant array of martyrs
and various other saints, made her appearance. Mary then took
her seat on the throne that had been erected for her. Moreover, as silence was observed in this holy gathering and as all
reverently stood about the throne, a certain woman who, despite her poverty, was decently dressed in a fur coat, fell at the
feet of the inviolate virgin and begged her to have mercy on the
patrician John, who was now dead. And when she repeated her
petition for the third time, and yet could not elicit any response, she added: 'My Lady and Queen of the World,' she
said, 'you should know that I am the same poor woman who
was accustomed to lie naked and trembling in the atrium of
your major basilica. But as soon as that man noticed me, he felt
sorry for me, and put this fur coat, which he had been wearing,
around my shoulders.'

(9) "Then the blessed Mother of God said to her: 'The man
for whom you are interceding is weighed down by a great burden of sins. But there are two things in his favor: first, that he
had a great concern for the poor, and, secondly, that with great
humility he was devoted to churches. Frequently he carried oil
on his own shoulders and provided fuel for the lamps in my
church.' And when the other saints testified in favor of this
same patrician, and together declared that he had done the
same for their churches, the Queen of the World at once gave

4. This reference is to Cardinal Humbert (+1061), the cardinal bishop of
Silva Candida or Santa Rufina. Cf. Lucchesi, *Vita* 1, 103.

orders that this patrician be brought before them. Suddenly a crowd of devils dragged in the aforesaid John, bound with penal shackles, and terribly wasted by the filth of the chains that were about him. Then Our Lady commanded that he be set free to take his place among the assembly of the saints. But she directed that the chains from which he had been released should be used to fetter another man who was still alive. Then the assembly of the saints broke up, and each of them went his own way and disappeared from the woman's view.

(10) "The blessed apostle Peter, however, went to his church, where he then met with all his successors, the Roman pontiffs, a choir attired in the festal vestments of their office. Consequently, blessed Peter, since he still appeared to be dressed in Hebrew garments, as he is everywhere depicted in paintings, then received the Phrygian cap[5] on his head, and like the others was vested in priestly attire. With that completed, in melodious song they began to chant the anthem that reads: "You are the pastor of the sheep," and with that led him to his place among the priestly choir. Upon arriving there, the prince of the apostles himself began the nocturnal office with the words: "Open my lips, O Lord."[6] In liturgical fashion he then chanted three psalms and a similar number of lessons and responses, assigned for the feast days of the apostles, and so when matins and lauds were finished, all carried out according to proper form, the bells of the church were rung, and at that the priest who had seen all this awoke, and his dream was ended.

(11) Moreover, the same bishop I mentioned above told me that as a certain monk daily passed in front of the holy altar of the blessed Mary ever virgin, he used to recite the customary antiphon, which begins: "Rejoice, O immaculate virgin Mother of God," and after each verse, repeated the greeting: "Rejoice." And so, one day while reciting this antiphon as he passed by, he heard a voice coming from the altar, that said: "You have wished me joy, may joy also be yours."

(12) Now that same bishop reported to me that a certain

5. The traditional papal headdress, which later became the tiara.
6. Ps 50.16, used in the breviary as the opening verse of the night office.

brother used to delight in reciting the office of the dead, not daily, nor certainly on a feast day of the saints, but when he was alone. After he had paid his debt to the human condition and stood before the tribunal of the heavenly judge, a swarm of devils violently began to accuse him of the crime of neglecting the rule established by the Church by showing his contempt for praying to God according to the usual ritual of the divine office. Then the Queen of the World, the ever blessed virgin Mary, backed by the company of all the choirs of saints, with one accord came to his assistance. "This man," they said, "was our chaplain and priest, in that he so often readily took part in the office of the dead and undoubtedly was at the service of us all. Therefore, God forbid that he should fall into the hands of these wicked ones, since when he was alive he strove so generously to help us." And so, at the prayer of the blessed Virgin and the petition of all the saints he was deemed worthy of joining their company. But the bishop who recounted this event was unaware of whether this brother had come back to us, or had told of these events to others who were still alive.

(13) I have written these things to you as a friend, venerable brother, since I take delight, whatever the occasion, in speaking with you, as if I were partaking of an elegant repast, and my heart always rejoices and ardently longs for the opportunity of writing something that is pleasing to you.

LETTER 169

Peter Damian to the monk John. The latter had upbraided him for wishing to relinquish his episcopal office. Damian defends his position, stating that as a bishop he had been so preoccupied with secular affairs that the interior light of contemplation had grown dim, and that he wished to return to his beloved solitude. He cites several *exempla* to reinforce his argument. The conclusion of this letter is lacking in the manuscripts.

(ca. 1070)

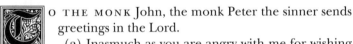 O THE MONK John, the monk Peter the sinner sends greetings in the Lord.

(2) Inasmuch as you are angry with me for wishing to relinquish my episcopal office, and advise me to look to the service I can render, with your leave I will say that you are not viewing the matter with the eyes of the spirit. Because I am surrounded by the darkness of so many secular interests, I am unable to see the brightness of the interior light, and cannot lift my confused and insensible mind to the contemplation of spiritual truths.

(3) About seven years ago, the abbot of the monastery dedicated to St. Peter on the outskirts of Perugia, resigned from the office committed to him, and turned over his duties to a superior provided by the authority of the Apostolic See. Judge Rainerius, an outstanding man, known for his persuasive eloquence, recently spoke to me about this matter which I now relate. "After this abbot," he said, "had given up the administration of the office he had abandoned, he daily celebrated two masses. My father," he noted, "who was already an old man whom the abbot had formerly invested as a monk, constantly served for him as he celebrated the liturgy. And so one day, after the abbot had read the gospel and was about to offer the heavenly sacrifice,

my father saw a lamb standing beside the altar. When of a sudden he was about to take hold of the lamb and remove it, he was seized by a fit of trembling, and did not dare reach out for it. And as they came to that part of the Mass when the Body of Christ was to be broken, he saw the lamb on the table of the altar, and while he gazed at it again with fixed attention, it promptly disappeared. When the venerable abbot became aware from my father's remarks that he had seen what had happened, he ordered him to keep the matter secret, and solemnly forbade him to tell anyone about it so long as the abbot was alive. Shortly afterwards, after completing a life dedicated to the pursuit of holiness, the abbot died, and only a few days later he who had seen the vision also ended his days and went to the Lord."

(4) To what else should this story inspire me, if not to abandon all interest in ecclesiastical office and to devote myself with total freedom of spirit to solitary contemplation? Yet, as this account was being related to me, at almost the same time I heard another story that, in my opinion, is also worthy of remembrance. Even though it does not refer directly to the matter at hand, it does not lack the element of giving praise to God, who is served by everything that I write.

(5) Richard, who at that time was the abbot of the monastery at Camporeggiano, told this story that he had heard from the incontestable accounts of several people. A certain man from the region of Lombardy, together with his wife, was on his way to visit the shrines of the blessed apostles. And when the traveler came to Lake Bolsena, he boarded a fisherman's boat to buy some fish. After returning to the shore, he discovered that he had lost his purse in which he had twenty-four shillings in the coin of Pavia. And when his wife bitterly complained at their cheap, coarse meal, and hounded him over his great loss, the good-hearted man calmly put up with this and tried to soften the blow his wife had suffered with comforting words. "We still have six pounds in the pennies of Lucca," he said, "and by spending only this sum we can have a decent trip. For the merciful God will bless us and compensate for our loss." Upon returning from their pilgrimage, it happened that

as the aforementioned man was renting lodging near the same lake, he was in good spirits, and said to his companions: "My brothers, since this lake did us great harm, it is only proper that with the help of God it should serve us an elegant meal on our way home." And turning to the bystanders, he said: "Who will sell me a fish for twelve pence?" A fisherman who was standing nearby at once spoke up: "I, indeed, have a very fine fish for sale, but if you want me to sell it to you, you will definitely have to pay me fifteen pence." Without the slightest hesitation he paid the man his money, and told his wife to prepare an excellent meal with the fish he had bought. When his wife was gutting the fish, she found his moneybag with twenty-four shillings in the coin of Pavia in the fish's intestine. At that, all who were present gave thanks together, and readily declared that whenever future ill fortune struck them, they would always place their hope in God. . . .

LETTER 170

Peter Damian to Judge Moricus. He advises the judge, as a safe-guard against perjury, to avoid frequent swearing, which was the practice among people of his region. It is far better to avoid swearing an oath altogether. He then exhorts the judge to practice almsgiving in support of the poor. As was his custom, Damian reinforces both sets of advice with striking *exempla*.

(1070)

O THE MOST prudent judge, sir Moricus, the monk Peter the sinner sends greetings in the Lord.

(2) Since, my dear friend, I am aware of your weakness, and that inwardly you are suffering from a nervous condition, I will forego presenting you with many precepts from Holy Scripture, and, satisfied with a light bundle, will not burden your shoulders with a heavy load. And so that my abbreviated remarks may comply with the topic itself, I shall confine them to the few things that I advise, so that while fearing to weary you with weighty matters, let me also be solicitous of your feeble condition by keeping my remarks to the minimum. I therefore exhort you, my dear friend, and reverently call to your attention, that in your charity you refrain from swearing an oath, a practice that people of your region sacrilegiously indulge in, and that you not overlook ministering to the needs of the poor in so far as your means allow. And so, from the first of these I protect you, as if I were saving you from being swallowed up by a yawning abyss, and toward the other I urge you on, as toward a mighty stronghold offering life-giving defense. For as Tobias says: "Almsgiving frees a man from every sin and from death and keeps him from going down into darkness."[1]

(3) But first of all let me say a few words about oath-taking.

1. Tob 4.11.

As I mentioned above, whoever violates his oath by forswearing himself, severs himself from the body of Christ as if he were actually cut away, and deprives himself of the sacraments of man's redemption. For when one takes an oath and according to the usual formula says, "This I will do, or surely not do, so help me God and this holy book of the Gospels," he makes an agreement with God on the condition that, if he does not fulfill what he has promised, he will never again be helped by God or by the holy Gospel. And just as at the time when he was initiated into Christ, and at the official catechizing of the priest renounced the devil and all his works, so like a deserter and a traitor he renounces God and his Gospel, thereby refusing to place his trust in him for the future, as if by some new agreement. And just as Laban built a cairn of stones between himself and Jacob,[2] and thus blocked one another by preventing their passage way, so by lying does he, as it were, place his false oath between himself and God.

(4) Moreover, he causes the book of the Gospels to be sealed against him, so that he is unable to open it as he blocks every approach to salvation that lies between it and himself. Of this book it is said in Isaiah: "All prophetic vision will become for you like the words in a sealed book that people will give to one who can read, and say: 'Come read this'; he will answer, 'I cannot,' because it is sealed."[3] What is this sealed book if not the holy Gospel, wrapped in symbolic statements and figures, and by a certain profound secret far removed from human understanding? This is truly the book of which John says: "Then I saw in the right hand of the One who sat on the throne a book, with writing inside and out, and it was sealed up with seven seals."[4] And what are the seals with which the book of the Gospels is said to be sealed up, but the seven mysteries by which, to be sure, the whole range of the Lord's providence is fulfilled, namely, the Lord's Incarnation, his Nativity, Passion, Resurrection, Ascension into heaven, followed by the Judgment and lastly his Kingdom? And so, with these seals the book of the Gospels is sealed up in such a way that unless Christ had

2. Cf. Gen 31.44–47.   3. Isa 29.11.
4. Rev 5.1.

opened it, no one would be able to have access to it. And thus the text cited above continues: "For the Lion from the tribe of Judah, the Scion of David, has won the right to open the book and break its seven seals."[5]

(5) Therefore, whoever takes a false oath should carefully consider that unless he repents and does satisfaction according to the canons, he so closes for himself the seven seals of the Gospel text, that neither the Lord's Incarnation and Nativity, nor his Passion, Resurrection, or Ascension, nor the Judgment or the Kingdom will ever be able to benefit him. All of these he totally rejects, and so far as he is concerned reduces them to nothing, for in violating his oath he renounces the assistance of the Gospel, and thereby also the help of God.

(6) And so, I do not think it out of place if I add here what Richard,[6] the prior of our monastery, a man of sterling virtue, told me only yesterday. "A man," he said, "from the territory of Perugia, who had come to the end of his days, willed his estate to his two sons and to the same number of daughters in a six-fold proportion, so that of the divided inheritance he left two thirds to the males, while the females received one third. After the man's death one of his sons also died, but the surviving brother, as if it were not enough that he did not divide his deceased brother's property with his sisters, made a claim to their portion by bringing a false charge against them. For the more one's possessions increase, so much greater is the cupidity of the owner. And then what happened? The case was brought to court, witnesses for the various parties came forward, the lawyers presented their arguments, the complaint was filed, the charge was heard, and legal claim was withdrawn by the opponents. At length, the parties met for further deliberation before the bench, allowing a certain priest, who favored the case of the man against his sisters, to claim that he was present when the dead man made his will. He took his oath, and so the case was solved, and on the testimony of one man the controversy was laid to rest.

5. Rev 5.5.
6. The prior of the monastery of St. Bartholomew in Camporeggiano; cf. Lucchesi, *Vita* 1, no. 28; 2, pp. 155–56 at *Epist.* 7, 17.

(7) But when the priest came forward to testify under oath for the man against the women, and had already placed his hand on the book that was set before him, suddenly a horrible serpent fell from the tree which overshadowed them, and, entwining itself about the book, encompassed it with the coils of its scaly body. All were thunderstruck, astonished by this obvious portent, and the priest especially became rigid with fear and abjured the oath that he had taken, not to serve the truth but merely to win human favor. And thus the ancient enemy who had spewed the poison of his ill will into the heart of the priest, causing him to swear falsely, visibly proved that he was present when this oath was taken, using the figure of the beast that is associated with him. The women's uncle, moreover, who knew about the affair, but to please their brother had suppressed the truth, upon leaving the court fell into a pit together with the horse on which he rode, and the animal, pinning him down, caused such serious damage to his whole body that he was almost at death's door. Thus divine providence clearly showed that anyone who is unwilling to stand up for the truth with constancy of spirit, will also deservedly suffer a bodily fall.

(8) Therefore, my dear friend, do not suppress the truth, but with all your strength defend it in every undertaking and dispute. Whoever resists the truth to gain human favor is indeed guilty of denying Christ, who is Truth itself.[7] Guard against false oaths, and if possible even restrain yourself from taking any oath. For just as one who has nothing to say, never lies, so for one who does not swear, it is impossible to commit the crime of perjury. For it is Truth itself who says: "Plain 'Yes' or 'No' is all you need to say; anything beyond that comes from evil."[8] And so, avoid perjury lest you be compelled to find the book of man's redemption closed against you.

(9) Nor should you forget what I said before: rescue your soul by almsgiving, and be constant in performing works of mercy. For the Lord says: "Give alms, and all is clean for you."[9] And again it is written: "He who is generous to the poor lends to God."[10] Therefore, support the poor, so that you yourself be-

---

7. Cf. 1 John 5.6.
8. Matt 5.37.
9. Luke 11.41.
10. Prov 19.17.

come the creditor and make God your debtor. Nor does almighty God prompt you to give alms, as if he were unable to provide food for his poor. But he rather shows you people who are in need, that he might set before you the means of your redemption. In fact, it is written: "A man's wealth is his ransom."[11]

(10) Again, the same Richard, our venerable brother who told the story recounted above, faithfully reported what I am about to say, just as he heard it. "Eight poor men," he said, "were recently on a pilgrimage to Jerusalem, and, since they had nothing at all to eat, spent a whole week without taking any food. While they wasted away from this protracted fast, they grew so weak and worn out from the difficulty of the long journey that they almost fainted. As they staggered about on faltering feet that could scarcely support them, suddenly a dog appeared with a cloth in its teeth in which bread was wrapped as in a sack. At once seizing upon the bread and giving thanks, they quickly devoured it, and, sustained by this food, they finished a trip of eight days, never stopping on the way.[12]

(11) Some time later when they were again suffering from almost intolerable hunger, three Saracens joined them as companions on their journey, each carrying a loaf of bread for his own meal. When it came time to eat, they sat down. Two of them ate their own ration without sharing a single piece with the hungry Christians. But the third Saracen broke one of the loaves that he carried into nine portions, and, keeping only one piece for himself, gave an equal share to each of the Christians who were with him.

(12) Later on as they were traveling together, they were attacked by ferocious lions that specifically pounced on just those who had eaten their bread without sharing it. At once they violently tore them to pieces, and, paying no attention at all to the others, voraciously devoured only these two men. Thus it happened that they who had eaten alone, were alone eaten, and those who without practicing charity had consumed their food like animals, were devoured by these wild beasts. Later, as they were walking along the seashore that was strewn with gravel,

11. Prov 13.8.
12. Cf. 1 Kgs 19.8.

they found a fish of enormous size, which they promptly hid in the sand because they saw horsemen rapidly approaching them. When these men came upon the scene and saw the gravel recently heaped together to form a mound, they wondered what it was, thinking that it was someone's secret burial place that presented quite a mystery. And so, their curiosity led them to open the mound, and at length in divine providence they saw that a dead man was buried there. And thus, abandoning what they had undertaken, they departed, while the pilgrims completed the digging and promptly turned this blessing of God's goodness into food for their journey. . . .[13]

13. The letter ends abruptly since it is incomplete in the MSS.

LETTER 171

Peter Damian to a sick man at the point of death. There is some
question whether this small piece is actually a letter or a liturgical *Commendatio animae*. The text is almost identical, with some
additions and subtractions, with the *Commendo te,* used as a
prayer for the dying since the eleventh century in the Roman
Ritual.[1]

(Not datable)

 COMMEND YOU,[2] dear brother, to almighty God,
and I entrust you to him who created you, so that,
when by your dying you have paid the debt to which
every man is subject, you may return to your Maker, who
formed you from the clay of the earth.[3] Then, when your soul
goes forth from your body, may the radiant company of angels
come to meet you, and may your judge, the senate of the apostles, release you.[4] May the victorious army of white-robed martyrs greet you, may the glittering throng of confessors, bright as
lilies, gather about you. May the jubilant choir of virgins receive
you, and may the embrace of the patriarchs enfold you in

---

1. *Rituale Romanum* (Rome, 1864), 130–31.

2. MS *Vat. lat.* 3797 is the only manuscript of Damian's letters that contains
the *Commendo te.* It is entitled, *Ad quemdam aegrotum,* which is struck through in a
later hand, and in the margin, also in a later hand, it is called the *Commendatio
animae.* Its presence in this MS strongly supports its authenticity, and the vocab-
ulary and style agree with those of Damian. One phrase particularly, *amoena
virentia,* finds an echo in his *Letter* 66 (Reindel, *Briefe* 2, p. 279, line 8), written
to Countess Blanche, where he speaks of *pratis iucunda satis amoenitate vernan-
tibus,* and in *Letter* 27 (Reindel, *Briefe* 1, p. 248, line 9) in the phrase *in aeterni vi-
roris amoenitate.* See also *Letters* 136 (Reindel, *Briefe* 3, p. 466, line 31) and 171
(Reindel, *Briefe* 4, p. 257, line 9). In all these he seems to parallel Virgil, *Aeneid*
6.638 (see edition of O. Ribbeck [Leipzig: Teubner, 1895], p. 512), and Prudentius, *Liber cathemerinon* 3.101 (CCL 126.14).

3. Cf. Gen 2.7; 3.19.

4. Cf. Matt 19.28; Luke 22.30.

blessed peace. And then, gentle and joyful, may the Lord Jesus appear before you, to assign you a place forever among those who stand in his presence.

(2) May you pay no heed to anything that is frightful in the darkness, that crackles in the flames, that is racked in torment. May loathsome Satan, together with his accomplices, give way to you and tremble before the angels who attend your arrival, and disappear into the vast abyss of eternal night. "Let God rise up and his enemies be scattered; may those who hate him flee before him, driven away like smoke in the wind. Like wax melting at the fire, let sinners perish at the presence of God."[5] And so, let the legions of hell be thrown into confusion and be overwhelmed with shame, and let the servants of Satan never dare to block your path.

(3) May Christ, who suffered for you, rescue you from punishment; may Christ, who was crucified for your sake, free you from excruciating pain; may Christ, who humbled himself to die for you, free you from death. May Christ, the Son of the living God, set you in the evergreen loveliness of his paradise, and may he, the true Shepherd, recognize you as one of his own flock. May he free you from all your sins and assign you a place at his right hand in the company of his elect. May you see your Redeemer face to face, and, standing in his presence forever, may you behold with blessed eyes Truth revealed in all its fullness.

(4) And so, having taken your place in the ranks of the saints, may you enjoy the sweetness of divine contemplation forever and ever. Amen.

5. Ps 67.2–3.

LETTER 172

Peter Damian to V—— and P——, clerics of the church of Faen-za. The thrust of this letter is to condemn the opinion that a couple contracting marriage during forbidden times need not separate so long as the marriage was not consummated. He opposes the implied conclusion that marriage is contracted not by mutual consent, but by intercourse. He also upholds the decision of spurious canons that a couple marrying during forbidden seasons must separate.

(Not datable)

 O SIRS V—— and P——, religious clerics of the church of Faenza, the monk Peter the sinner offers the service of his fraternal charity.

(2) Your brotherly concern has complained to me, that certain people, who are disturbing the regulation of ecclesiastical discipline and, in the words of the prophet, have preferred their own body to God,[1] contract marriage during the season of Lent. But to evade the sentence of the canons, after taking a wife and celebrating marriage, they claim that the one thing lacking was intercourse. Added to your complaint is the more serious fact that some individuals who, to all appearances, seem to be spiritual men and claim to be learned in the Scriptures, try to excuse those [who have acted as you have described]. For while the authority of the canons decree that those who have been married in the period from Septuagesima Sunday to the octave of Easter, within three weeks before the feast of St. John, or from the Advent of the Lord till after the feast of the Epiphany, must separate, these learned individuals ordain that legal marriage is had only by intercourse, and declare that such

---

1. Cf. Ezek 23.35.

persons who have married during these aforesaid times, and have not had intercourse, need not separate.[2]

(3) But anyone who has the slightest acquaintance with sacred Scripture would readily understand that this is most absurd and at the same time most frivolous. For if they are correct in saying that marriage is legally established by intercourse, why is it that the sacred canons decree that marriage be never consummated without the public celebration of marriage? Do the canons require this so that the husband might take his wife to bed in public? But since this would be so indecent and shameful, that in all the ages the human race has existed, we read of no one ever attempting this, except two men, namely, Paris and a certain philosopher,[3] how could canon law order something that even the unbridled lust of the pagans has deemed most disgraceful? Moreover, if marriage is solemnly constituted only by carnal intercourse, how is it that a widowed person is permitted to contract a second marriage, but is forbidden by the canons from entering third and fourth marriages?[4] Is it because after a man has taken a second wife, he is denied the right of ever taking her to bed, which is absolutely ridiculous? I might further add that if intercourse constitutes marriage, as often as a man sleeps with his wife, so often does he undoubtedly contract marriage.

(4) Wherefore, if one has intercourse a hundred times, not only does he commit the crime of multiple marriage, which is contrary to canon law, but incurs the guilt of being married a hundred times.[5] Whoever ventures to affirm this will doubtlessly be considered insane. Obviously, intercourse which is indeed permitted by law, does not constitute marriage, but is rather an act of marriage. According to the decree of Pope Leo, "not

2. Burchard IX, 4 (*Ex conc. Hilerdensi*, c. 3, apocryphal; PL 140.816A); cf. Ryan, *Sources*, no. 289, p. 130.

3. For Paris, cf. Virgil, *Aeneid* 2.602 (ed. Ribbeck, p. 310); Cicero, *Epistulae ad Atticum* 1.18.3 (ed. D. R. Shackleton Bailey [2 vols.; Leipzig: Teubner, 1987], 1.38). The second reference is so vague that it defies identification.

4. Burchard IX, 23 (*Ex decreto Hormisdae;* PL 140.818D), but actually this canon is from Benedict Levita, *Capitularia* III, 406 (MG LL II, 2, 127).

5. Burchard IX, 20 (PL 140.818C; text = Martin of Braga, *Capitula* 80: CJC I, 1142 ad C. 32, q. 7, c. 9).

every woman who has relations with a man is that man's wife, just as not every son born to a father is that father's heir." And somewhat farther on he says: "There is no doubt that such a woman has no relation to marriage, in whom it is clear the sacrament of marriage did not exist."[6] From these words, therefore, one can certainly understand that the sacrament of marriage is one thing, and that carnal sacrilege is something quite different. For that which is carried out according to the canons is a sacrament, but whatever is unlawfully performed contrary to the canons, is a sacrilege.

(5) Again, by reason of the time factor, one and the same action may be judged to be either helpful or harmful. Thus, if someone should prune his vines in the dead of winter, he will destroy his vineyard; and one who sows in the summertime, wastes his seed grain. But if the soil is cultivated at the proper time, it is at length prepared to receive the seed. Anyone who hires stone masons to work during a snowstorm, invites disaster; and he who cuts down trees in the springtime when the sap is running, to build a house or to join the wooden panels of a ceiling, wears himself out by toiling in vain. And to apply these principles to the sacraments, anyone who ordains clerics outside the appointed times, certainly does not advance them in orders, but places an obstacle in their path that hinders them from ever being ordained. And anyone who indiscriminately, and not at the proper time, administers the sacraments of confirmation or baptism, is not considered to have confected a sacrament, but is guilty of sacrilege.

(6) And thus, since these sacraments of the Church require their proper times, and achieve their effectiveness from the appropriateness of the time frame assigned to them, how is it that only marriages can be effective if they disregard the prescribed time periods? For as Solomon says: "Everything has its season, and everything under heaven its time."[7] And a little farther on: "A time to weep and a time to laugh; a time for mourning and a

---

6. Burchard IX, 1, 24 (PL 140.815A–B; 819A); Jaffé, 544; *Collectio Dionysio-Hadriana* (PL 67.288A–B).

7. Eccl 3.1.

time for dancing; a time to embrace and a time to refrain from embracing."[8] And so, those who dance and laugh when it is time to weep; who engage in embracing when it is a time to refrain from embracing; just as they pervert the proper time order, for them pleasure will rightly be turned into bitterness, joy into sorrow, glory into confusion, and marriage will be changed into prostitution. For since it is guaranteed by law that at harvest time or in the season when grapes are gathered, charges are not to be brought forward in court, or legal affairs concluded, and by reason of time it is established that whatever then is decided in a court of law should be considered invalid, how is it that the Lenten season does not nullify marriages which the authority of the canons condemns? Do the sacred canons have less force than legal sanctions? It is said that the substance of marriage consists in intercourse, and if that is lacking, marriage cannot be called a sacrament.

(7) Therefore, according to this opinion, the Blessed Virgin Mary was married to a man by reason of intercourse, since, as we know from the Gospel report, she agreed to be married[9] to her husband Joseph: "Before they came together," it says, "she was found to be with child by the Holy Spirit."[10] But because the evangelist does not clearly use the word "marriage," therefore you perhaps do not believe me when I say that the Blessed Virgin was married. So, let me cite one of the expositors, who explains just what happened. For Bede says in his explanation of Matthew: "We should first take note of the words: 'before they came together.' The words 'coming together' do not mean intercourse, but the time of betrothal which usually preceded it, when she who was first betrothed became a wife. Therefore, the phrase 'before they came together' means: Before they had properly celebrated the solemn rites of marriage, she was found to be with child by the Holy Spirit. Certainly, according to the order of things I referred to, they later came together

8. Eccl 3.4–5.

9. For a discussion, see Irven M. Resnick, "Marriage in Medieval Culture: Consent Theory and the Case of Joseph and Mary." *Church History* 69.2 (2000): 350–71.

10. Matt 1.18.

when, at the command of the angel, he took his wife home with him."[11] And Ambrose also says: "Let it not disturb you that Scripture frequently uses the word 'wife.' For it declares that the celebration of the betrothal is not a despoiling of virginity, but the public witness of the marriage."[12]

(8) And so, since it is as clear as day that the Blessed Virgin Mother of God did not marry, and still, according to the statement of Scripture, she undoubtedly entered into solemn marriage, how can one say that when intercourse is lacking, there can be no marriage? On the contrary, I freely attest that intercourse can be had without marriage, and that a union without intercourse can rightly be called marriage. For at times there are celibate marriages, there are those that are properly called virginal marriages.[13] In such cases the wife is so united with her husband by marital agreement, that the desire for a heavenly marriage completely precludes a carnal union. Tradition has it that blessed John the evangelist was removed from such a marriage by the Lord, and that while he remained virginal, the union which he disdained was still called a marriage.[14] And it was to such a marriage that the blessed apostle seems to invite his hearers, when he says: "And now for the matters you wrote to me about. It is a good thing for a man not to touch a woman; but because there is so much immorality, let each man have his own wife and each woman her own husband."[15] But while first declaring that it is a good thing not to touch a woman, and then decreeing that because of immorality each man should have his own wife, the wise teacher undoubtedly proposes celibate marriages, so that if only by so doing we are able to escape the snare of immorality, we should not seek carnal intercourse in marriage. For it is clear that from the beginning union in marriage was instituted to bear children and to beget posterity.

11. Bede, *Homilia* 1.5, *In vigilia nativitatis Domini* (CCL 122.32–33).

12. Ambrose, *De institutione virginis* 6.41 (PL 16.316 B–C), but not verbatim.

13. On marriage without sexual intercourse, see Dyan Elliott, *Spiritual Marriage: Sexual Abstinence in Medieval Wedlock* (Princeton, NJ: Princeton University Press, 1993).

14. See *Scholion* (PL 145.665–68); Bede, *Homilia* 1.9, *Sancti Iohannis evangelistae* (CCL 122.62).

15. 1 Cor 7.1–2.

(9) Therefore, so far as the history of the world is concerned, the purpose of marriage is the procreation of children. Yet, just as the earth is cut through only by the plowshare, but that this can happen, other necessary parts of the plow are employed; only the strings on a cithara and on other similar musical instruments are adapted to producing melody, but that they may be so adapted, there are other parts in the structure of the instrument that are not struck by the musician. Thus there are other purposes in addition to that of begetting children, both for promoting the sacrament of marriage and for the integrity of the human race, such as the assembly of marriage attendants, the equipment needed for an outstanding celebration, betrothal gifts, documents and lists describing the dowry and marriage portion, and other similar items. All of these together are called the marriage. And from of old, as said above, all these things pertained only to the procreation of children, but now as the world grows old, and since there has shone forth the teaching of him who proceeded from a virgin and is himself undefiled, all of this is done to avoid immorality. Formerly, for the promotion of a more ancient mystery, it was said: "Cursed be the man who is without offspring in Israel."[16] But now it is said: "Husbands, love your wives, as Christ also loved the Church."[17] And the apostle continues: "Now is the time," he says, "when married men should be as if they had no wives."[18] And again: "I should like you all to be as I am myself."[19]

(10) Moreover, as I said above, he who declares that one should marry a wife but should not have relations with her, does so, not to eliminate offspring, but rather to obstruct the flood of fornication. Nor does he wish to avoid swelling wombs and squalling infants, but desires to have an unsullied marriage bed and a celibate life of conjugal continence. And when he said: "But if they cannot control themselves, they should marry,"[20] and in another text: "You may come together again: otherwise, for lack of self-control, you may be tempted by Satan,"[21]

16. This text is not found in the Vulgate.
17. Eph 5.25.   18. 1 Cor 7.29.
19. 1 Cor 7.7.   20. 1 Cor 7.9.
21. 1 Cor 7.5.

he obviously shows that he avidly desires mutual chastity among those who are married, but reluctantly permits them to have carnal relations.

(11) Therefore, in view of what was previously stated, it is obvious that whoever denies that marriage can exist without intercourse, obstinately opposes the apostle, through whom Christ is speaking. He it was who wished that all would follow him in living continently, and yet advised each to have his own wife to avoid falling into impurity. Consequently, let these wise fools with their senseless mouthings be ashamed, as they stubbornly assert that a man need not separate from a woman whom he married during the Lenten season, but with whom he has not had intercourse. They, moreover, at times rush into such madness that they will deny any obligation to abandon a woman known to have been lured away by a man on Good Friday, the very day on which our Lord was crucified. And while they impudently construe such action as a legal marriage, by their clever arguments they merely confirm their sacrilegious concubinage. In fact, as the Lord was enduring his crucifixion, this man was absorbed in the pleasures of befouling lust. And while the whole world was dying with its Redeemer, as members truly united with their head, he was engaged in the obscene desires of an animal in heat.

(12) But now let me briefly relate what happened in my time on this day of the Lord's crucifixion. In the city of Ravenna certainly many animals were slaughtered on that day by the merchants in the meat markets, but by the vote of the senate, and especially by the decree of the venerable hermit Martin, they were all thrown to the dogs. What, therefore, would the good people who zealously served God have done, had they seen a newly wedded wife passing by in her bridal attire, if they had discovered that crowds of friends had abandoned the adoration of the cross to take part in the wedding dance?

(13) But tell me, you people who are making these novel claims, if it should happen perchance that a man had relations with his wife during the Lenten season, would you impose a penance on them without dissolving the marriage, or would you compel the parties to separate after dissolving the union by

obtaining a divorce? But note that canon law prescribes that anyone who sins with his wife during this period should reform his life by undertaking only forty days of penance.[22] How then can you say that marriage is contracted only by intercourse, and, contrary to the opinion of all sacred writings, judge that both actions are the same, namely, that beyond all doubt canonical authority nullifies marriages performed at illegal times, but attacks intercourse with the imposition of only a minor penance? Tell me, I say, speaking with your permission, if marriages are to be considered validated by intercourse alone, why are those contracted contrary to the precepts of the law condemned to the point of divorce, while intercourse is confronted with only a slight amount of penance? For if both are the same, just as they are no different in regard to sin, so too they should not be subjected to an unequal sentence. Indeed, where the cause is the same, the punishment for both should be the same.

(14) Furthermore, what is to be thought of this situation where it is commanded under canonical sanction, that if virgins who are not on their guard, should take as their husbands the very men who violated them, they might be reconciled with the Church after one year of penance, just because it was only marriage that they abused?[23] For if marriage is nothing more than sleeping together, why are virgins who practice prostitution said to have violated marriage, since certainly they did not violate intercourse, but rather fulfilled it? For surely if marriage rights consist only in intercourse, then foul houses of prostitution should not be condemned, but rather be honored as places of distinction, and foul-smelling brothels should become temples of marriage. Have we come so far with the subtleties of our philosophers, that marriage laws are to be held in the same esteem as the pleasures of obscene concubines? Are we to value the slough we call a house of ill repute to the same degree as we do an unsullied marriage bed?

---

22. Burchard XIX, 75 (PL 140.1000C), from the *Poenitentiale Ps.-Bedae*, c. 5, n. 2 (F. W. H. Wasserschleben, *Die Bussordnungen der abendländischen Kirche* [Graz, 1851], 262); *Collectio IX librorum* IX, 37 (PL 138.438).

23. Regino II, 151 (PL 132.312B); Burchard IX, 14 (PL 140.817B).

(15) And now, to speak with great indignation, is secret intercourse to be held in the same light as the public, and therefore honorable, celebration of marriage? Consequently, let shrewd cunning be thrown into disarray, nor should one be confident of joining by a multiplicity of words such acts that truth has set apart. Furthermore, let blameworthy presumption be curbed, lest what now secretly begins to thrive through indiscreet daring, afterwards grow on all sides through the vice of cohabitation. Let illegal marriages be dissolved, so that ecclesiastical discipline may continue to exist in all its vigor. Repeal whatever was agreed to in defiance of the law, lest this cancer that now arises among us increase with evil stealth, and spread from one member through the whole body of the Church. And thus let episcopal authority block this daring presumption, so that the Christian religion may not be tossed by the waves and whirled about by every fresh gust of teaching[24]—which God forbid—but immovably persevere according to the norms of apostolic tradition. Blessed be the name of the Lord.

24. Cf. Eph 4.14.

LETTER 173

Peter Damian to his disciple Bucco. The monk has asked whether God used good or bad angels to punish men for their sins. Damian replies, citing examples from the Old Testament and from the *Acts* of the martyrs, that at his pleasure God used both.[1]

(Not datable)

ETER TO HIS dearest son Bucco.

Your regard for me has led you to inquire whether it is the good or the bad angels by whom almighty God chastises the sins of offenders, and whether he is accustomed to inflict the punishment of sudden death or of some great misfortune. To this there is indeed an easy and obvious response. For if we pay close attention to sacred Scripture, we discover that retribution is administered by both kinds of spirits, just as the supreme Judge disposes.

(2) But lest my short reply not relate to this important matter, I will say that Sodom was destroyed by good angels. For if they had been hostile forces, blessed Lot would never have venerated them, nor, as we read, would he have received them reverently as his guests. "I pray you, sirs," he said, "turn aside to the home of your servant, and spend the night there."[2] The angel, moreover, who killed seventy thousand men when David took a census of his people, was undoubtedly a good spirit. For Scripture speaks of him in these words: "The angel of the Lord, speaking through the lips of God, commanded Gad to tell David to go to the threshing floor of Ornan the Jebusite and to set up there an altar to the Lord."[3] A reprobate spirit, to be

---

1. The text of this fragmentary letter is found only in the *Collectanea* of John of Lodi, preserved in MS Vat. lat. 4930, first printed by Gaetani: PL 145.909C–910D.

2. Gen 19.2.   3. 1 Chr 21.18.

264

sure, would not have ordered an altar to be built, nor would the devoted prophet have humbly obeyed him.

(3) Moreover, those angels were also holy, who, as reported in the second book of Maccabees, struck down Heliodorus as he was attempting to carry off the money deposited in the sacred temple, beat him with terrible blows, caused him to become blind, and left him for dead. And Scripture continues to speak of them in this fashion: "They saw a horse," it says, "splendidly caparisoned, with a rider of terrible aspect; it rushed fiercely at Heliodorus and, rearing up, attacked him with its front hooves. The rider seemed to be wearing golden armor. There also appeared to Heliodorus two young men of surpassing strength and glorious beauty, splendidly dressed. They stood on either side of him and scourged him, raining ceaseless blows upon him. He fell suddenly to the ground, overwhelmed by a great darkness, and [his men] snatched him up and put him on a litter."[4]

(4) But Scripture more frequently demonstrates that God also applies his scourge to men through the agency of reprobate spirits. For an evil spirit would seize King Saul and cause him to be overwhelmed by madness.[5] And Satan struck blessed Job, not only with bodily affliction, but also in the loss of his children.[6] Moreover, as sacred history records, the demon Asmodaeus killed the seven husbands of Sarah, the daughter of Raguel.[7] Hence it was written: "He loosed upon them his indignation, wrath, and troubles, which he sent by wicked angels."[8] It is evident, therefore, that the impulse of God's justice is applied to us both by good and by wicked angels, as is attested by these and many other citations from sacred Scripture. But since all such punishments and adversities of divine justice are administered by angelic service, it is the free choice of almighty God alone to decide when he will employ good, and when he will use wicked angels.

(5) But that we may not digress through a long list of examples, St. Cecilia used the threat of a good angel's wrath, while

4. 2 Macc 3.25–27. 5. Cf. 1 Sam 16.14–15; 18.10.
6. Cf. Job 1.12. 7. Cf. Tob 3.8.
8. Ps 77.49.

the blessed martyr Agnes called upon an avenging evil spirit. The former, indeed, served notice on her spouse Valerianus: "I have as my lover an angel of God, who guards my body with great zeal. If he should be even slightly aware that you are touching me with impure love, he will rouse up his fury against you, and you shall lose your comeliness and your youth in its full flower."[9] The latter, however, informed the prefect that his son was strangled by an evil spirit: "He," she said, "whose will your son tried to carry out, received the power to do with him what he would."[10]

(6) Consequently, from the clear evidence of the Old and the New Testament we learn that divine retribution is dispensed not only by evil spirits, but also by good angels. For any master of a household captures wild animals and repels thieves, sometimes by employing dogs, and at other times by using his servants.

9. *Passio sanctae Ceciliae virginis et martyris*, ed. B. Mombritius, *Sanctuarium seu Vitae Sanctorum* 1 (1910), p. 333.

10. *Vita S. Agnetis auctore S. Ambrosio*, II, 10, *AA SS*, p. 716; cf. *Epistolae ex Ambrosianarum numero segregatae* 1 (PL 17.739).

LETTER 174

Peter Damian to bishop V—— and to his canons, sent perhaps to the same bishop V. of *Letter* 115.[1] This is a pastoral letter, warning his correspondent to guard against the spiritual dangers occasioned by our five senses. His advice applies all the more to those who are responsible for others committed to their care. Those in authority are equally accountable for the sins of their subjects. In this piece we have an excellent example of Damian's mystical-allegorical interpretation of Scripture.

(Not datable)

 O THE MOST reverend bishop, sir V—— and to the holy canons of his church, the monk Peter the sinner offers his service.

(2) In an army that is equipped for battle, horns, clarions, tubas, and war trumpets are carried, so that by their resounding blast the guards on watch around the camp may be alerted, and the fighting men may arm themselves against a hostile night attack. We also, who have sworn to serve in the heavenly army, and have gathered to do battle against the potentates of this world and the superhuman forces of evil,[2] must arouse one another by our mutual clamor, so that the nocturnal invader may not discover us overwhelmed by unseemly slumber, but be in fear of always finding us prepared and ready to go into action. For we are arrayed in a city that is seen to have five gates, since we live in a body girded with five senses.

(3) And so, we obstruct these gates with bars, and use bolts, locks, and spikes when we carefully guard the gateways of our senses from invading vices and from the vanities of the world. For then our Pentapolis remains safe and unmolested, secure

1. Cf. Lucchesi, *Vita* 1, 62. See also FOTC, MC 5.306.
2. Cf. Eph 6.12.

behind its own fortifications, nor do [its warriors] arrogantly rush out to attack the enemy, or open its defenses as the hostile forces attempt to invade, and thus as our spirit stands firm on the brow of Mount Sion, it searches for the things that are above and does not condescend to seek for dissolute carnal pleasure. It yearns for "the Jerusalem that is on high, a free woman who is also our mother,"[3] but treads with disdain upon her who is in servitude, with her children. Otherwise, if, like the men of Gomorrah, one goes out into the wooded vale, which is now the salt sea,[4] that is, if a man throws himself into the abyss of a fruitless life, if he seeks for the brine of earthly wisdom, he is soon overthrown by the enemy that has won the victory, because he did not stay within bolted walls in his own city. Did not the prophet bolt the gates of this city of ours when he said: "The man who stops his ears to hear nothing of bloodshed, who closes his eyes to the sight of evil—this is the man who shall dwell on the heights"?[5] And does not the Lord guard the access to our taste, when he says: "Keep watch on yourselves: do not let your minds be dulled by dissipation and drunkenness."[6] Of the sense of smell the apostle says: "We are indeed the good odor offered by Christ to God for those who are on the way to salvation."[7] But on the contrary, a vile odor hung on the breath of those who said: "Let us have perfumes to our heart's content, and let no flower of spring escape us; let us crown ourselves with rosebuds before they can wither."[8] And our sense of touch ought to wish for the same objective as that of the sense of taste. For what the prophet says: "Taste, then, and see that the Lord is good,"[9] is the same as what John remarked: "That which we felt with our hands concerning the word of life."[10]

(4) Moreover, the battle that we wage against our five bodily senses is mystically signified by the five kings of Midian. "Let some men among you be armed for battle," said Moses. "They can fall upon Midian and exact vengeance in the Lord's

3. Gal 4.26.
4. Cf. Gen 14.3.
5. Isa 33.15.
6. Luke 21.34.
7. 2 Cor 2.15.
8. Wis 2.7.
9. Ps 33.9.
10. 1 John 1.1.

name."[11] When they made war on Midian, as sacred history relates, and were victorious, they slew all the men and their kings—Evi, Rekem, Zur, Hur, and Reba, the five kings of that people.[12] Evi, to be sure, has the meaning "bestial" or "wild."[13] We stab this king within us with our spiritual dagger, when we cut away our wild habits, when we excise from our hearts the madness of bestial violence. For when the Lord says, "How blessed are the gentle; they shall have the earth for their possession,"[14] how can you obtain the blessedness of the meek unless you curb the wildness of the bestial spirit within you?

(5) Now Rekem, or, as the ancient version has it, Rocon, means "uselessness."[15] What else can we call whatever is done in the world to foster desire for the world, unless we speak of it as Scripture does: "O the emptiness of those who are empty, and all is emptiness."[16] Emptiness, indeed, begets empty people, and those who are empty do vain, or empty, things, since the world, which passes away, causes people whom it deceives to become empty, and men turn the world, which they madly love, into emptiness. And so, the knight of God slays this king, the true Israelite cuts him down, if he does nothing that is superfluous, nothing useless, or that does not have a purpose, but gravely and reasonably tries to carry out the commands of God's law.

(6) And now, the third king of the Midianites is called Zur (Sur), which rightly has the meaning "wall," or "strong," or also "narrowness."[17] What should we here understand by a wall or something strong, except the obstinacy or stubbornness of an unyielding spirit? But if it is said to mean narrowness, this too is not far removed from the vice of hardheartedness, since one who is hard and obstinate in forgiving a neighbor's faults is constricted by narrowness of soul, since he lacks the capacity to love. And the prophet says of this love: "Your commandment

---

11. Num 31.3.   12. Cf. Num 31.8.
13. Cf. Jerome, *Nom. hebr.* 12.24.   14. Matt 5.4.
15. Cf. Jerome, *Nom. hebr.* 29.26.
16. Eccl 1.2; cf. Augustine, *De civitate Dei* 20.3 (FOTC 24.253), and elsewhere; Sabatier II, 353, n. at v. 2. Damian's use of the Latin phrase *Vanitas vanitantium* reflects the pre-Vulgate version employed in patristic times.
17. Cf. Jerome, *Nom. hebr.* 14.29.

has no limit."[18] Or, it may also have this meaning, that the dire straits of damnation follow from hardness of heart. Consequently, Solomon says: "Happy the man who is always scrupulous in conduct, but he who hardens his heart falls into evil."[19]

(7) And following this, the fourth king of Midian is called Hur (Bur), which is said to mean "irritation."[20] With that, you see that the names of these kings are shadows and images of vices. For those who carry heavy burdens through their gates, who bring disturbing sins from without, and carry them through the portals of their senses into the secret confines of their heart, undoubtedly excite God to anger, and provoke him to pronounce an avenging sentence against them. Hence it is written: "Dissemblers and crafty men provoke the wrath of God."[21] And of such men it was often said to Ezekiel: "For they are a provoking house."[22] And the psalmist says: "How long, O God, will the enemy taunt you? Will the adversary pour scorn on your name for ever?"[23]

(8) But on the other hand, Reba (Rebe), which has the meaning "well ordered,"[24] appears here only as irony, or in a sense opposite to its proper meaning, since the one who is said to be well ordered, is, on the contrary, subject to disorder and confusion. For everyone who is prone to vice, even though superficially he pretends to live an orderly life, fosters in his heart the darkness of confused and disordered ideas.

(9) And so, the five kings of the Midianites symbolize our five bodily senses, because every vice that presides in the body depends on these senses. We must therefore destroy them and cut them down with our swords when they rise to do battle against us, when they continue to lead us into sin. Did not the Lord command us to kill these kings and cut them to pieces with the sword of the Spirit, when he ordered us to tear out our eye or cut off our hand or foot if they were our undoing? "It is better for you," he said, "to enter into life with one eye

18. Ps 118.96.
19. Prov 28.14.
20. Cf. Jerome, *Nom. hebr.* 31.4, s. v., "Ur": "provoking to anger."
21. Job 36.18.   22. Ezek 3.9.
23. Ps 73.10.
24. Cf. Jerome, *Nom. hebr.* 29.27.

or maimed, than to keep both eyes, hands, and feet, and be thrown into hell."[25] These, then, are the kings of the Midianites, but Midian should be understood to mean "of the judgment."[26] For whoever fail to be ruled by the law of the Spirit, but obey their carnal senses, prove that they are destined not for mercy but for judgment, as it is said of a certain man who had no faith: "He who does not believe has already been judged."[27] On the other hand, it is said of him who listens to the voice of the Savior: "He does not come up for judgment, but passes from death to life."[28] Everyone should mightily strive to be engaged in holy deeds and should struggle to purify and sanctify himself in all things. In so doing, he never ceases to chastise and judge himself. For he who perfectly evaluates himself, need not await judgment. But to judge oneself perfectly means to avoid doing what is reprehensible, and fearfully to re-examine his actions that were considered blameless.

(10) Moreover, anyone who acts in this fashion truly destroys the kings of the Midianites, overthrows the Amalekite princes, and keeps himself untainted by the plague of vice. And thus it was that the same sacred history records: "And the children of Israel went forth and came to the fountain of judgment, which is Kadesh, and killed all the princes of the Amalekites and also those of the Amorites who lived in Asasonthamar (Tharansem)."[29] Now Kadesh has the meaning "sanctification."[30] And so, in a spiritual sense we slay all the Amalekites and Amorites in Kadesh, which is the fountain of judgment, when we engage in sanctifying our life with good works, and still judge ourselves to be wicked and blameworthy. Although we take pains always to live beyond reproach, we never cease finding fault with our deeds by carefully taking them into strict account. And we should note that both the fountain of judgment and Kadesh, which signifies sanctification, are one and the same place, because it is true that every just man finds fault with himself as he lives a holy life, and by judging and blaming

25. Mark 9.43–48; Matt 5.29–30; 18.8.
26. Cf. Jerome, *Nom. hebr.* 8.18–19.
27. John 3.18.   28. John 5.24.
29. Cf. Gen 14.7.   30. Cf. Jerome, *Nom. hebr.* 4.4.

himself he becomes more and more holy. In this fashion the life of the saints is found wanting in their own esteem, and still it is judged to be beyond reproach in the deeds that they perform. Hence the principal city of the kingdom of Sihon is called Heshbon,[31] which is said to mean "thoughts."[32] From this we may gather that the major part of the devil's power reigns in the realm of thoughts.

(11) Now Sihon signifies the spirit of wickedness. But Heshbon is taken from the authority of Sihon, and its ownership is given to the Israelites, when our thinking, which had been swollen with the disease of pride to the point of being judged as blameworthy, bows down in true humility as a result of the gift of grace, so that it now judges its own deeds, which in its arrogance it had formerly extolled, and after diligent examination humbly finds them blameworthy. Consequently, with the devouring sword we overthrow the Amalekites and the Amorites in Kadesh, which is the fountain of judgment, because then we lay low the barbarism of all vices, then we victoriously engage the powers on high, if we live upright lives and still judge ourselves to be guilty and subject to sin, saying with the apostle: "If we claim to be sinless, we are self-deceived and the truth is not in us."[33] And then Heshbon, which we said can be interpreted to mean "thoughts," is compelled to come under the authority of the Israelites, when our soul is delivered from pride and from every worldly desire, and is handed over to the love of the kingdom of heaven. The knights of Christ can never desert the battle against their thoughts, because the righteousness of our deeds does not make us free, if the soul armed with virtues does not resist its evil thoughts.

(12) It was indeed sufficient for those living under the Old Law, if only their external deeds were morally good; but once the awesome voice of the Gospel was heard, we were commanded also to struggle vigilantly against our thoughts, even as we divested ourselves of evil deeds. "You have heard that our forefathers were told: 'Do not commit adultery.' But what I tell you is

---

31. Cf. Num 21.26.
33. 1 John 1.8.

32. Cf. Jerome, *Nom. hebr.* 17.26.

this: If a man looks on a woman with a lustful eye, he has already committed adultery with her in his heart."[34] So it was, that John the Baptist, who represents the Old Law, was said to have worn a garment of camel's hair about his waist.[35] But our Savior, who is the author of the Gospel, was seen by John standing among seven lamps of gold, robed down to his feet, with a golden girdle around his breast.[36] Now what is meant by the garment of camel's hair about the waist, if not the command given to our forefathers: "Do not commit adultery"?[37] And what does the golden girdle around the breast signify, if not the word that was spoken to those who profess the Christian faith: "If a man looks on a woman with a lustful eye, he has already committed adultery with her in his heart"?[38] Thus also God's voice gave this command through the prophet: "O Jerusalem, wash the ill will from your heart; how long will you retain your evil thoughts?"[39] And elsewhere he says: "I have listened and heard nothing good from anyone."[40] And Solomon said: "A holy and disciplined spirit will have nothing to do with falsehood, and will withdraw itself from thoughts that are without reason."[41]

(13) Therefore, let us take up the sword of the Spirit and fight without respite against the swarming thoughts that are attacking us. We have read that when the priest Phinehas saw an Israelite lying with a Midianite woman, he suddenly took up a spear[42] and pinned the sacrilegious pair of fornicators together through the genitalia.[43] This deed would have instructed the people [of Israel]. But you, who are taught to be proficient in another kind of war, in which the physical sword is removed from your hands, take up the sword of the Spirit, and if you should see your Israelite senses lying in a Midianite brothel, that is, wallowing in lascivious and seductive thoughts, do not

34. Matt 5.27–28.
35. Cf. Matt 3.4.
36. Cf. Rev 1.13.
37. Exod 20.14.
38. Matt 5.28.
39. Jer 4.14.
40. Jer 8.6.
41. Wis 1.5.
42. The Latin word used here is *sirosma,* a variant of *siromastes;* cf. Charles de Fresne DuCange, ed., *Glossarium mediae et infimae Latinitatis* 7 (Paris, 1883–1887), 496, where the meaning is given as "lance" or "javelin."
43. Cf. Num 25.7–8.

have mercy or hesitate, but strike at once and pierce them through without delay. Cut open the very womb, that is, the secrets of nature, and, penetrating deeply, thrust into the very source of sinning, so that it will never be able to conceive or give birth to poisonous offspring that might contaminate the Israelite camp. Let the sword of the Spirit, I say, destroy the very birthplace of sinning, that it may extinguish the wanton pleasures of our indulgent flesh.

(14) While this mode of action is necessary for all according to each one's capacity, it is especially important for those who are in positions of authority and are charged with directing the lives of the brethren. For them it is truly imperative that the fire of episcopal zeal be enkindled in combating the vices of their subjects, that with Phinehas they may possess the dignity of the eternal priesthood. But if they suffer from slothful negligence by disregarding those who have sinned, stripped of their priesthood, like Eli they will be thrown to the ground and break their necks.[44] Consequently, when the people of Israel joined in the worship of the Baal of Peor in the wilderness, and shamefully succumbed to the harlots of Moab, the Lord was furious with the Israelites, and said to Moses: "Take all the leaders of the people and hang them on gibbets in the full light of day, that my anger may be turned away from Israel."[45] Why is it, that when the people fell into the depths of lust, vengeance was meted out to their leaders? The subjects transgress, and the rulers are hung on gibbets? Surely, there is a difference here between the one who sins and the other who is flogged. The reason is that the guilt of the subjects redounds to the dishonor of their leaders, and the fault committed by the sheep is ascribed to the negligence of the shepherd. And note how dreadful is the lot of those in authority, that they are punished not only for their own offenses, but also for those of their subjects. And Moses accuses them, because the law of God indicts them for negligence and sloth. He hanged them in the full light of day, because they were brought forth to be tried and to be accused by the light. "All those who commit evil deeds," as the

44. Cf. 1 Sam 4.18.
45. Num 25.4.

Lord says, "hate the light and avoid it, for fear their practices should be shown up. But those who act truthfully come to the light."[46] He, indeed, comes to the light, who reveals his secret sins by way of a sincere confession.

(15) Therefore, the pastors of churches should make sure that they beget children in Israel. But they should not rear just any kind of offspring, but sons who will mature to fight bravely the battles of the Lord. Moreover, anyone who uses his established office of preaching to incite others to join in the fight, but does not himself take up arms, is like the man who sounds the trumpet for battle, but does not personally dare to engage the enemy. Such a man does not beget male offspring, since he is an inactive father. Such a one, surely, was prefigured by Zelophehad,[47] who had no sons, but at his death left five daughters. Now Zelophehad has the meaning of "shade on his face."[48] For anyone who preaches about brave deeds, and fails to live like a man, takes shelter, as it were, under the trees of edifying words and hides in the shade on his face, lest he appear dishonorable, since he does not take to the field of battle because of his sloth and cowardice. And thus, this man for his part begets not sons but only daughters, and five of them at that, since he trains his followers not to exert their vigor and spiritual daring, but to live a life of undistinguished ease. And since he fails to take pains in supplying them with eagerness for spiritual combat, he compels them to devote themselves to external affairs, to serving the needs of their five bodily senses.

(16) Therefore, my dear friends, barricade the gates of your senses against the forces of attacking vices, and open them to the army of spiritual virtues. The soul of the knight of Christ should be spread out like a net to trap the flow of worthless thoughts, and, receiving the urgings of the Holy Spirit, should enclose them like fish. Let the prowler in the night find you strong and alert, that he may not break into the stronghold that you protect, I mean, of course, that he not gain entrance into your heart. May he always see the triumphal banner of the cross flying high against him, and may he not, which God for-

46. John 3.20.   47. Cf. Num 26.33.
48. Cf. Jerome, *Nom. hebr.* 20.23.

bid, take from you the spoils of victory, but quickly disappear as he takes flight. Always press forward and conduct yourself with honor, and yet weigh each action as you take strict account of it in your heart, so that as you now stand trembling before your own tribunal, you may appear undaunted before that final and inevitable judgment, not at length to be found guilty, but to receive the reward of glory.

LETTER 175

Peter Damian to the monk Honestus.[1] This letter is reconstructed from two fragments preserved in the *Liber testimoniorum (Collectanea)* of John of Lodi. These bits are not consonant with *Letters* 1 and 27, also addressed to Honestus.[2] In one fragment he
speaks of the danger of a hostile attitude toward correction; in
the second he addresses himself to problems found in Luke's
Gospel.

(Not datable)

"THEY HAVE HATED him who rebuked them in the
gate; and have loathed him who speaks the whole
truth."[3] And in the next verse the prophet says to
them, "You shall build houses of hewn stone, and you shall not
live in them."[4] He, indeed, rebukes a person in the gate, if he
chastises someone for his fault, and, in so doing, prods him on
his way to his heavenly homeland. But he who detests the one
who has corrected him, does not dwell in the house that he
himself had built, since even though he had erected a building
of good works, he was not worthy to live in it, because he refused to enter through the door of rebuke. And he who did not
choose to enter by the narrow gate of adversity, will find it impossible to inhabit the pleasant atmosphere of the inner court-
yard.

(2) Blessed Luke, who is symbolized by a bull calf, because
the bull calf was usually slaughtered as a sacrifice, is the only
evangelist who reports the three canticles: first, that of Zechariah; secondly, that of Mary; and thirdly, the canticle of Simeon.

---

1. The recipient of this letter is identified in the titles of the two fragments
found in the *Collectanea.*
2. See FOTC, MC 1.37–83, 247–54.   3. Amos 5.10.
4. Amos 5.11.

And since none of the other evangelists cites a canticle in his own account, only Luke, who alone represents the figure of the victim prescribed by the Law, reports these various canticles: first, that of the priest; then, that of the virgin; and finally, the canticle of the just old man. Thus he shows that before all others in the Church, he should be held worthy of the office of chanter, who had previously offered himself to God as a true sacrifice. He therefore sounds dry and taut, not wet and limp like one who is flowing with pleasures. When alive, to be sure, a sheep bleats; but when it is dead, it sings; and a dry harp string produces a clear tone, while a moist one sounds dull. Those, therefore, who leave the world, should be most careful and intensely fearful, lest in their flight from the snares of secular affairs, they become more deeply implicated in the bonds of a soft and disordered life. For even though they offer God something that is good, the sacrifice of the donor is not received unless he who makes the offering presents himself, so to speak, as a token of his own devotion. Thus it was that Cain wasted his sacrifice, because he had failed first to offer himself.[5]

5. Cf. Gen 4.5.

Peter Damian to the abbot G<ebizo>. He chastises Gebizo for his pride and disobedience in deserting the priorship of Fonte Avellana. After being properly elected, Gebizo begged to be relieved of his office because of ill health, but then took up the duties of abbot in a monastery built by his brother. Damian contends that it was not illness that prompted the move, but the desire to advance to abbatial rank in another monastery outside the hermitage of Fonte Avellana. After citing Gebizo's own words and the canonical legislation against him, Damian urges the abbot either to return to his responsibilities at Fonte Avellana, or to become a simple monk under the authority of another.

(Not datable)

O BROTHER G<EBIZO> the monk Peter the sinner sends greetings.

(2) What you have done, brother, appears to be an ominous and portentous thing, and the road you are now following as an inexperienced traveler is impassable. Clearly, at my command, even at my request, and after being promptly elected by the brothers, you accepted the governance of the hermitage, and then, after declaring that you were ill and weak and unequal to assuming such great responsibilities, you rejected the burden that had been placed upon you. But now, created abbot in another monastery, you evidently demonstrate that you are unwilling to hold office under another's authority, lest you produce offspring in some other's name. And while attempting to extend the fortune of your own family, you disdain the idea of raising up issue for your deceased brother. You thus imitated Onan, the son of Judah, who, according to the account in sacred history, when "going in to his brother's wife, spilled his seed on the ground, so as not to raise up issue for his brother." But take note of what follows: "Therefore," Scripture

says, "the Lord took his life, for what he did was wicked in the Lord's sight."[1]

(3) Indeed, you loathe the idea and shudder at the thought that the subjects of Gebizo should be called the disciples of Peter, and as one who seeks his own glory and disdains others, you blush to share your reputation with anyone else. As we know, it is decreed by canon law, that when a husband is impotent and is unable to have intercourse with his wife, he may not abandon and divorce her and enter a second marriage.[2] It would surely be pure fantasy, if, after being unable to have relations with his first wife, he should hope to succeed with the second. In your case, too, if you have the strength to rule a community there in the other house, you were also able to do so here. But while you were vigorous enough to assume the direction of this community, you took refuge in adultery and moved into the governance of another one. And so, you are not allowed to retain the wife you now have, since after turning against your legitimate spouse, you are now living with a whore, especially since canonical authority again ordains that if one transfers from one church to another, let him lose the one that he despised, and in no way be allowed to retain the church that he newly acquired.[3]

(4) Obviously, you are striving to achieve great reputation for yourself, and reject the idea of producing offspring to enhance another's glory. So it was with him who, as next of kin, had the right to take Ruth as his wife. But he said: "I yield my right as next of kin to Boaz, for I must not cut off the posterity of my own family."[4] This man, surely motivated by vainglory, sought to increase his posterity in his own name. Boaz, however, a good and honest man, made light of enhancing his own fame, and was content merely to observe the commands of

---

1. Gen 38.9–10.

2. Burchard IX, 44 (PL 140.822A–B), citing an apocryphal letter of Gregory (33, q. 1, c. 2); see P. Fournier, "Études critiques sur le Décret de Burchard de Worms," *Nouvelle revue historique de droit français et étranger* 34 (1910): 66, 107; Ryan, *Sources*, no. 255, p. 119.

3. Burchard III, 48 (PL 140.681B), with citation from the canons *Ex Concilio Meldensi*, c. 30, in MGH Cap II, 2, p. 406; Burchard I, 74 (PL 140.568A), from the *Collectio Dionysio-Hadriana, Decret. Leonis*, c. 38 (PL 67.294C–D).

4. Ruth 4.6.

God's law. But note that not even the former's name is remembered, despite his effort to have his memory perpetuated in his posterity, while the latter's fame is recorded with glory, not only in the roll of the fathers, but even in that of the patriarchs. The former lost the glory of his posterity for which he labored, while the latter received the name of father, which he had made light of in his observance of God's law. The former is not remembered for having any offspring at all, while the latter became the father of powerful kings. And finally, the former, in striving to be remembered in his posterity, failed to win a reference in history, while the latter, who made no effort to bear children under his own name, by providing for the fertility of David's line, begot the Savior of all the world.

(5) Refrain, my brother, refrain from this arrogant posturing and from exalting yourself so obviously in your pride. For when pride has struck root in the heart of any man, even though at times it is covered with a certain golden veneer of self-induced humility, it will never be totally restrained from showing a glimpse of itself or from erupting secretly. Call to mind, dear brother, that recently while you were sitting in chapter with the community, you erupted in these words as one giving counsel: "Father," you asked, "is there not a reward in store for us if we give our support in building a monastery?" And this you said, not to solve a knotty problem, since none was at hand, but that you might prepare for what you were then going to say: "Yet who is not aware of this, except one who knows nothing of duty and affection?" But that your gushing remarks might now flow more freely, you then added: "My brother was recently instrumental in dedicating the monastery of St. Lawrence, which had been built by him, and as generous benefactor endowed it with twelve liturgical vestments." What business was it of ours to hear what your brother had given to such a sacred place, or to know what his offering had cost him, except that you should appear noble and superior because of your brother, and that he might be regarded as rich and generous in view of his gift?

(6) It was in the same vein that shortly afterwards, making up the story out of whole cloth, you continued: "My brother

was wedded to the only daughter of a certain count," and then you immediately added: "I say the only daughter, because that lord had no other children." So that shame would not be detected on your face, because you feared to be discovered in a falsehood, you then remarked as if you were letting out the breath that had swelled within you: "Nor would my brother have married her, if there had been other heirs to the property of the parents." You did not say this in so many words, but you made it clear to us that we should come to this conclusion. For no matter what a man proclaims with his tongue, God, the searcher of hearts,[5] listens only to the secrets of the mind, and in the ears of the hidden judge, it is not the noisy voice but the clamor of the heart that resounds.

(7) This is the reason for the prophet's words: "Your ear has heard their heart's desire."[6] This, too, is why Daniel said of the proud king Nebuchadnezzar: "And the king exclaimed: 'Is this not Babylon the great that I have built as a royal residence by my own mighty power and for the honor of my majesty?'"[7] To whom, I ask, did this arrogant and boastful man reply with words of inflated pride, but to his own exalted thought that had already resounded in his mind? Moreover, that spirit of perdition who is reported to have said, "I will scale the heavens; I will set my throne high above the stars of heaven; I will sit on the mountain of the covenant in the far reaches of the north; I will rise high above the cloud banks and make myself like the Most High,"[8] did not give utterance to those words with his lips, since he was not of flesh and blood, but as a tyrant gave vent to all this in sacrilegious thoughts. If, therefore, this lofty angel fell without hope of redemption, not because he spoke against the Creator of the universe, or had done certain evil deeds, but only because he had swelled with pride in the wickedness of his thoughts, how does it profit us to prostrate ourselves like humble men in our garb or speech, but inwardly to pride ourselves above other men by reason of our illustrious ancestors, or of our exceptionally lofty wisdom? So, we should strive to speak

5. Ps 7.10.
6. Ps 9.17.
7. Dan 4.27.
8. Isa 14.13–14.

modestly and to be seen as humble men. Let us tear deeply rooted pride from our heart, and soon, if it be absent from our purpose also, humility will be evident in all that we say. For when the liquid dries up in the cask, no one is likely to drink delicious wine from his cup.

(8) Indeed, who can make fine flour from bran? Or, who can produce sparkling silver from a vein of iron? And what is more, to use the figure from the Gospel, "can grapes be picked from briars, or figs from thistles?"[9] In the same way, in the verse that follows, "a bad tree never yields good fruit."[10] Truly, in this case the tree must be understood to mean the will, and not the person. For the same human person is able to perform good deeds as well as bad, just as from the same soil figs come forth as well as thistles. But just as a bad tree never bears good fruit, so also from a proud will, which is undoubtedly evil, pure and unblemished humility can never emerge. And just as when the root is damaged, all the branches of the tree will surely become dry, so too from a proud spirit, even if temporarily some good work seems to grow, when the moisture of the earth is exhausted, it will shrivel up because of the arid and stony soil. "The seventy-two came back jubilant," as the evangelist Luke reports, "and they said: 'In your name, Lord, even the devils submit to us.'"[11] And what was the reply of him who searches the secrets of the heart? "I watched how Satan fell, like lightning, out of the sky,"[12] as if he would say: Take care, lest while the evil spirits are subject to your command, your minds be weighted down by the yoke of pride. For if Satan because of his pride irrevocably lost heaven, which had been his, a proud man can never find that for which he hopes.

(9) To be sure, when Joab stoutly fought the Ammonite king at Rabbah and laid siege to that royal city, he sent messengers to David and invited him to come so that the victory would be ascribed to his name. "I have attacked Rabbah," he said, "and the city of waters is about to be taken. You had better muster the rest of the army yourself, besiege the city and take it; other-

9. Matt 7.16.   10. Matt 7.18.
11. Luke 10.17.   12. Luke 10.18.

wise I shall destroy the city, and the name to be proclaimed over it will be mine."[13] A military man was happy to confer the victory he had won on the king to enhance the glory of his fame, and should a servant of God disdain to award his teacher the patronage of his brothers who are subject to him? Herod and Philip named the cities they had built by their own effort, one for Augustus, the other for the emperor Tiberius,[14] and should we who have renounced the trappings of this life, and, what is more, have vowed to become dead to the world, lust after the faint glory of empty fame, and burn with desire for the idle words of trifling praise?

(10) Beware, brother, lest your spirit take offense at what I am saying, and go to pieces like dust under the blows of correction, lest you be exactly that for which I am rebuking you, and that in the process [your fault] be more clearly observed. Pride, indeed, causes the human soul to become like glass, so that in its lack of patience it finds it impossible to bear the blow of correction. It is called glass because one can see through it,[15] and so, if it were strong and solid, it would surpass all other metals; but since it is easily broken, it sells at a low price. In like manner, he who by his impatience is broken when assailed by correction, even though possessing other virtues, he demonstrates that he does not have firmness and strength. That is why the Lord spoke through the prophet in reference to the proud people of Israel, afflicted by the disease of impatience: "The house of Israel has become dross to me."[16] Obviously, if the dross of any metal is beaten with a pounding hammer, it promptly breaks up and is reduced to dust. And so, that your soul may not become dross in the sight of God, it should calmly bear the blows of friendly correction.

(11) But now as I conclude my letter by making you aware of my decision: either return to the office that you recently turned down, or, content to promote your own salvation, live as a monk under obedience to the prior. May your legitimate efforts

---

13. 2 Sam 12.27–28.
14. Cf. Josephus, *De bello Judaico* 1.10; *De antiquitate Judaica* 18.3.
15. Cf. Isidore, *Etymologies* 16.16.1.
16. Ezek 22.18.

as a faithful prior either grant you success in the formation of your spiritual sons, or may your submission in sincere humility exalt you in the sight of your Redeemer, who humbled himself for your sake.

LETTER 177

Peter Damian to the priest Ubertus. Professing to be not only a devotee of ancient custom, but also a student of contemporary observance, he replies to special questions on baptism and the sacrifice of the Mass. The problems are relatively unimportant, and Damian gives his interrogator scant attention. His questions lend themselves more to oral discussion than to a formally dictated letter. The author's fidelity to the normative practices of the Roman Church deserves special attention.

(Not datable)

 O THE DEVOTED priest, sir Ubertus, the monk Peter the sinner expresses his bond of personal charity in the Lord.

(2) I have no doubt, venerable brother, that your minor questions arise from the fervor of the spiritual zeal that nobly motivates you, but since the bearer of your letter is prepared to return, I find it necessary to prepare only a brief response. This is especially so, because the solution of your problems does not require a lengthy discussion, since all of them are so obvious that anyone who is aware of the norms of the Church, will find no difficulty in them at all. For my part, I am not inclined to introduce new customs into the Church, but am intent on observing those that were begun by the Fathers. And since we received faith from the apostles, and from apostolic men we learned to preserve order in the Church, so we do not change the type of discipline handed down to us from our ancestors, just as we keep intact the very foundations of the faith. Hence, the apostle said to Timothy: "[I write this] to let you know how you ought to conduct yourself in God's household, that is, the church of the living God, the pillar and bulwark of the truth."[1] For at the pres-

---

1. 1 Tim 3.15.

ent time it is not lawful for the latest members of the Church to choose what seems most important to them, but it is imperative to observe whatever was ordained in ancient times, especially that which the Roman Church maintains. Now, heresy is called a "choice,"[2] and deservedly those bear the name of heretic, who presume to choose whatever seems better to them, and refuse to abide by those things that were established by the holy doctors.

(3) I, however, since I profess to be a disciple of holy men not only of ancient times, but also of the present, and do not claim for myself a doctor's chair, am not formulating a new regulation in these matters about which you inquire, do not issue a rule of law, but simply make known to you either what I was accustomed to hear in the Roman Church from the custodians of the Apostolic See who were my teachers, or what I learned in other churches from frequent visits there.

(4) And so, following the custom of the Roman Church, I have always mixed chrism alone with the sacred baptismal water, and have never observed wine or oil mixed in this way. Moreover, the text that is read on Holy Thursday, and which also bears the title: "General instruction for the preparation of chrism," seems to say that we are to add nothing but holy chrism to the baptismal water. Among other things it states: "The water of baptism is prepared with the oil of sacred chrism, and it becomes a fountain of heavenly grace."[3] Now, since the author of this text has previously said all that is necessary to say about holy oil, when he comes to baptism, he makes no mention of oil and states that baptismal water is prepared only with chrism; it is obvious beyond the shadow of a doubt that he wishes only what he mentions to be added to the water. For if he had wanted wine or oil to be poured into the water, in speaking of chrism he would not have remained silent about them.[4]

(5) In celebrating holy Mass, moreover, I have learned of

2. It was a commonplace that the word "heresy" derived from the Greek term for "choice." Cf. Isidore, *Etymologies* 8.3.1.

3. Since this custom differs from that currently observed in the Church, one must examine a missal or ritual of the eleventh century to confirm Damian's position.

4. Chrism is made from a mixture of olive oil and balsam resin. Once it has been blessed by a bishop, it is employed in various sacramental rites. Early in

this customary rule in well-disciplined churches, and hold it to be correct, that we omit the purification of the chalice at the end of Mass if we hope to offer the sacrifice of the Mass again the same day.[5] Otherwise, whenever we offer the holy sacrifice, we always follow the custom of concluding the Mass by purifying the chalice. Also, whether we are fasting or have eaten, we are not to change this rule of purification. But what you observe, namely, that some say that after one has purified the chalice, he cannot be said to be fasting, and by bringing up these frivolous trivia they try to cause controversy, you must here be reminded of this statement of the apostle: "Have nothing to do with foolish and reckless speculations. You know they breed quarrels, and the servant of the Lord must not be quarrelsome, but kindly towards all."[6]

(6) And so, let it be enough for you to hear this short reply regarding the custom now maintained in the Church, nor should you demand that further reasons be supplied you. Indeed, this matter needs further elaboration, and that is more easily achieved by discussing it orally than by putting it in writing. Nor should you wonder that this brief letter, written in such haste, does not satisfy you, or also that it fails against the rule of elegance. Question the bearer of this letter, since it was almost noon when he reached our mountaintop, and he had this short document in his hands before sunset. You should still look into the matter of baptism, to see whether perhaps I have forgotten something that is maintained in the Roman Church. I beg God's goodness, venerable brother, to come into the sacred recesses of your heart and illumine it with the rays of his brilliance, that the key of David that opens the book sealed up with the seven seals,[7] may also open for you those things that are still closed, and with its power loose those that are bound.

---

the history of the Church it came to be used in baptism, during which the baptizand's head is anointed with chrism. Damian's point here is simply that it is unnecessary (and contrary to ecclesiastical custom) to add wine or other substances to the chrism of baptism. For another reference to chrism and baptism, see *Letter* 146.10 (FOTC, MC 6.159).

5. Damian here gives evidence of the contemporary practice of bination, i.e., celebrating Mass twice on the same day.

6. 2 Tim 2.23–24.   7. Cf. Rev 3.7; 5.5.

LETTER 178

Peter Damian to the former abbot A——. This abbot had been justly expelled from office for notorious crime. Continuing to do harm to the monastery and to its monks, he has now threatened still greater violence. Damian's decision: If the abbot does not desist from this persecution, he will be judged contumacious and will suffer excommunication. But if he allows the monks to live in peace, he may yet win God's grace.

(Not datable)

O THE FORMER abbot, sir A——, the monk Peter the sinner, greetings.[1]

(2) Since your disgraceful deeds, brother, have increased to such an extent that their notoriety has quickly spread among the people, in all justice you were consequently deprived of the office of abbot. But because it was reported to me that you continue to harm the monastery and its monks, and threaten still greater evil, I warn you to desist at once from this madness, and expiate the evil you have done by performing a fitting penance. But if you persist in your obstinacy, and do not promptly abandon this foolhardy mode of action and allow the Church of God and its servants to live in peace, be assured that you will suffer divine punishment, and will be condemned, excommunicated, and declared anathema by the authority of the Apostolic See. But if, on the other hand, you wish to live in harmony with the brothers and permit them to remain undisturbed, you can recover the grace of almighty God, and will always enjoy my confidence in you.

1. This short letter, previously overlooked by the first editor, C. Gaetani, was discovered in an eleventh-century manuscript in the Biblioteca Medicea-Laurenziana in Florence, and published by A. Campana in the *Rivista di storia della chiesa* 1 (1947): 90.

LETTER 179

Peter Damian to G——, a nobleman, a letter of consolation to one who was suffering from ill health. Without hope of future eternal happiness, for which physical trials are a preparation, our afflictions would be unbearable. He should weigh the comparative values in the following pairs of words: trouble and glory, momentary and eternal, light and heavy. The long view of human existence gives us strength to endure temporary distress. Incidental to his advice, but nevertheless noteworthy, is his brief discussion of contemporary animal husbandry and medical practice.

(Not datable)

 o sir g——, a member of the nobility, the monk Peter the sinner offers his service in fraternal charity.

(2) You have asked me, my dear friend, to send some words of consolation to you by mail, and to sweeten your bitter spirit by supplying you with soothing suggestions in the midst of the many blows that you are suffering. But if your sense of prudence has not been lulled to sleep, consolation is at hand, since your very hardships undoubtedly demonstrate that God is instructing you as his son so that you may receive your [eternal] inheritance. For what is clearer than the remark of Solomon when he said: "My son, if you desire to be a servant of God, hold fast to justice and the fear [of the Lord], and prepare yourself for testing"?[1] Indeed, wherever there is fear [of the Lord] and justice, the testing under each adversity is not a bullwhip used on a slave, but rather the chastisement inflicted by a father. And so, when blessed Job said, as the blows of the scourge were assailing him: "that he who has begun, may be pleased to crush me, that he may let loose his hand and cut me

---

1. Sir 2.1.

off," he at once continued: "And that this may be my comfort, and that, afflicting me with sorrow, he spare me not."[2]

(3) This very chastisement is truly a great comfort to those whom God has chosen, because by bearing up under these temporary blows, their steps grow stronger in the firm hope that they will attain the glory of everlasting happiness. For as Scripture attests: "The Lord does not twice pass judgment for the same offense."[3] Consequently, evil men, who do not mend their ways while receiving punishing blows, even though they are compelled to suffer in avenging flames after their afflictions in this life, are in no way sentenced twice. This is true because their twofold tribulation in God's just decree is continued in such a way, that what was begun in this life is made still more galling in the life to come. And just as the lash is only the beginning of the torments of hell for those who are hardhearted and obstinate, so surely for the good and upright of heart the same blows are the means of gaining heavenly reward.

(4) Assuredly, the craftsman hammers the gold that he might beat away the dross; again and again he rasps it with the file so that the gleaming metal may shine more brightly. "The furnace tests the work of the potter, and just men are tried by affliction."[4] Similarly, blessed James says: "My brothers, whenever you have to face trials of many kinds, count yourselves supremely happy."[5] Indeed, they are esteemed to be truly happy, who for their sins are charged with temporal suffering in this life, and for the good deeds that they have performed are granted everlasting rewards in heaven. What a fortunate exchange it is to be punished with temporary distress here below, and later to rejoice in the pleasant surroundings of eternal light; now to endure bodily vexation, and afterwards to be transported into glory worthy of an angel. In this happy condition, no weakness afflicts us, no tremulous old age slows our gait. We are not tormented by the loss of wealth, nor inflamed by the urge to acquire it. On the contrary, we enjoy the undiminished vigor of perpetual youth, and the conspicuous beauty

2. Job 6.9–10.   3. Cf. Nah 1.9.
4. Sir 27.6.   5. Jas 1.2.

of the blessed glows with such unchangeable brightness, that the gracious charm of life remains forever at its peak. And since all that we desire is always at our beck and call, no fear of loss disturbs our peace as we live securely in never-ending enjoyment.

(5) Wherefore, my dearly beloved brother, as you are beset with the biting lash and encompassed by blows of heavenly chastisement, let no desolation depress your spirits, no murmur or complaint escape your lips, no lament or sadness overwhelm you, or faintheartedness cause you to become impatient. On the contrary, always let your face reflect your serenity, let joy be in your heart, and thanksgiving be poised ready on your tongue. Praiseworthy indeed is the providence of God, who for a moment afflicts his own so that he might protect them from everlasting pain. He oppresses one that he might lift him up, amputates that he might heal, and casts one down, that he might exalt him once again. For one who performs good deeds and endures evil in return, [will find that] whatever just reward is denied him on earth will be increased many times over in heaven.

(6) Moreover, when bodily physicians despair of their patients' health, they allow them to eat indiscriminately as often as they wish. But for those whom they expect to recover, they firmly forbid the food they desire, because it will do them harm. Furthermore, they prescribe unpleasant medicine for them, that the bitter draught may make them well and produce the sweetness of good health. Therefore, why should we marvel if almighty God, the physician of souls, allows the guilty ones, who are destined for everlasting death, to live as pleasantly as they choose, but restrains those whom he selects [for eternal life] by the strict severity of his law?

(7) Similarly, we allow animals that are soon to be slaughtered to live more freely and to feed more generously. But we pay little attention to the leanness and poor condition of those we set aside for breeding and increasing the stock. Vines and fruit trees of various kinds, moreover, must undergo pruning, but those that are sterile and will eventually be thrown into the fire, we allow to branch out as wildly and diffusely as they will.

(8) Therefore, do not envy the happiness that evil men enjoy in this life, but rather be sorry for them. In fact, since they do not deplore their own lot, you should grieve for them. Such men, to be sure, are like dumb animals that eat on their way to the slaughterhouse, that indulge their passions as they hurry along to their death. But be glad that you must undergo hardships and depression, and with all your being rejoice in the Lord. For since now, as I might put it, you are held down by the inadequacy of useless wings, you will later be rewarded as you take away with you a hoard of precious gold, as Paul promised when he said: "Our troubles that are now slight and short-lived, will have as their outcome an eternal glory in us which far outweighs them."[6] Carefully examine these words of the apostle and diligently meditate on them, for whatever you must suffer is short-lived and light; so that you may patiently bear the burden that is said to be light,[7] and be confident that whatever is short-lived will quickly pass away.

(9) Nor should you fail to notice, moreover, how aptly and exactly God's words agree with one another so that after speaking of afflictions that are temporary and light to bear, he at once adds that they will yield an eternal weight of glory. And so, you should think about and compare these correlatives with each other: suffering and glory, temporary and eternal, light and weighty. Rejoice, therefore, and be glad that the suffering you endure is short-lived, and the glory that awaits you is eternal. Everything that you bear is light, all that you look for is heavy. Rejoice, I say, since in exchange for affliction you will receive glory; for what is light, something weighty; and for the temporary, an eternity will be yours.

(10) Consequently, amid hardships and trouble always lift up your eyes to him who after your afflictions is prepared to cherish you within the sweetness of his embrace, who after storms and tribulations will set you among the delights of heavenly peace, and will wipe away the tears from your eyes with the cloth of everlasting consolation. "And God will wipe all tears from the eyes of his holy ones."[8] Constantly dwell also on these

6. 2 Cor 4.17.   7. Cf. Matt 11.30.
8. Rev 7.17; 21.4.

other words of the apostle, and while you are stricken, rejoice in the Lord with all your being: "More than this," he says, "let us even exult in our [present] sufferings, because we know that suffering trains us to endure, and endurance brings proof that we have stood the test, and this proof is the ground of hope. Such a hope is no mockery, because God's love has flooded our inmost heart through the Holy Spirit, who is given to us."[9]

(11) With these and other texts of Holy Scripture, my dear friend, reinforce your spirit with patience, and happily look forward to the joy that will follow sadness. May hope encourage you in joyful expectations, and an ardent love inflame you, so that your soul, filled [with desire], may forget what the body has suffered as it yearns to possess the interior vision it has contemplated.

9. Rom 5.3–5.

LETTER 180

Peter Damian to bishop W———. This long fragment, appearing for the first time in Damian's letter collection, is preserved only in the manuscript of the *Liber testimoniorum veteris et novi testamenti (Collectanea)* of his disciple, John of Lodi. It addresses the problem of the universal salvific quality of Christ's crucifixion. Despite God's will to save and redeem all men through the cross, many are still unredeemed because through ill will or vanity they refuse to drink of the cup of immortality that was placed in their hands.

(Not datable)[1]

ND YET, THERE are certain fools who totally deny that our Redeemer was crucified for the salvation and redemption of all people. Accordingly, in a few words let me give them my reply. Because of the wound of original sin, by which through Adam the corrupted nature of all humanity succumbed to the necessity of death, and the disease that involved every type of concupiscence insolently broke its bonds, the death of our Savior occurred as the only true and efficacious remedy. He, indeed, who was free from the necessity of dying, and who, as one uniquely without sin, wished to die for sinners, while remaining without any debt [of his own], paid death's debt for us. Therefore, relative to the greatness and effectiveness of the price, and in so far as it pertains to the condition of the human race, the blood of Christ is the redemption of all the world.[2]

(2) And still, those who leave this world without faith in

1. In a superscription to this fragment there is the following statement: "In the letter to Bishop W., where he speaks of the letter of Bishop Transmundus, that bore this bishop's seal." Bishop Transmundus is otherwise unknown. See Lucchesi, *Clavis*, 48.
2. Cf. Eph 1.7; Col 1.14.

Christ and without the sacrament of regeneration, are unable to participate in this redemption. Consequently, since all are rightly said to be redeemed because of this one universal nature and one universal condition that were truly assumed by our Redeemer, but since, on the other hand, not all are rescued from captivity because of their depravity, the right to redemption undoubtedly belongs in a special way to those from whom the prince of this world has been driven out,[3] so that they are no longer instruments of the devil, but members of Christ. Among all men there is not a single one whose nature was not assumed by our Lord. Even though he was born in a form like that of our own sinful flesh,[4] still every other man is born possessed of that sinful flesh. Therefore, God, the Son of God, who without sin participated in human mortality,[5] granted to mortal sinners that those who participated in his birth would escape from the fetters of sin and from those of death as well.

(3) And so, just as it did not suffice for the renewal of mankind that Christ was born as a man, unless men were reborn in him by the same Spirit from whom he had his being, so it is not enough for men's redemption that Christ the Lord was crucified, unless they die and are buried with him in baptism.[6] Indeed, the cup of immortality that is the product of our infirmity and the power of God, possesses the quality of profiting all men; but if one does not drink from it, he will not be cured. Therefore, one who says that the Savior was not crucified for the redemption of all the world, does not take into account the power of the sacrament, but reflects the incurable vanity of unbelievers, who are damned.

(4) Consequently, in so far as it reflects the fact that the Son of God took upon himself our common nature and condition, and in so far as it pertains to the force and power of the price that he paid, it is proper to say that our Savior was crucified for the redemption of all the world. But since the death of Christ has failed to benefit many who continued to live in their impious ways, it is correct to say that the redemption of the world is

3. Cf. John 12.31.   4. Cf. Rom 8.3.
5. Cf. Heb 4.15.
6. Cf. Col 2.12; 2 Tim 2.11; Rom 6.4–8.

something foreign to them. Although this redemption is perceived to be something specific and appropriate to the saints and to those chosen by God, it does not derive from human effort, but is a unique gift of the Savior. To this point, the apostle urges that prayers and intercessions be offered for all men,[7] which is regularly and carefully practiced in all churches. That of these, many are lost, is undoubtedly the fault of those who perish; but that many are saved, is the gift of him who is the Savior. That the guilty one is damned, follows from the blameless justice of God; but that the sinner is justified, depends on the incomprehensible grace of divine mercy.

(5) Now, we know of many people who would say that some have been deprived of the preaching of the Gospel, so that they would not be saved as the faith was announced to them. But if it can be proven that from the time when the Gospel first began to shine throughout the world, there was no one at all to whom the grace of Christ was not announced, it cannot justly be claimed that some did not hear what demonstrably had been preached to all. Otherwise, if we can find people to whom the Gospel was not made known, it cannot be said that this happened without God's decree. Yet it is monstrous that this decision should be judged reprehensible by man, because the human intellect is unable to understand it. Wherefore, we come to the proper conclusion about this decision, if we do not protest against God's decrees, by which he abandons those who deserve to be abandoned, and if we give thanks for his mercy, by which he acquits those who do not deserve to be freed. The latter, in fact, would have remained obstinate in their sins if the mediator between God and men had not intervened by a more generous grant of grace in the secret economy of God. We may therefore be assured that his most sacred blood so imbued the sacraments of human salvation, that it purified all those who were on their way to accepting grace, converted the old leaven into the unleavened bread of sincerity,[8] and through the grace of regeneration renewed a world that had been corrupted by the plague of original sin.

7. Cf. 1 Tim 2.1.
8. Cf. 1 Cor 5.8.

INDICES

INDEX OF PROPER NAMES

Lucchesi, Giovanni, 7, 81, 92, 218, 241, 249, 267, 295
Luke the Evangelist, 144, 277–78, 283

Macarius, monk, 61
Mainard, abbot of Pomposa, 15
Mainard, bishop of Gubbio, 84
Mainard, monk of Sitria, 66
Manso, abbot of Monte Cassino, 86
Marinus, monk, 57
Marozia, 240
Martha, 211
Martin of Braga, 256
Martin, hermit, 261
Martin, monk, 94
Mary, 125, 167, 211, 228, 239, 241–43, 258, 277
Melchiadis, pseudo, 169
Michael, the archangel, 5, 81
Michal, 137–38, 196
Mombritius, B., 266
Moricus, judge, 247
Moses, 23, 38, 50–51, 62, 65, 105–8, 114, 117, 129, 144, 153, 156, 158, 203, 211–12, 215, 217, 268, 274

Naaman, 213–14
Nehemiah, 42–44, 54
Nero, Claudius Tiberius, emperor, 80
Nicholas, pope, 143
Niermeyer, J. F., 6

Onan, 279
Origen, 112
Ornan, 264
Otto I, emperor, 85

Paul the Deacon, 80
Paul, apostle, 6, 12, 25, 54, 94–102, 114, 116, 133, 137, 167, 214, 215, 220, 241, 293
Peter Damian, vii, 3–4, 7, 15, 59, 72, 76, 79, 84, 88, 92, 94, 103, 131, 142, 159, 162, 170, 217, 228, 233, 236, 244, 247, 253, 255, 264, 267, 277, 279, 286, 289, 290, 295
Peter de Burgo, 135

Peter the rhetorician, 170
Peter, abbot, 90
Peter, abbot of Vicenza, 59
Peter, apostle, 25, 81, 83, 94–95, 99, 100–102, 116, 137, 139, 141, 165, 166–67, 241–42, 280
Peter, archpriest, 159
Peter, monk. See Peter the rhetorician
Prudentius, 253

Rachel, 9, 33–36, 95–96, 149, 207
Raguel, 40, 265
Rainaldus, bishop of Como, 240
Rainerius II, marquis of Monte S. Maria, 3
Rainerius, judge, 244
Rameses, 110
Reba, 269
Rebecca, 71
Regino of Prum, 189, 262
Reindel, Kurt, 15, 77, 80, 85, 93, 115, 253
Rekem, 269
Resnick, Irven M., 71, 258
Reuben, 23, 32
Richard, abbot of Saint Vanne de Verdun, 77
Richard, of Camporeggiano, 4, 5, 245, 249, 251
Rufinus, 112
Ruth, 280
Ryan, J. Joseph, 163–64, 166, 189–91, 217–18, 256, 280

Sabatier, P., 269
Sallust, 144
Samson, 142
Samuel, 57, 138, 168
Sapphira, 171, 172
Sara. See Sarah
Saracen, 251
Sarah, 265
Sardanapalus, 61
Satan, 79, 81, 86, 120, 254, 260, 265, 283
Saul, 57, 74, 96, 138, 196, 265
Scholastica, saint, 131, 134
Sennacherib, 194
Shimei, 62
Silvester, 45

INDEX OF SACRED SCRIPTURE

Old Testament

New Testament